NORTH AMERICAN SUN KINGS
Keepers of the Flame

By

Joseph B. Mahan

With An

Expository Statement

By

Cyclone Covey

ISAC PRESS
Institute for the Study of American Cultures
Non-Profit Educational
1004 Broadway
Columbus, GA 31901

1992

Library of Congress Catalogue No. E99.Y9M34 1992
ISBN 1-880820-03-X   975'.004975-dc20
CIP 92-35595

Printed in the United States by Sewell Printing Service, Inc. ● Composition by Repro Services, Inc.
Atlanta, Georgia

This Work
is
D E D I C A T E D
to My Wife
Dr. Katherine Hines Mahan

who has contributed materially to its content and to my will to pursue it to completion.

and to My Father
Joseph Buford Mahan, Sr.

Whose support and understanding set me initially on the road to seek the knowledge that is its core.

Acknowledgement

It is my desire to record my appreciation to my friend, Samuel W. Brown, Jr., Chief of the Yuchis, and my three major professors: Ellis M. Coulter and Arthur R. Kelly, of the University of Georgia, and Hugh T. Lefler, of the University of North Carolina, for turorage, scholarly example, and encouragement which they provided me in the formative stages of this work.

I wish also to express gratitude to scores of friends, casual acquaintances, and others I never knew personally who have helped in assembling the information this book contains. My greatest regret is that many of them have not lived to see its completion.

Preface

This work is intended to trace the genealogy of a Native American dynastic line and its subsidiary branches which once governed diverse peoples who occupied North America south of the Great Lakes and from the Mississippi Valley to the Allegheny Mountains and the Savannah River. Recognized by their subordinates as children of the sun, these potentates maintained their hereditary positions by virture of their powers—physical, intellectual, and mystical—through several millennia and survived until the second half of the twentieth the horrendous vicissitudes arising from the intrusions of Europeans in the early sixteenth century.

This is a beginning effort to bring together information pertaining to this subject utilizing whatever research methodology I have had available, whether it be historical, archaeological, ethnological, or rote-learned oral tradition.

These are the areas in which I have had sufficient training and experience to feel confident in the conclusions I have drawn. I have also made use of the pioneering epigraphic studies by Dr. Barry Fell, the results of which have contributed substantially to a fuller understanding of information I have gleaned from other disciplines.

Understanding of the significance of this history of North American peoples is expanded to an incalculable degree in the expository section, "The Implausible Union of Ankh & Thunderbird," in which Cyclone Covey has analysed the extent and particulars of their identity with ancient peoples of Europe, Asia, and Africa and the kinship of their sun and moon religion with better known manifestations of it, including that of Egypt, Persia, the Indus Valley, and Central Asia.

The major area that is lacking is comparative linguistics to make this an exhaustive investigation. A competent study of all the languages known to have been spoken by the people I have introduced needs to be undertaken, especially if the study were pursued to its logical conclusions regardless of barriers such as oceans and vast distances. The possibility of language diffusion across these barriers, generally assumed inpenetratable, has not been considered until very recently. I have not even attempted such a study as I have no competence at all in that specialized area.

I have tried to make the narrative "reader-friendly" in that I have generally gone from the known to the unknown, have introduced persons, circumstances, and concepts and have sought their antecedants, causes, and continuity from the present backward through four centuries.

It has been my aim to achieve sufficient understanding of these elements to project some of this understanding still further into the periods of the American past which until now have been known only through the investigations and interpretations of the archeologists. No matter how competently and thoroughly done, without the aid of written notations these investigations can only reveal the barest outline of numerous and complex cultures

Chapter 1

A Sun King Goes "as the Sun Goes"

It was a sad and eerie occasion January 3, 1958, a counterpart of ceremonies reaching back to remote antiquity.

I was one of six "white" friends bearing the copper casket of Samuel W. Brown, Jr., Chief of the Yuchi Tribe of Indians, to its grave prepared in the Sapulpa, Oklahoma city cemetery. The sun shone suddenly near the end of a wintry day which had been cloudy, cold, and windy with occasional flakes of snow.

Weather bulletins on the local radio broadcasts had reported the progress of a snowstorm sweeping southward across the plains of Nebraska and Kansas which, it was logical to believe, would reach this section of northeastern Oklahoma in the early evening. People who had assembled earlier in the day for the funeral services at the Little Cusseta Indian Baptist Church near Bixby feared that there would be bad weather for the ceremonies at the grave, scheduled for four o'clock.

The older men reassured the people expressing concern: "The sun will shine. She always does when one of her children goes home." I was less confident than they but I did remember Chief Brown's oft-repeated statement: "We come as the sun comes and we go as the sun goes."

I had met the elderly chief the previous June while he was on a visit to his ancestral homeland in the Chattahoochee Valley along its river which separates the states of Georgia and Alabama. I saw his picture with his two daughters in the Columbus (Ga.) *Ledger-Enquirer* one Sunday morning. I read that he was the hereditary chief of the Yuchi tribe and that he and his two daughters had spent the past few days in Seale, Alabama. They had come to visit the area where their ancestors had lived for many generations and to see certain specific sites associated with the forced removal of their people to the West in the 1830's. I also learned that the visitors were scheduled to leave that morning for their home in Mathis, Texas.[1]

As I was then teaching history and cultural anthropology at the University of Georgia's off-campus center in Columbus, I found this news of particular interest. My area of speciality had long been the origin and history of the aboriginal peoples of the Southeast: Cherokees, Creeks, Seminoles and several smaller tribes among whom were the Yuchis, the tribe I knew least about because very little had been published about them. Now it seemed that a visit with the chief offered an opportunity to learn something more about these people.

I began immediately to search the telephone directory for a motel in Seale as the Browns were reported to have been staying in one there. My wife, in her characteristic practical manner, suggested that I drive as quickly as possible the fewer than twenty miles to the small Alabama town, where there was probably only one motel anyway. I found Chief Brown and his two daughters, Dorothy Jean Brown and Jewell Brown Caton at what was indeed the only motel in Seale. In my excitement, I introduced myself as an "expert" on the Southeastern Indians to the obvious amusement of the elderly chief. "Which ones?" He asked and then: "What do you know about the Yuchis?"

"Not very much," I admitted and undertook to excuse my ignorance by explaining that "The Yuchis have never talked to anybody." I meant anthropologists, who for most of the previous century, with notebook and camera in hand, interviewed and observed all the American Indians who could be persuaded to cooperate.

---

[1] The Columbus (Ga.) *Ledger-Enquirer*, June 23, 1957.

Chief Brown with daughters Jewel Brown Caton (r) and Dorothy Jean Brown soon after their arrival in Alabama, June 1957. (Colum-bus Ledger-Enquirer*).*

"That is not true," the old man replied firmly. "I have been talking all of my life. The trouble has been I could not find anyone who would listen."

This exchange began a pleasant and productive relationship in which I undertook to be the person he had never found to "listen" to him as he attempted to record a lifetime of information about his people. I did not realize at the time but later became convinced that he made his first trip "home" to Alabama and Georgia so late in his life in the hope that he could find someone trained in historical methods who might pursue research into Yuchi history.

During the months following this June visit, which he extended three additional days to visit Columbus and see the exhibits on Southeastern Indians I was helping to prepare for the new Columbus Museum of Arts and Crafts. Chief Brown and I communicated often by letters, phone conversations, and tape recordings. I asked questions and he answered to the extent and depth he felt I was capable of assimilating and using. Very soon I learned that much of the Yuchi version of Southeastern Indian history directly contradicted what I had been taught in graduate history and anthropology courses or had read in available books on American Indians.

Chief Brown, his daughter Dorothy Jean Brown and nephew Samuel H. Brown, spent two weeks in Columbus that October so he could take part in ceremonies sponsored by the cities of Columbus, Georgia and Phenix City, Alabama in the first annual "Port Cities" Day, intended to promote the construction by the U. S. Corps of Engineers of a series of dams making possible a nine-foot navigation channel from these cities to the Gulf of Mexico. The chief of the "hometown" Indians had been invited to preside at a formal peace ceremony to help call public attention to the event and incidentally clear the record of long-ago misdeeds on the part of the Anglo-Americans including the seizure of the Yuchi homeland. The result was a public relations success exceeding the most optimistic expectations.[2]

During this second visit in the East, the Chief had time to meet a great many local people and was invited, with his daughter and nephew, to meals in the homes of several new friends. On these occasions, the chief displayed a charisma and social savoir-faire that was unaffected and beguiling. There was a kindness in his demeanor which I discovered, made him trustful of others. On his first visit to our home, he was welcomed by our playful, half-grown collie, whom for some long-forgotten reason, my wife, Katie, or I had given the not very appropriate name "Poochie."

---

[2] *Ibid.*, October 27, 1957; The Columbus *Ledger*, October 29, 1957.

"What is his name?' Chief Brown asked as he attempted to keep the canine greeting from becoming too enthusiastic.

Inspiration came to me and I seized the opportunity to play a mild practical joke on my venerable guest. "We call him 'Poochie,' " I said, "but his name is actually *Timpoochee*." (Timpoochee Barnard was perhaps the best known Yuchi among his own people and his Anglo-American neighbors at the time of the removal.). I thought Chief Brown would sense the humor I intended in this name-pun.

That was not the case. The old chief beamed and expressed pleasure at our having named our beautiful dog for his renowned fellow tribesman, who was also his father's great uncle. With this unexpected response I clearly could not with any degree of grace admit I was merely joking. The dog was suddenly renamed and for the rest of his long life his name was really short for that of the famous Yuchi. Frequently thereafter, both in telephone conversations and letters, Chief Brown would inquire about "Timpoochee."

I worked with the Chamber of Commerce personnel making elaborate preparations, which Chief Brown directed by mail and phone, for the peace-making ceremony which was to be part of the Port Cities observance. The three arbors of a Yuchi "Square Ground" were constructed under Chief Brown's direction in a city park on the bank of the river. They were situated one each at the center of the south, west, and north sides of a sixty-foot square. This replicated the Yuchi ceremonial ground, site of all religious and inter-tribal activities. The post-and-pole structures were covered with green willow boughs to shade long split-log seats. The ground inside the square was scraped clean of all vegetation and carefully packed to form a smooth, hard surface.

When ceremonies began on a bright October afternoon, the Yuchi chief, resplendent in a red-tipped, white feather crown, woven beaded sashes, and black silk "hunting coat," occupied the center seat in the west or "chief's" arbor. He carried an ancient twelve-feather eagle tail fan symbolizing his rank as king and micco (priest). At his instructions, the Stars and Stripes flew from a flagpole attached to the center support post of this arbor. The Chief was flanked by the mayors of Columbus and Phoenix City. In this arbor and the two flanking it, sat an impressive array of dignitaries including the commanding general of the Infantry School at Fort Benning, two Congressmen representing local districts in Georgia and Alabama, members of the two state legislatures, members of the two city councils, the two chambers of commerce, and other civic and business leaders of the bi-state area.

On the east side of the square, benches had been placed at the request of the chief for the convenience of ladies and other special guests. Behind them stood Fort Benning's Infantry School band. Hundreds of onlookers surrounded this extraordinary assemblage.

At the center of the square was a Sacred Fire circle some eight feet in diameter covered with white sand. On this white area lay four sections of logs extending from the center to the outer edge with each pointing to one of the cardinal directions. A fire burned vigorously at the junction of these logs. It was obviously intended for some other function than merely provide heat on this sunny October day in South Georgia. East of the fire stood a sizeable earthenware vessel beside which lay a gourd dipper on a large piece of bark.

Facing the fire from in front of the west arbor was a man with russet complexion dressed in red hunting coat, ribbon-decorated leggings, beaded sashes and a red turban from the rear of which hung white crane feathers. In his hand he held a rattle made from a small coconut shell. This was Samuel H. Brown, nephew of the chief, who was serving the function of the square ground chief.

At a motion from the chief, the band played the *Star Spangled Banner*, the crowd cheered and the ceremony of peace-making began. The square ground chief raised the coconut shell rattle toward the sun and began shaking it in rhythm and, to its accompaniment, chanting a prayer in the Yuchi language. As he sang, he danced around the fire, which he circled four times. When he had finished, the mayor of Columbus welcomed the Yuchis and other guests. He spoke of a time now one hundred and twenty years past when there had been war between the people of this area and the Yuchis and told the chief that the people of Georgia and Alabama had assembled in a spirit of

Using traditional five-gar-teeth implement, Samuel H. Brown scratches his uncle, Chief Brown, in ancient ritual opening the peace-making ceremony, October 1957. (Columbus Ledger-Enquirer*).*

Wired for sound and shaking a coconut rattle, Chief Brown instructs his nephew and four acting pole boys at the beginning of the peace ceremony, October 1957. (Columbus Ledger-Enquirer*).*

peace asking that the old wrongs of that era be forgiven, that the animosities so long remembered be forgotten and that peace and brotherhood be restored between the two peoples.

The Yuchi chief stood to a thunderous applause, raised his hands toward the sun and waited for silence. When he could be heard, he said a prayer in his native language to *Cohantoney*, the ''Breath-Master,'' which he repeated in English. He then spoke eloquently of the ''Old People,'' his ancestors who had occupied land along the Chattahoochee and throughout the eastern part of the country for many centuries, how they had considered this land their mother and had always been careful to take only what was needed from her and never to hurt her. He said the Earthmother nestled her children in their ''last great sleep,'' while she continued to provide for the needs of their living children. It was his hope that the newcomers to the land that had been the Yuchis' for so long would love and protect it as his people had done. He was grateful to the present occupants, the Chief said, for inviting his people back so they could visit the land of their ancestors.

As I stood beside his casket in distant Oklahoma a few months later, I was aware of the sharp contrast with the recent October day. I wondered if his body would rest as securely as it would have in the homeland where his mother the Earth sheltered so many generations of his forbears.

Following his speech to the people in Columbus, the Yuchi chief explained the meaning of the sacred ''medicine,'' the *pardeh*, which he was about to share with them. He told them that this was one of the gifts given to the *Zoyaha*, his people, by the Breath-Master at the time of Creation, that it was one of their seven sacred medicines and that it produces a spirit of goodwill and brotherhood. It is part of the spiritual and physical cleansing all right-living Yuchis undergo at the annual festival of the new corn in July. All who wished to do so were invited to take one small swallow of the decoction in the crockery jar beside the Sacred Fire drawing its strength since early morning from the rays of the sun.

Chief Brown ended this invitation, as he ended all of his formal statements, with the proclamation, ''*Zopathla*,'' Chief of the Yuchis, I have spoken!'' It is significant here that in the Yuchi language *zo* is ''sun'' and *pathla* is ''king.''

Beginning with occupants of the west arbor who were served by the Chief himself, almost every person present in the arbors drank a little of the ''white drink'' from the same goard dipper as it passed to them. When they had finished, it was passed to occupants of the seats on the east side. Finally, those standing on the outside were invited to file to the center of the ground and receive their portion. It was interesting to me to learn that the plant whose root produces this medicine is the white button snakeroot, a synthetic version of which was the famous ''tranquilizer'' which had recently come into great popularity as a treatment for stress and various mental illnesses.

There was little sun symbolism visible at the Chief's funeral, except a general concern expressed by several people that the sun should be shining for the burial. There was more that was traditional Yuchi, however, including a complete service with ancient hymns sung in the ancestral language. At the grave, four of Brown's closest associates, representing the four town kings, stood in turn beside the grave and made, respectively, symbolic presentations of offerings of the items that were formerly placed in the grave;. These were venison, sofkee (boiled cracked corn), tobacco, and shell. A beautiful new quilt in a traditional Yuchi pattern was placed on the casket before the metal vault was lowered over it. A small cedar bough was dropped into the open grave.

That was not all of the symbolism present, however. An American Legion color guard stood nearby and a bugler sounded ''Taps.'' Suddenly a firing squad took position and fired toward the setting sun rather than over the grave as is customary. A Yuchi man beside me whispered, ''In the old days, an arrow was shot toward the sun.'' I happened to know that an arrow represented the sun spirit in ancient art in many areas.

As is customary in Yuchi funerals, members of the deceased's clan filled the grave. Just when the last shovel of dirt was placed, I looked toward the sunset. At that instant the final red segment of the solar orb sank below the horizon. I knew that the latest of the Zoya had gone as the sun goes. I hoped that he would not be the last of this ancient dynastic succession.

Chapter 2

The Continuing Tradition

I have been conditioned through extensive formal education in historical and ethnological research methods to suspect data obtained from oral tradition. I have never accepted this premise without reservation, however. Personal experiences have convinced me of the accuracy of detail in stories transmitted by word of mouth. Growing up more than half a century ago in a small rural community in North Georgia provided these experiences. I am aware, through my initiation into the Masonic Order, of the effectiveness of learning orally-transmitted historical details and ritualistic lore by rote. My observation of the accuracy of oral transmission by the Yuchis over unbelievably long periods has convinced me that this can be a most effective means of preserving knowledge precisely.

Although I was thus predisposed, nothing I had experienced or learned had prepared me to believe at first the volume and astounding accuracy of the vast store of traditional knowledge Chief Brown possessed. Much of this knowledge he said had never been recorded by any means except human memory. This was a matter of concern to me when I made his acquaintance. Governed as I was by the prevailing concept of "the American Indian" that his historical and cultural traditions were eroding at an increasing rate in each generation, I was unprepared to accept totally contrary evidence even in as authorative a form as Chief Brown's statements.

In my first conversation with the Yuchi chief my academic conditioning came out in my comment that I wished to help record Yuchi traditional knowledge "before it is lost." The crass nature of this remark came home to me in the old man's reply, "I hope you won't say that to my people as we have worked all our lives to preserve our heritage." Its fallacy was further apparent later in the comment of another Yuchi, Madison Bucktrot, of Bristow, Oklahoma, who commented to me, "We have never been able to understand how telling the white man anything would help to preserve it."

The concept of my learning Yuchi tradition and culture values for their intrinsic worth and not simply to record them for posterity grew gradually. I came to realize that there are two correlated principles in the Yuchi system of transmitting esoteric knowledge to neophytes, whether younger Yuchis or interested aliens like me. One of these is that the person seeking knowledge must have learned enough already to understand what may be imparted to him. The other is that the neophyte must ask for the knowledge. It is never imposed upon anyone. Eventually, it became apparent to me that this idea was inherent in the Yuchi name, *Cadaley* (Hunter), which Chief Brown conferred on me.

These principles and my personal limitations guided and restricted what the Chief could tell me to expedite the writing of this history. Nevertheless, the information he was able to impart in the six months we were acquainted was impressive and varied. The surviving physical record of his effort is in the letters and tape recordings he prepared for me. These repose in the history archives in the Simon Schwob Memorial Library at Columbus College. They provide much of the factual basis for this chapter. They are supplemented by letters and other documents in the Samuel W. Brown, Jr. Collection; in the Oklahoma Historical Society Archives. An additional record is my own memory, reinforced by the tutorage of several Yuchi friends during the past thirty years and more, by my experiences on the Square Ground at Kellyville, Oklahoma, by my research into pertinent written sources, and by the understanding that comes from a synthesis of all I have learned.

Thus, based on Chief Brown's statements and details gleaned from the foregoing sources, a summary of the history and cultural heritage of the Yuchis follows.

Their original name was *Zoyaha Wano*, "which was the governing word, as it is of today, from their starting point." They were also called the *Yustafa Wano*, "Upper People" or "First People." The

Jewel Brown Caton, successor to her father as Yuchi Chief, explains to Mr. and Mrs. D. Abbott Turner details of traditional tribal costume in a mural in the Columbus Museum, 1962. (Columbus Ledger-Enquirer).

element *wano* in these names means "people" and *zoya* is "sun-filled." The syllable *ha* is a first person nominative ending identifying the speaker as belonging to the people named. Thus the name *Zoya* properly has the ending *ha* only when it is spoken by a Yuchi of *Zoya* descent. The second name, Yustafa Wano, also denotes descent from the moon. They with the Zoya constituted a united people, who were later called the *Shawano*.

The leader of this union had a "tribal town, a big one at *Coshafa*." This name breaks down into *Co* (man) and *sha* (eagle-serpent) plus *fa*, an ending denoting "place." This name is symbolized by the drawings of composites of men and eagles and men and serpents which are prominent in the aboriginal religious art of eastern North America.

Before the middle of the seventeenth century A.D. the Zoya and Yustafa Wano (Shawano) were the cohesive central component which formed a common bond among all the peoples of Eastern North America south of the upper shores of the Great Lakes except, perhaps, the areas in the Northeast controlled by the confederated Iroquois tribes. The united peoples were divided into four groups known to themselves as the *Ispogogee, Kispogogee, Muscogulgee,* and the *Muscovee*. They were known collectively as the *Shawano* or *Shawanogee*, which means eagle-serpent people or eagle-serpent-earth people. The group most closely related to the *Zoya* called themselves *Zoyaha*. Those descended from the *Yustafa* were the *Chiyaha*, "People of the Eye," i.e. Moon. Both called themselves *Yugeeha*, "sky-earth," people. Descendants of both are the people known today as the Yuchi.[1]

The Shawano had their own large towns and areas of direct control. However, many of them lived dispersed in other areas where they constituted a special priesthood attending the sun kings and ministering to the religious and medical needs of the surrounding populace. They were the *Inihas* among the Algonquin peoples and the *Miccos* among the Muskogeans. The Cherokees called them the *Ani-Kutani*. Among the latter, this privileged group became oppressive and their unregulated, self-indulgent way of life highly resented. Those *Kutani* resident in the tribal towns of the mountain-dwelling Cherokee were massacred in a popular uprising about the year 1760, during a war with the

[1] Joseph B. Mahan, *The Secret, America in World History Before Columbus* (Columbus, Ga.: Published by the Author, 1983), pp. 26, 27.

South Carolina colonists. "Old Hop," or *Canachechi*, the last Cherokee king, whom the English called "Emperor," died about the same time. Although he was aged and ill, the English suspected that the rebels killed him too.[2]

In my study of the Cherokee before 1957, I had come to the same conclusion. I did not know the identity of these people, however until I put together a statement by Brown with other facts about the people who call themselves the *Sha-la-gi* or "Duck-Earth" people. The Chief asked me one day what the Cherokee people call themselves. I told him. Whereupon he commented, "They gave us a lot of trouble once." I then remembered that Old Hop was *Canachechi* (spelled variously) of Echota (sometimes *Chote*). This appears to be *E* (tobacco) *zo* (sun) *ti* (the sacred medicine), a name strongly suggesting Yuchi influence. Echote was the "Beloved Peace Town" on the Little Tennessee River in what the English called the "Over Hill" division of the Cherokee territory. Its name was given about 1817 to the new capital town of the Cherokee Nation in northern Georgia.

Old Hop and his predecessor, Moytoy, were both called "Emperor" by the English. None of his successors was ever designated as such. James Adair, a contemporary observer, implied in his *History* that the English had Old Hop removed and *Ataculacula* installed in his place because the emperor was receiving support from the French.[3] Perhaps it was not to the British interest to allow any tribe to have so powerful a leader as these native "emperors." However, the dynasty survived among the Cherokees for more than half a century. The principal chief, who served them from about 1805 until his death in 1827 was called "Pathkiller" or *Pathla*, the Yuchean word for "king."

In the early twentieth century, John R. Swanton, chief ethnologist of the Bureau of American Ethnology, investigated the identity of the *Ispokogis*, who were said to have been associated with the town of Tukabatchee since ancient times. He learned that:

Two Ispokogis came down from above, approached the ball ground and saw that there were people there and that it was good, so they remained with the people. One of these people made a dugout canoe, and, when it was completed, he got into it and began floating up into the air. But when it was some distance off, he looked back and saw all of the people standing still and gazing after him. Then he said "I can not leave them." So he came back and, when he landed, the other Ispokogi lay down and died. The surviving Ispokogi remained with the people after that, and with reference to this event the word was that "There shall be a link of brothers, life without ending." This meant that when one Ispokogi died there should always be another to take his place.[4]

From a report by Benjamin Hawkins, President Washington's agent to the Creeks, Swanton reported that "They have in this town, a micco of another family, the Is-po-co-gee Micco, the ancient name of the town." He also quoted a fuller account of the miraculous arrival of these people from the sky which one Tukabatchee Mico told to Gen. Ethan Allen Hitchcock in 1842. In this story "seven persons of both sexes were sent down from heaven in very old times; later they attempted to return, but one of them, thought to have been a man, died whereupon the others came back." These people taught the Tukabatchee "how to make a fire and how to worship the Great Spirit. They also brought certain plates from heaven which they gave the chiefs."[5]

On one occasion, Chief Brown was talking to a group of school children in the Columbus Museum. Someone asked him what his "Indian name" was.

"I have several," was the reply. "My mother called me '*Coo-wee*,' (Little Bird);" Most of my people call me Willie; sometimes they call me *Zopathla*. The Creeks call me *Micco Fushudgee*; (Bird

---

[2] Joseph B. Mahan, "Identification of the Tsoyaha Waeno, Builders of Temple Mounds" (Chapel Hill: University of North Carolina, Doctoral Dissertation, 1970), pp. 188–190.

[3] Samuel Cole Williams, *Adair's History of the American Indians* (Johnson City, Tenn.: Watauga Press, 1930), p. 32. (Cited hereinafter as *Adair's History*)

[4] John R. Swanton, "Social Organization and Social Usages of the Indians of the Creek Confederacy," *Forty-Second Annual Report of the Bureau of American Ethnology* . . . (Washington: United States Government Printing Office, 1928), pp. 65–66.

[5] *Ibid.*, 505–506.

Tail) *Yoholo* (king) or *Ispogogee Micco.*'' The children were visibly impressed by the variety of the old man's names. I was suddenly aware of just how very much history was embodied in this one man.

The name *Ispogogee* was familiar to me from my reading of Southeastern Indian history. I remembered the quotation just given in which the name is identified with the Upper Creek town of Tukabatchee. As is clearly stated, the Ispogogee were identified by the residents of that town as the people who came from the sky in a ''boat'' and gave the people there the sacred fire, the medicines, and knowledge of much else that was useful. It was also the Ispogogee who had remained with the Tukabatchees as their miccos. When I heard Chief Brown apply the name *Ispogogee* to himself, I began to reconstruct the relationship of Yuchis with older Muskogee groups, among whom the Tukabatchee were the ancient head town. Important to all of this were the ''Tukabatchee plates.''

In the year 1742 Old Bracket, an elderly member of the Tukabatchee tribe told the Scottish fur-trader James Adair about certain copper and brass items buried under the chief's arbor on the Square Ground in his tribal town. There were seven of these, two brass and five copper. Some were circular and some were in the shape of large axes, Brackett said. He said also that these had been given to his people in ancient times by the Great Spirit and that they were taken up each year during the annual festival of the new corn and paraded with special ceremonies around the sacred ground. In these ceremonies men bearing one plate each followed the town king in a procession around the sacred fire. They all carried ''white canes with swan feathers at the tip.'' Adair included this information in his *History of the American Indians* with a drawing of two of these plates. On one of the plates Adair showed is inscribed the Roman diphthong, /E. Others were said to have ''writing'' on them.[6]

Old Bracket's account of the *five copper* and *two brass plates* under the beloved cabbin in Tuccabatchey-square.

    The shape of the five copper plates; one is a foot and half long and seven inches wide, the other four are shorter and narrower.

The largest stamped thus   The shape of the two brass plates, —about a foot and a half in diameter.

Drawing of two of the Tukabatchee plates from Adair's History.

Almost a century later, the reverential care with which these sacred items were handled when the Tukabatchees were forced to leave their ancestral town and migrate to the west was recorded by the Alabama historian, Albert Pickett:

> When the inhabitants of this town, in the autumn of 1836, took up the line of march for their present home in the Arkansas territory, these plates were transported thence by six Indians, remarkable for their sobriety and moral character, at the head of whom was the Spoke-oak Micco. Medicine, made expressly for their safe transportation, was carried along by these warriors. Each who took one had a plate strapped behind his back enveloped nicely in buckskin. They carried nothing else, but marched on, one before the other the whole distance to Arkansas, neither communicating nor conversing with a soul but themselves, although several thousands were emigrating in company; and walking, with a solemn religious air, one mile in advance of the others.[7]

There is information from several sources which links these relics with the Shawano or the Shawnees. Walter Lowrie, a Missionary allowed to see them in 1852, stated that ''Muskogee tradition affirms that there were more of these plates possessed by them at former periods, of different kinds, some of which had letters or figures, but that the number was diminished by the custom of placing one or more of them with the body of a deceased chief of the pure or reigning blood. The

---

[6] Williams, *Adair's History*, p. 179n.

[7] Albert Pickett, *History of Alabama*, 2 Vols. (Charleston: 1851), vol. 1, pp. 86–87.

plates remaining are placed in the hands of particular men. They are guarded with care, and are kept from being touched by women."[8]

Henry Rowe Schoolcraft, in his massive six-volume *History, Condition, and Prospects of the Indian Tribes of the United States*, quotes an account by R. M. Loughridge, Creek missionary and joint-author of a dictionary of the Creek language, who was allowed to see the plates. He related:

> The old Chief Tukabatchee Mikko, came out and said that I could see them, on condition that *I would not touch them*. They profess to believe, that if a person who has not been consecrated for the purpose, by fasting or other exercises, six or eight days, should touch them, he would certainly die, and sickness or some great calamity would befall the town. For similar reasons, he said it was unlawful for a woman to look at them. The old chief then conducted me into the square, or public ground, where the plates had been laid out for my inspection. There were seven in all, three brass and four copper plates.

> The brass plates are circular, very thin, and are, respectively about twelve, fourteen, and eighteen inches in diameter. The middle sized one has two letters (or rather a double letter) near its centre, about one-fourth of an inch in length; thus /E very well executed as if done by a stamp. This was the only appearance of writing which I could discern on any of them.

> The four copper plates (or strips) are from four to six inches in width, and from one and a half to two feet in length. There is nothing remarkable about them. Like the brass plates, they are very thin, and appear as if they had been cut out of some copper kettle or other vessel.[9]

Swanton wrote in 1914 that the plates had been kept in a box back of the mico's seat. At that time he talked to the chief of the town about them and was told that even the chief could not handle them without becoming sick. The ethnologist wrote that "when I drew outlines of the plates from my memory of Adair's figures he recommended that I tear them up and throw them away or ill would certainly befall me before I got home."[10]

One day, after I knew Chief Brown's relationship to the town of Tukabatchee, I asked him if he had ever seen the famous Tukabatchee plates. "Oh, yes," he said quite casually without elaboration. I could not gather sufficient courage to ask if he knew where they were at that time.

The Shawano were leaders in a secret organization known in the nineteenth century as the Order of the Four Roads which accepted members on an individual basis and provided training contributing to the intellectual and physical growth of the neophyte. Women were accepted as members. This organization was similar to the Freemasons in so many details that many people thought it had been patterned on this order. It was known to exist among some forty tribes and related to the Great Medicine Society which had members throughout the Algonquin and Siouan tribes of the old Northwest.

Knowing I was a Mason, Chief Brown spoke to me about the secret organizations of which the Yuchis had been part in greater detail than he would have otherwise. Nevertheless, what he had to say in this regard was carefully weighed and imparted only to the limited extent he felt absolutely necessary for me to understand the role of these organizations in tribal relationships. More precisely, perhaps, he told me only enough to allow me to learn more on my own.

On several occasions he told me bits of information from which, augmented with details I have since learned elsewhere, the following narration can be pieced. Chief Samuel W. Brown, Sr. led a company of Yuchi men to join the Union Army after the band of Confederate renegades known as Quantrell's Raiders attacked the Yuchi settlement, destroyed many of their homes, stole their horses

---

[8] Swanton, "Social Organization," 506.

[9] Henry R. Schoolcraft, *Information Respecting the History, Condition, and Prospects of the Indian Tribes of the United States: Collected and Prepared under the Direction of the Bureau of Indian Affairs per Act of Congress of March 3, 1847*, 6 Vols. (Philadelphia: Lippencott, Grambo & Co., 1853–1857), vol. III, pp. 87–90.

[10] Swanton, "Social Organization," 510.

and other property and killed some of the people including Brown's mother, Suttah. The Yuchi leader was commissioned a captain in the U. S. Army. While in the Army he became acquainted with several Masons and joined that order. After the end of the war, Brown was one of a small group of Masons to organize the first lodge of the order in what was to become Oklahoma.

One day Chief Brown visited the Columbus Museum. C. Dexter Jordan, chairman of the museum board of directors, was showing him his treasured three-volume original edition of the McKenny and Hall *History of the American Indians* with its magnificent lithographs printed in the 1840's from portraits of Indian leaders who had visited Washington from time to time since Thomas Jefferson's administration. The Yuchi chief obviously enjoyed seeing them and studying the clothing and accessories of the subjects. He pointed out the portrait of Timpoochee Barnard to me.

The portraits of the Creek chiefs held his attention for a long time as he commented on leaders whom his father had known personally, including *Opothleyoholo* and *Manawah*

He turned the pages commenting on such things as face paint and ear ornaments. He said some people were shown with too much paint or in incorrect configuration. Others had several silver tear-drop pendants hanging from the rims of their ears when they "should have had only three." Mr.

Portrait of Timpoochee Barnard from McKenney and Hall.

TIMPOOCHEE BARNARD
AN UCHEE WARRIOR.

PUBLISHED BY F. W. GREENOUGH, PHILAD

Jordan and I watched and listened intently to this remarkable demonstration of traditional knowledge. Eventually the chief lingered over one page for a while. He looked to see if I was watching. He pointed to the page saying: "This man is wearing everything just as he should. Read about him when you have time." I did so and this is what I read:

> TAIOMAH. at the head of a secret society which has long existed among the Sauks and Foxes, and may be considered a national institution. The meetings of this body are in a spacious lodge erected for this purpose, the entrance to which is guarded by a sentinel, who admits none but the initiated. They are understood to have a ceremony of initiation which is solemn and protracted, and a secret that may not be divulged without fatal consequences. Candidates for admission are subjected to careful trial and scrutiny, and none are received but such as give undoubted evidence of courage and prudence. Women are eligible to membership . . .

> They have a peculiar dress, and a mode of painting, and like our Freemasons, from whom the order may have been derived, exhibit themselves to the public in costume on certain great occasions . . . . When a young man proposes to join this society, he applies to a member to propose and vouch for him. This application is communicated to the head man of the Order, who in a few days, returns the answer, which is simply affirmative or negative, without reason or explanation.

> If accepted, the candidate is directed to prepare himself. Of this preparation we have no knowledge, but we are told that a probation of one year is imposed previous to the initiation. The society is sometimes called the great medicine of the Sauks and Foxes; it is said to embrace four roads or degrees—something is to be done or learned to gain the first degree; a further progress or proficiency leads to the second and so on. Admission is said to cost forty or fifty dollars, and every subsequent step in the four roads is attended with some expense. There are few who have attained the honors of the fourth road.

> These particulars have been gathered in conversation with intelligent Indians, and embrace all that is properly known, or, rather, believed, on this curious subject. The traders have offered large bribes for the purpose of obtaining information in regard to the mysteries of the society, but these temptations and the promises of secrecy failed alike to lead to any disclosures. Many of the tribes have similar institutions.[11]

Following his October 1957 visit to Columbus, Chief Brown prepared a tape-recorded statement thanking the people of Columbus for their kindness and hospitality to himself, his daughter, and nephew. In this he referred to the time when there was "no Alabama, Georgia, Mississippi, . . . only one people." He said this had been the case when the Yuchis lived in this area. In fact, he said, "this was true of all the eastern seaboard states long ago with many people living together as one people." Here he was referring to the socio-religious inter-tribal confederation described above in this chapter as it existed before its destruction by the raiding Iroquois in the mid-seventeenth century. This sad episode will be dealt with more adequately in a subsequent chapter.

In another tape made about the same time Brown spoke of his ancestors' having come from the Bahama Islands. He told the story in these words:

> I heard many times from the older people who have handed down to me the story of a people that were known by a different name than they are known today—the Yuchi people. They were called, back in ancient days in their own way, *Zoyaha* people. They said that there was a great black fire that came from the west and destroyed everything in the path for sixty miles in width or more; and that they saw another one. There were three of these fires; the first one was from the east and the other one from the north. After this black one from the west came through and destroyed everything, they took the north that the east one would guide them to safety. And

---

[11] Thomas L. McKenney and James Hall, *History of the Indian Tribes of North America with Biographical Sketches and anecdotes of the Principal Chiefs. Embellished with one Hundred Twenty Portraits, from the Indian Gallery in the Department of War, at Washington*, 3 Vols. (Philadelphia: Published by D. Rice and A. N. Hart, 1855) pp. 29–30.

Taiomah, a Musquakee brave, head of the Order of the Four Roads. McKenny and Hall lithograph, courtesy Thornton F. Jordan.

they landed through this place where they were cut off from the mainland of where they were going north; and that's where they landed.

Dorothy Brown was helping her father make this tape. She asked him, "Where do you think they were located when this thing came about?" His reply was:

Well, it seems like today it would be on the Bahama Islands or the Andros Islands, not far from what would be the Everglades of Florida now. And after they established themselves there for some time, they builded their sacred grounds, in the terms of today, worship grounds.

I had not known him very long before I came to understand that Chief Brown did not waste time on small talk, that the comments he made, seeming purely to entertain, and the stories he related that appeared intended for amusement were all carefully selected to elucidate some subject he wanted his listeners to know in greater detail. Sometimes the connection between the story and its intended import was not clear, however. Sometimes the moral seemed purposely obscured so it required conscious effort. Knowing this, I made mental and, when possible, written notes of what seemed even the most inconsequential of the old chief's comments.

One good example of an apparently unassociated comment of Brown's which became meaningful to me later concerned the blossom of the dogwood tree. In a conversation which I believed to be intended to answer questions from me, I asked if he could tell me something about the town of *Cutifachechi* where DeSoto met the lady ruler.

To my surprise, the question appeared to be ignored as the Chief pointed to one of the handsome black leather boots he was wearing. I saw they had embossed floral designs on the sides.

"Do you know this flower?" He asked.

"It's a dogwood," I replied.

A story followed in which my friend told of having the boots made at a fine shop in San Antonio. "I am very fond of dogwoods," he explained, "So I told the young man taking my order that I wanted these blossoms on my boots. He had no idea what I was talking about, so I had to draw them for him."

I looked closely and admired the boots and designs, commenting that the Chief had done a fine job drawing dogwoods. With that the conversation ended, apparently without my question being answered. The conversation passed to another subject and the identity of the sixteenth century town was left undetermined.

Later, my long-time friend, Rufus George, was helping me design an exhibit on Yuchi culture in the Columbus Museum. He suggested a frieze of dogwood blossoms. "What is the significance of this bloom," I asked him.

"You have seen the sacred fire on the Square Ground," he told me. "That is the King's Ground and the fire is the mother of all the other fires. The dogwood blossom shows the four sections of the white circle which the four logs create and the red center of the flower represents the fire itself." Suddenly, the symbolism and the identity of Cutifachechi were both clear to me. The identity was further confirmed when I read John R.; Swanton's statement that the name, which he considered to have belonged to the Cussetas, had something to do with *dogwood*.

The Cussetas were close to the Yuchis in association and friendship, although not in cultural or ethnic heritage. By their own account the Yuchi town of Apalachicola adopted them when they came into the Southeast in relatively recent times. In one of his taped statements, Chief Brown declared unequivocally that these were the only people to whom the Yuchis ever gave all their seven medicines. In this same taped conversation he left no room to doubt the close association between his people and the Cussetas. He said:

> I want to mention here that there are some things that I think and believe truly from the older people that spoke the languages. Fortunately, I happen to know some of them and one is about the connection of the Cussetas and the Yuchis. Their history I believe I know pretty well from the older people. They were friends in the early days in that country. You will find them allied together most everywhere you look on the map and they were friends when they went west and also friends until today. The Yuchis adopted these people into their ceremonial grounds and they're the only tribe of all the different tribes that ever had a right to use any part of our medicines that were given to them by our Yuchi people.

Chief Brown always spoke of the Cussetas with fondness and it was in their church that he directed his funeral be held. This, he said was because "everyone, the Creeks and Yuchis, the Christians and non-Christians," who wished to come would feel welcome there.

A story of Chief Brown's concerning the Cussetas illustrates the relationship of various sacred fires to the fire of the Yuchis. He said that on two occasions these people had let their fire go out. Both times a group of the younger men had wanted to relight the fire and keep it going. It was the Yuchi chief's obligation to help them, so they had come to ask Chief Brown to kindle their fire and teach them what they must know to maintain it. Both times, they became careless in a few years and let it go out. Eventually another group got together and came to Chief Brown for help. "I went with them," Brown related, "and helped them get the fire going. This time I got them together and lectured to them on the absolute need not to lose it again. This is the last time I will be able to help you," he told them . . . "I won't be here next time."

A somewhat similar story concerned the Cherokee Green Corn ceremony:

"It was about 1917 soon after my father had turned the chief's seat over to me. Several of the older Cherokee men in one of their settlements came to see me and asked for help in getting the Green Corn ceremony going again. I was interested in knowing more about the Cherokees and their history, so I agreed to go and help them. I had a new Ford automobile, so, on the day they were to meet, I drove over the bumpiest road I had ever seen to the place they had told me to come.

"I finally arrived and found several of the old men sitting in the area they had cleared to serve as the dance ground. Eventually more came and I got them together to decide how we were going to proceed. I asked if anyone knew the songs to accompany the ceremony. One or two of them knew some parts of each, but nobody knew all of the songs. I knew that they had once known them and the rituals that accompanied them, but they had long since been forgotten.

"There was not time to teach them how to do everything, even if I had known the Cherokee Green Corn songs. There had to be a fire, so I improvised. 'Get the matches,' I told them. We got the fire going and I led them round and round the fire and we had a sort of Green Corn ceremony."

In writing this chapter, I have tested my own memory to determine just how much and how accurately I am able to remember details from statements by the Yuchi chief I heard more than thirty years ago. Admittedly, they were more memorable and were much more forcibly impressed on my consciousness than remarks heard in everyday, casual conversation. Also, I have been able to reinforce my memory through notes made at the time, letters from Brown and his daughter, Dorothy, tape recordings, and other means. The result has been that I am convinced that human memory is a highly efficient instrument for storing and recalling information. My memory has proved accurate in the instances I have been able to check it against the written or recorded version of specific data. Thus, I believe it is reasonably so in instances in which verification is not available. Encouraged by this assumption, I am offering additional bits of history Chief Brown imparted to me incidentally as well as purposely, but of which I now have no other record except memory or, in some instances, the inclusion of the information in *The Secret* from memory a decade ago.

The fact that the Yuchis had "always" had cows, bees, chickens, sweet potatoes, and peaches seemed beyond doubt in Chief Brown's mind. It seemed, also, that he was convinced that I should be aware of this in order to refute statements to the contrary that permeated the published material on the Southeastern peoples generally. He emphasized this belief on several occasions and usually in a very effective manner. The cow's skull atop the ball pole on the sacred ceremonial ground demonstrated the presence of cattle in precolumbian times. My suggestion that this must have been a buffalo's skull in earlier times, brought a sharp retort that the Yuchis had *always* known the difference between a cow and a buffalo.

The bee was no less important in the chief's understanding of Yuchi culture. He informed me that it had important symbolic meaning and there is a tape in the Columbus College archives collection on which he told of his delight at seeing bees on the bank of Yuchi creek as he sat in the sun one day and thought of his ancestors who had lived there. Bees in the intricate beadwork on the belt in the Columbus Museum which Sakasenney wore to Oklahoma in 1836 signify their importance to the Yuchis.[12]

It was not true, the chief knew, that all the foods that had become traditional with Yuchis had been part of their diet before European contact. "Who were the German people who came to live near the Yuchis on the Savannah River?" he asked me one day. "The old people said they were friendly and kind and gave us the cabbage."

---

[12] Mahan, *The Secret*, 27.

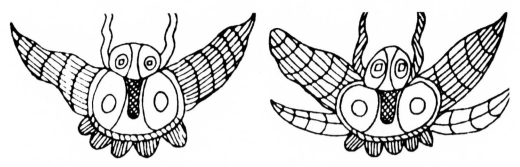

The Bee in Southeastern art: design from Mississipian Period pottery vessel. (Sun Circles, Pl. 36).

Stylized insects (bees?) on beaded belt worn concealed under his shirt by Sakasenney on the forced trek to Oklahoma in 1836, now in the Columbus Museum. Columbus Museum photo.

The Bee in Minoan art. A gold ornament showing bees in a style clearly resembling those from the Southeast. Photo, Arthur Evans, Palace of Minos.

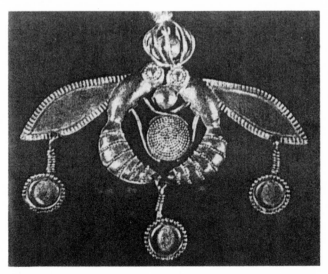

"Those were the Salzburgers," I told him. Their role in Georgia history is well known. I did not know until much later the intimate association these peaceful Austrian Protestants had for a while with the Yuchis. Only in 1980 did I learn this with the publication of the journal of one of their number, Philip Georg Fredrich von Reck.[13]

The chief knew from direct, unbroken tradition the nature and scope of the priestly organization, the Order of the Four Roads, among his people. He stated emphatically, however, that he could not and would not attempt to explain the intricacies of a body of knowledge so vast that in learning it the old priests and medicine men had literally spent a long lifetime of study and hard work. He said he could only relate generalities and principles which would serve as guides for anyone—future generations of his own people or whomever—wishing to undertake the arduous task of understanding the full scope and philosophical implications. Speaking of the manner in which the traditional knowledge was organized and learned by neophytes, called "hunters," Chief Brown said:

They had about 136 degrees, out of all the things of the woods, the prairies and they simplified it down to thirty-six degrees and that's what I had to learn. Some of them never learned it. They got it down to twelve and that represented the eagle with his twelve tail-feathers.

---

[13] Kristian Hvidt, ed., *Voyage, Drawings, and Journal of Philip Georg Fredrich von Reck* (Savannah: Bee Hive Press, 1980).

Chapter 3

Written and Oral History

Much of the history Chief Brown related centered around locations and events of 1835 and 1836 involving the forced expatriation of the Yuchis from eastern Alabama, the last remnant of their ancient domain in the Southeast. His remarkable familiarity with this tragic period in the history of his people had resulted from time he spent as a youth with his great-uncle, *Sakasenney* or Little Bear, the brother of his paternal grandmother, *Suttah*. Little Bear described localities that were important to the Yuchis and those associated with the removal in such vivid detail sixty years after he had last seen them that his young listener was able to locate and recognize them after another sixty years had passed.

These scenes included the "horseshoe-shaped" falls on Yuchi Creek with a stone fish trap at their foot[1] and the high, cliff-like banks of blue and white marle a quarter of a mile downstream.[2] Included also was the site of Fort Mitchell within the stockade walls of which Sakasenney and the other "hostiles" were incarcerated after they surrendered to the soldiers and were awaiting departure. At Fort Mitchell also is the old military cemetery where Timpoochee Barnard is buried. I eventually learned he was Chief Brown's collateral ancestor as well as the namesake of the Mahan collie.

When the day came for their departure, Sakasenney and the other captives marched eighty miles to Montgomery to be herded aboard a steamboat for the torturous voyage down the Alabama to Mobile, thence along the Gulf shore to New Orleans and then up the Mississippi and Arkansas to Fort Smith. There those who survived were put aground to make any way they could the last leg of their journey one hundred miles west to the area assigned them on the Canadian River. The Columbus newspaper reported that:

> On Saturday last, about twelve hundred of these deluded beings, who have surrendered or been taken prisoners, left Fort Mitchell for Arkansas, many of them in chains, and all guarded by a detachment of United States soldiers. They will go by land to Montgomery, where they will take shipping to their destined homes.[3]

On his two trips to Alabama in 1957, Chief Brown visited all of these sites and told me of events associated with them that he had heard in his youth. He told how the Yuchis had fought hardest of any of the people who had desperately tried to defend their homes in the "Creek War," during the late spring and summer of 1836. He had been told that the men and boys made their final stand in the area between the Big and Little Yuchi creeks, and that they had taken the sacred medicines for

---

[1] Because they were located in an inaccessible wooded area, Chief Brown was unable to visit these falls on his first visit to the area in June 1957. When the owner of the property, Hillery R. Mott, learned of the impending second visit of the venerable chief the following October, he had a road cut through the woods for more than a mile from his home to the base of the cascade. When the Chief came to visit him on that second visit, Mr. Mott had a sofa placed in the bed of his pickup truck and Chief Brown, his daughter Dorothy, and Mrs. Mott rode to the falls in genuine comfort.

[2] These are the high banks at the foot of which Chief Brown was told certain ceremonial items were buried. After his death, friends he had made in Alabama and Georgia formed the "Coweta Memorial Association," the purpose of which was to purchase this landmark and 100 acres of ground adjacent to it where the Chief had said the last ceremonies were held in the area. This was done and presented to the Yuchi Tribe as a memorial to their late chief and the members of their tribe who defended the spot so valiantly in June 1836. Three bus loads of Yuchis came from Oklahoma for the ceremonies on the site on Sunday, June 8, 1958, at which local community leaders presented the deed for the land to Samuel H. Brown, nephew of the Chief, who accepted it on behalf of the tribe. The land is still being held for use on behalf of all Yuchis.

[3] The Columbus *Enquirer*, July 7, 1836.

Hillery R. Mott signs deed to the 100-acre tract of land presented to the Yuchi people in memory of Chief Brown, June 1958. Onlookers are (l to r) Joseph Mahan, Roy L. Smith, president of the Coweta Memorial Association, purchaser, and Mrs. Mott. (Columbus Ledger-Enquirer).

the last time in the East on the flat area at the top of the marle banks on Yuchi creek. When the ceremony ended, Chief Brown said, the people responsible for them buried their ceremonial items at the base of the cliff as it had become clear that there was no way to escape. Capture of the Yuchi "hold-outs" is recounted in the Columbus *Enquirer* (June 25, 1836).

The recorded history of the last days of the Yuchis in their old homeland resides principally in files of the Columbus newspaper for the years 1835 and 1836 and in records of the United States War Department for the same period in the National Archives. These were the months when events climaxed as the result of tensions that had been building for more than twenty years, following the War of 1812. The Treaty of Ghent, signed January 1815, established that the United States was the dominant power in the American Southeast, militarily, commercially, and politically. No longer were American ambitions in the region to be restrained in any way by the British, the French, or the Spanish, although four additional years were required to convince the Spanish to "sell" Florida to the United States. After that, the Indians posed the only deterrent and it was generally believed in the South that they constituted only a temporary obstacle to the westward march of the American frontier.

A decade earlier Thomas Jefferson had grown keenly interested in the Old Southwest (Gulf States and Mississippi Valley) as the result of his skillfully orchestrated purchase of the vast Louisiana Territory from Napoleon. In his characteristic blend of intellectual idealism and political practicality, he conceived a plan for transporting the Indian tribes of the region to territories west of the Mississippi. There, he believed, they could continue to live in accordance with their native culture free from contaminating influences of Caucasian Americans. Whatever its theoretical merit, Jefferson's plan had no chance of effective implementation at any time or even of being undertaken for a quarter of a century.

The powerful Cherokee tribe, soon to develop into a "nation within a nation," the Creek Confederacy, and the Chickasaws and Choctaws were rapidly adopting the tools and way of life of their European-American neighbors and attaching themselves ever more firmly to their ancestral lands, comprising in Jefferson's time the Tennessee River drainage in East Tennessee, the Appalachian mountains in western North Carolina, all of Georgia except the area east of the Oconee and Ocmulgee rivers, all of the later Alabama territory except a small area around Mobile, and the Territory of Mississippi along the Gulf of Mexico and the Mississippi delta to the mouth of the Yazoo river.

Georgia was the first state to put into effect a plan to require the Federal Government to assume responsibility for removing the resident natives from their lands within her borders and thus encourage the implementation of Jefferson's visionary resettlement program. There was little chance to put it into effect, however, except for the Convention of 1802 between Georgia and the Federal Government. Under the terms of this agreement, signed at Milledgeville, the State Capital, Georgia ceded to the Central Government all her claims to the lands in the future states of Alabama and Mississippi. Dating from the original charter of George II to the Colony of Georgia, the land comprised the approximate northern one third of each. In return, the United States assumed claims against the state growing out of the fraudulent sale of land within this territory, agreed that the western boundary of the state would be the "high water mark on the western bank of the Chattahoochee river," and promised to remove the remaining Indian tribes from within Georgia borders as soon as it could be "reasonably done under peaceable terms."

In fulfillment of the latter condition, the United States acquired two tracts by treaties with the Creeks in 1802 and 1804, but no more during Jefferson's administration. His successors for the ensuing twenty years felt less than enthusiastic over the idea of removing the Indians by force from land that had been the home of their people for centuries. Justification for removal weakened as the result of Christian missions to the major tribes. Beginning with one to the Cherokees undertaken by the North Carolina Moravians in 1801, the missionaries spread the virtues and handicrafts of "civilization" among the increasingly receptive subjects of their efforts.

The only people to put the migration plan into effect during Jefferson's administration were a small group of Cherokees who migrated to Texas in 1805 in the belief independent of the President, that their lot would be better with the Spanish than with their new Anglo-American neighbors in the Southern Appalachians. The other tribes had no intention of migrating or even of surrendering more land to the encroaching Americans. The same was true of the powerful Shawnee and their Algonquin allies in the Old Northwest Territory beyond the Ohio.

The native tribes took encouragement from the presence of friendly Spanish and British traders in Florida and British influence issuing from Canada. Many of their number seized the opportunity to annihilate the unwelcome intruders on their ancestral lands and joined forces with the British when the War of 1812 broke out. The result of this war, which ended in 1815, was the withdrawal of the British from the Southeast and transferral of their Canadian trading activities to the land west of the Lakes. The French no longer controlled the vast Louisiana Territory. Their position in Florida had so weakened that the Spanish sold the territory to the United States in 1819 and left the Indians to defend themselves against the Americans.

The Southern tribes had attempted to remain neutral when the war began in 1812. The Shawnees, Sauks and Foxes, Miami, and other Algonquins of the trans-Ohio region were not so inclined, however. The Shawnee leader Ticumseh undertook to organize a pan-Indian alliance extending from the Great Lakes to the Gulf of Mexico strong enough to destroy the American settlements west of the Alleghenies. He was not successful to the degree he had hoped, but a large contingent of the Creeks, Yuchis, Seminoles, and Cherokees formed the "Red Stick" party and prepared themselves for war against the Americans and any Indians who might be allied with them.

They were soundly defeated by forces from Tennessee and Georgia supported by contingents of Cherokees and Creeks at the Battle of Horseshoe Bend in 1814 and were forced to relinquish a large area of tribal lands across southern Georgia between the Altamaha and Chattahoochee Rivers. This seventy-mile-wide stretch of "Pine Barrens" was intended as a barrier between the Indians and whichever European power might eventually obtain Florida.

Meanwhile, without resorting to war, the Georgians had managed to have the Federal Government negotiate a series of treaties with the confederated Muskogean tribes and the Cherokees in compliance with the Agreement of 1802. By 1819, when the Cherokees let go an area east of the Chattahoochee in Northeast Georgia, the Creeks controlled only the Georgia land between the Ocmulgee and Chattahoochee Rivers and the Cherokees that portion of the state north and west of the latter river. There the Cherokee boundary remained until the final cession of all tribal lands under the 1835 Treaty of New Echota.

The Creeks relinquished their remaining lands within the State in the 1821 and 1825 treaties at Indian Springs, the latter of which President John Quincy Adams declared fraudulent. A tense situation resulted when Georgia Gov. George M. Troup, ordered the state surveyors to proceed to lay out lots in a small section which Georgia claimed that was not included in the treaty. The governor's orders defied the President's threat to send the Army to arrest them if they entered the disputed region. This impasse was resolved by the consolatory intervention of several Congressmen and Senators who arranged for the President to call all concerned parties to Washington to sign a new treaty which would include the disputed territory. This was done and the Treaty of Washington of 1826 resulted.[4]

The Creeks involved, including many Yuchi families, moved across the Chattahoochee into territory that, presumably, was to be theirs in perpetuity. The home abandoned by one of the Yuchi families at this time is now relocated in Westville Village. It was the home of the Wells family for almost 150 years after the original owners were forced away following the Treaty of Indian Springs of 1825. In 1975, members of this family gave it to the Georgia living history museum to preserve as a unique historic relic. They had retained the word-of-mouth history of the traditional-style structure and the significant information that it was part of a Yuchi settlement known as "King's Town."

The 1826 migrants to Alabama settled into communities and cleared individual farms to begin life as farmers in the general style of their intruding neighbors. The situation lasted until the Creek Treaty of 1832 was signed on March 24 of that year. This pact ostensibly was intended to help the Creeks and Yuchis safeguard improvements they had made on tribal lands held in common and make it easier to take up the ways of "civilization."

The treaty provided allotments of 320 acres to each head of a family and 640 acres to each of the tribe's "chiefs and headmen." The individual reserves were located so that members of the same tribal division, called a "town," could live together on a compact body of land which would include their improvements. The treaty guaranteed the confederacy against intrusions on its lands and against forcible removal. Lands not included in the individual allotments could, presumably, be occupied by white settlers, but the allotted lands provided a permanent home for all native residents who did not choose to sell their allotments.

The shamelessly illegal but ingenious deals, conspiracies, and circumventions devised and put into operation by land speculators to obtain possession of the Indian allotments involved connivance of politicians in the adjacent states of Georgia and Alabama, forced the somewhat reluctant cooperation of the Federal Government and Army, and methodically provoked the Indians into

---

[4] Kenneth Coleman, ed., *A History of Georgia* (Athens: The University of Georgia Press, 1977), p. 100. (Map of the various Georgia cessions).

attacks on encroaching settlers. In four years' time these efforts succeeded. The frustrated, desperate Indians had been forced into a "war," which would justify their "conquest" and forcible removal to join their kinsmen already in the Arkansas Territory.

Mary Elizabeth Young researched the foregoing details and vividly narrated these shameful events a century and a quarter later in her book, *Redskins, Ruffleshirts, and Rednecks*.[5] This revealing book, which became available three years after Chief Brown's death, substantiated details he knew about the period from the stories related to him by Little Bear and other eyewitnesses.

Young did not relate one story that the Chief told me asking that it not be mentioned during the peacemaking ceremony in 1957. He did not want to rouse old antagonisms unnecessarily, he said. The story concerned the hanging of his two great-uncles, *Sincohah* and *Tisoso*, the brothers of Brown's grandmother, *Suttah*, which has already been mentioned above.

One day many years after hearing of the episode, I was reading typescripts of stories from the Columbus *Enquirer* by Joseph Peddy bound into a volume , *The Creek War, 1835-1837*. Under December 1, 1836, I read the following verification of the story Chief Brown heard from his great-uncle and relayed to me.

Six Creek Indians were hung in Girard, Alabama, on Friday last, convicted at the last term of Russell Superior Court for murder etc. The Indian who killed young Fannin some months ago, and a Chief, were included in the number. The Chief declared that the others were innocent, but that he was guilty of the charges preferred against him; he however acted in accordance with instructions given him by Neah-Emarthla and Neah-Micco, who it will be recollected have been permitted to go unpunished, and are now safely and quietly reposing in the forests of Arkansas. They met their fate with what might be termed true Indian philosophy, having sung several songs & given the well known "whoop" before taking the fearful leap. We have been told by those who witnessed the scene, that it was one of an effecting character, and well calculated to draw forth the sympathies of the white man in behalf of these deluded and unhappy people.[6]

The chief who was executed that November day in 1836 was *Tisoso*, or "Flint." He was also *Zopathla*, a position which he inherited through his father, Casenney Barnard who migrated to Arkansas in 1832. It was Barnard's wife, Yupaha, through whom Barnard's descendants inherited the right to the title "Birdtail King." Her brother was *Fus- Hudgee Micco*, "Bird-tail King," who died in 1862 while in the Union Army serving in the Indian contingent led by *Opothleyoholo*. In 1867 Samuel W. Brown, the son of *Suttah*, the sister of Tisoso and the niece of the latest *Fushudgee*, assumed the role and titles of "Sun King" and "Bird Tail King."

---

[5] Mary Elizabeth Young, *Redskins, Ruffleshirts, and Rednecks, Indian Allotments in Alabama and Mississippi* (Norman: University of Oklahoma Press, 1961),pp.73—113.

[6] The Columbus *Enquirer*, December 1, 1836.

Chapter 4

History Written on the Sacred Ground

"If you learn the meaning of everything on the Square Ground, you will find that nothing has been lost; all you need to know in order to understand our history is written on the sacred Ground in the ceremonies we carry on there."

These words spoken by Chief Samuel Brown, Jr. in 1957 have remained true. Now, as then, the two delineated squares lie side by side to form a rectangle bordered by a low earth ridge which has grown from the accumulation of the dirt scraped from the ground in July each year to make the surface smooth and clean for the ceremonies which accompany the kindling of the new fire. One square lies to the east of the other. In the center of this is an earthen mound in the shape of a flattened cone about five feet in height. In the center of the western square is the spot on which the sacred fire burns for the duration of eight days and nights of ceremonies and during those held at other times each year. In the centers of the south, west, and north sides of this square stand the bough-roofed pole frames called "arbors" covering the seats occupied by the men and boys when they are not actively engaged in the dances and rituals that comprise the ceremonies. Nothing of its physical form has changed in centuries, perhaps millennia! Thus, it seems believable that little of its meaning has been lost either.

So great a degree of continuity in any ceremonial activity, which must depend on the cooperating effort of many individuals, comes only from their shared devotion to whatever is the central purpose of the activities. In the case of the Yuchi the motivating aim is to assure the well-being of their people which is inextricably dependent upon the preservation of the sacred fire and the ceremonies and beliefs surrounding it. The requisite devotion results from understanding of and belief in this purpose and the conviction that it is worthy of continuation. It has been clearly apparent to me that this is true of the several families who have maintained the King's Ground near Kellyville, Oklahoma during the more than thirty years I have visited there periodically.

Maintaining this ground requires more than simply keeping the place clean, repairing the arbors, and replacing their leafy covers each year. There is an encircling ring of fifteen similar, somewhat larger structures of poles and tree limbs which, augmented by canvas tents, are the temporary Square Ground maintenance of; residences of these families for the eight days of ceremonies. These must be maintained also. This is only a small part of what is required. Living as they do subject to twentieth century American economy, family members must meet the demands of jobs, maintain their regular households, shop for groceries, and transport equipment and supplies to and from the Ground.

All of this is much more time consuming and infinitely more expensive than it was thirty years ago. Moreover, there is more cost than of feeding a family and visiting relatives at an extended series of day-long outdoor picnics. There is the traditional obligation to feed all visitors who may happen to arrive on the premises and make them welcome. The principal motivation for participating families to make this effort every year is a strong belief in the ancient Yuchi teaching handed down through numberless generations that the sacred fire must be maintained for the good health and well-being of the people and to save it "to relight the sun at some future time of trouble when it will go out."

Through three decades since I first visited there, inevitable changes have occurred: we have all grown older and Yuchi leaders have left their responsibilities to younger people who, in turn have passed them on to a still younger generation. Many of the people I have known through the years are no longer living. Evidence of change in the age and status of the individuals through so long a period dramatically appears when the lines form on the ceremonial square each year into the human chain that winds its way through the intricate designs of the ritual "dances."

The long Yuchi line being led by Melvin George (l) and Calgowee Littlebear about 1985. . (ISAC Research Center photo).

Above: Constructing the ceremonial arbors on the Yuchi Ground in Alabama, June 1963. (Columbus Ledger-Enquirer*).*

Right: Erecting the ball pole on the Yuchi Ground in Alabama, June 1963. (Columbus Ledger-Enquirer*).*

When I saw this chain for the first time, in 1960, I was impressed by the systematic manner in which the lines formed with the younger people following their elders from the chief of the ground and his helper at the head to children as young as three years following at the end of the line. I recognized that this was no chance order but the result of a longstanding pattern. I was no less impressed in 1990 when I saw even longer lines forming in precisely the same manner. The startling truth was that the children of the earlier year were now near the head of the line, some leading it on occasion.

The three men, Rufus George, George Watashe, and Albert Rolland, who served as my principal mentors on my early visits to Kellyville, informed me that the pattern of younger people following those more knowledgeable than they was not accidental. This was the way neophytes learned, they said. Without ever saying so explicitly, my teachers conveyed the idea that I should do likewise when I took part in the ceremonies. They told me that this line was in fact an unbroken chain of Yuchis, each one linking hands to people older and younger, which extended backward in time to Creation and is intended to reach indefinitely into the future—truly an effective means of assuring cultural continuity!

In those earlier years I took my place near the end of the line. When I could, I followed someone who demonstrated mastery of cadence, form, and verbal content and imitated these as exactly as possible without any knowledge of meaning or understanding which came more slowly than would have been the case had I participated in the rituals since childhood and meanwhile been exposed to other aspects of Yuchi culture. Albeit slowly, my awareness grew appreciably nonetheless.

From time to time, one or another of the three men who seemed to have assumed responsibility for helping me learn would make a casual statement on the order of, "This is the King's Ground," "The arbors are covered with willow when we are able to get it," or "You should read the twenty-third chapter of Leviticus." I took due note of these comments and read the Bible passage. Having done so, I was convinced that Jehovah had indeed admonished the Hebrews to observe an annual religious ceremony that was the same as the one in which I had been participating with the Yuchis. This conclusion strengthened when I read that the Chosen People were to reside in tabernacles or booths for eight days. I had no doubt remaining when I remembered joining the men and boys on a sortee into the woods to cut a small tree to shoulder as I followed a serpentine line in the "Lizard Dance" with which the series of events opens at nightfall the evening before the "Day Dances." At times during the ritual we held our leafy burdens over our heads and shook them violently. In Leviticus I read: "And ye shall take in the first day the boughs of goodly trees . . . and ye shall rejoice before the Lord your God seven days."

At times when I appeared to be ready more elemental theological information forthcame from my mentors. I soon realized, however, that this was only when two of them were together and never by one alone. I knew that maintaining this safeguard is a practice common to those entrusted with esoteric information. So I was pleased at the confidence they evidently had in my integrity and ability to learn. I was also reassured in my faith in the accuracy of the information preserved in the oral tradition of the Yuchis.

At last I comprehended:

1. The two squares together represent the earth and the sky, the union of which is basic to the Yuchi religion.

2. The eastern square is the earth and the central mound is the "mound of emergence," from which came the children of Mother Earth and to which they return at death.

3. The western square is the place of the sky-dwelling spirit which is present in the sacred fire and is represented by the sun in the daytime and the moon at night. The circle around an equilateral cross, at the center of which the fire flames, is the symbol by which this spirit is represented here as it has been in many eras and many places.

Left: Design on a Mississippian period pottery vessel duplicates precisely the figure traced by the dancers in the Yuchi rituals of opening and closing the door into the spirit world. (Funderburk, Sun Circles and Human Hands, *Pl. 34.*

Made in the shape of a running feline, this ceremonial axe from Crete is decorated with the spiral design common in Minoan art. (Reproduced from Evans Palace of Minos*).*

Right: Dog effigy vessel excavated in 1936 from a site within the city of Columbus by Isabel Garrard Patterson is decorated with the same spiral pattern painted on its two sides. (Columbus Museum photo).

4. The designs formed by the human chains in the rituals are intended to be seen from above. From this perspective they convey meaning that is apparent to anyone knowledgeable in Yuchi traditions. For example, some of the dances wind into a tight spiral and then reverse as the line retraces its circular route to return to a straight line. At the beginning of the ceremony on the day the new fire is started, the line makes its way to each corner of the eastern square where it traces this intricate pattern as participants repeat the "whoop" or spirit call. This is the ceremony of "opening the door," presumably to allow spirits of departed Yuchis to join the ceremony. The dance is repeated without whoops at the completion of the night dances at dawn on the following morning. This time it is called "closing the door." The spirits are returned to their place of abode in another realm to await next year's call by their living descendants.

This intertwined spiral is the design painted on the sides of the dog effigy pottery vessels found with several burials excavated from the Bull Creek site in Columbus and on the Flint River near Butler, Georgia. Four excellent examples of these vessels are now on exhibit in the Columbus Museum. It is difficult not to conclude that the pottery designs also symbolize the path into and out of the spirit world. The liklihood of this being true is strengthened by the association with the dog. Canines traditionally have led souls into the underworld in many cultures, notably in Egypt where the jackel god Anubis performed this function.

It is worthy of notice that this precise design appears on painted pottery made on the island of Crete during a long period designated Minoan II and III.[1]

In another of the chain designs repeated at various times during both day and night ceremonies, the line circles the fire until it forms a multi-ring spiral around the central cross and circle which surround the fire. This is a design often seen on Mississippian period pottery, as is the in-and-out, continuous spiral described above. The significance of this design as a symbol representing the Yuchis is clear. It contains their continuous human chain centering on the spirit in the sacred fire. Use of the design was widespread on ceremonial pottery during the archaeologically defined period.[2]

Much of the recorded history of the Sky-Earth people is no doubt present in such physical features as the tall "ball pole," which stands southeast of the ceremonial ground with a cow's skull mounted on top. This emblematic object strongly suggests in context that it represents the earth awaiting a union with the sun. It is suggestive of the cow goddess of pre-Sumerian *Al Ubaid* and the cow-headed *Hathor* of Egypt. These thoughts occurred to me when I first saw this prominent feature. I dismissed them as pure supposition, however, until years afterwards when I had come to understand that the nighttime "Green Corn" dances and their accompanying songs are actually hymns to the "Queen of Heaven." On one occasion when an especially capable leader announced he would lead one of the best known Yuchi songs, he walked to his place beside the fire as the line formed behind him composed of men and women, one following the other. He then began singing: "Ho! *Inana*, Ho, *Inana*!" He was addressing the diety of the night, the "Queen of Heaven," using the name by which the ancient Sumerians knew her!

There is even more evidence of continuity from ancient times in a diagram of the double ground which Chief Brown drew on a June day in 1936, perhaps to illustrate a verbal explanation to someone he was teaching. He labelled the sketch "Traditions of Americans, Euchee code of Arms, Mound Works." He signed and dated it June 21, 1934. The document was found among his papers after his death more than twenty years later.

There can be no doubt that the sacred ground forms the basis for this diagram. The perspective is from the west arbor identified as "Pathla," or king. Behind this arbor is a clear representation of the Zoya as the "moist drop of blood," referring to the account of their origin from a drop of the sun's blood which mixed with the earth.[3] The earth is represented apparently by four steps ascending toward the sun. The line from the sun passes through a simplified drawing of a serpent, or an

---

[1] Sir Arthur Evans, *The Palace of Mino: A Comparative Account of the Successive Stages of the Early Cretan Civilization at Knossos*, 4 vols. (New York: Biblo and Tannen, 1964), passem; Mahan, *The Secret*, p.72.

[2] Emma Lila Funderburk, *Sun Circles and Human Hand, The Southern Indians Art and Industry*, (Luverne, Al.; published by Emma Lila Funderburk, 1965) pls. 117, 127.

[3] Mahan, *The Secret*, p. 110.

accurate drawing of a human sperm, showing the Yuchis' descent from the "Sun or mother." It is notable that the symbol /E is here clearly associated with the sun. It is the same as the symbol on one of the brass disks that were among the ancient metal plates from the town of Tukabatchee to be discussed in chapter nine.

The principal features of the two squares are all easily recognizable in the Brown drawing. There are the encircled cross of the fire, the two medicine pots to the east on each side of the center line. There are the north and south arbors, labelled "Henehahs" (Princes) and "Tustenugees" (Warriors) respectively. In the eastern square in shown the mound, with a symbol above it which is identical to the Cretan linear A character for the syllable *ma*. This is also the word for "moon" in several ancient languages.

A decade ago I undertook to identify the other symbols the "code" contains.[4] Several of these are identical to letters or other phonetic symbols from the Old World. Two of them at least, the cow's head, and the "ox hide" are identical to Minoan hieroglyphs. I discovered that "Eight of these symbols are characters among the twenty-two shared by the Hebrew and Greek alphabets." Since I wrote that statement I have discovered that there is much greater significance to these symbols than was apparent at that time. It can now be stated unequivocally that the myth of the Yuchis—and of many other people—is written on the ceremonial ground and that this records a close relationship in ancient times to peoples of the Aegean, Eastern Mediterranean, Egypt, and the Near East. This relationship and more of the record preserved on the Yuchi Ground will be discussed in detail in subsequent chapters of this book.

---

[4] *Ibid.*,114−119.

Chapter 5

History on a Buffalo Hide

Muskogean peoples, specifically the Tukabatchee, told of messengers who had brought them their fire and taught them rituals with which to attend it. Two of these were the Coweta and Cusseta, whose relatively recent migration into the Southeast is well recorded in a history which *Chekilli*, acting king and chief of the Upper and Lower Creeks, narrated on a visit to Savannah in June 1735. It was written down in symbols on a buffalo hide under Chekilli's direction immediately after it was delivered.[1]

With the king were representatives from the eight towns that then comprised the confederation and thirty-nine other warriors and young men. The delegation had come at the behest of *Tamachechi*, aged king of the Yamacraw, who had greeted the colonists personally two years earlier on the same day they arrived at Yamacraw Bluffs, the site chosen for the new colony.

Peter Gordon who accompanied the governor of the colony, James Edward Oglethorpe, and the first settlers in the landing on February 12, 1733, wrote in his journal that about "one hour" after they had come ashore, "Tomo Chachi" and a small band of the Yamacraws came to welcome their new neighbors.

Oglethorpe returned the courtesy by visiting the king in his village and by inviting him for a more formal visit to the new settlement. This visit, which occurred a few days later on February 22, was an occasion of considerable ceremony on the part of both host and guest. Gordon described the events in detail noting particularly those accompanying the arrival of the Indian king:

> Before the King and other Chiefs, marched two warriors carrying long white tubes, adorned with white feathers, in their left hands, and rattles in their right hands, which was cocoa nutt shells, with shott in them, with which they beat time to their singing as they marched along, . . . When they came near the place where Mr. Oglethorpe was, the two warriors, who carried the rattles in their hands, advanced before the King and other Chiefs singing and playing with their rattles and putting themselves in many antike postures. Thane, they came up to Mr. Oglethorpe and the other gentlemen and waved the white wings they carried in their hands, over their heads, at the same time singing and putting their bodys in antike postures. Afterwards, they fixed a lighted pipe of tobacco to the tubes which they held in their hands, and presented it to Mr. Oglethorpe, who having smoaked several whiffs they thane presented it to the other gentlemen, who observed the same method which Mr. Oglethorpe had done. Thane they afterwards presented the same pipe to their king and two of their Chiefs, the King and each of the Chiefs smoaking four whiffs, blowing the first whiff to the left, the next to the right, the third upwards, and the fourth downwards.[2]

The "peace pipe" was often smoked in conferences and treaty making between colonial officials and native leaders in what appears to have been a standard ceremony. It was never described more clearly, however, than by Peter Gordon on this occasion.

Upon his arrival at Savannah two years later, Chekilli also engaged in ceremony. He made a talk to the English governor which, according to an eyewitness, "was handed over to the Interpreter, Written upon a Buffalo-skin and was, word for word, as follows:[3]

---

[1] The Phillips Collection, Papers of the Earl of Egmont, the Hargett Library, University of Georgia, Athens, vol. 14201, pp. 1–12, 127–128. (Cited hereinafter as Egmont Papers).

[2] Ellis Merton Coulter, ed., *The Journal of Peter Gordon* (Athens: University of Georgia Press, 1963), 44.

[3] The original buffalo hide has been lost, but the English translation was preserved in a copy sent to the Earl of Egmont, President of the Board of Trustees of the Colony. It is in the "Phillips Collection, Papers of the Earl of Egmont," in the Hargett Library, University of Georgia Library, Athens.

At a certain time the Earth opened in the West, where its mouth is.the Earth opened and the Cussitaws came out of its mouth and settled near by. But the Earth became angry and ate up their children; therefore, they moved further West. A part of them, however, turned back, and came again to the same place where they had been, and settled there. The greater number remained behind, because they thought it best to do so. Their children, nevertheless, were eaten by the Earth, so that, full of dissatisfaction, they journeyed toward the sunrise.

After a long period of migration during which they encountered many unusual phenomena including a red, bloody river where they lived two years they came to a mountain which gave forth red smoke and thundered. This mountain made a noise like singing and they named it the King of Mountains.

The narration continues at length recording various peoples they met and the fires that came to them. A white fire came from the east which they did not accept at first, nor did they take a blue fire which came from the west. At last a red and yellow fire came from the north. This they mingled with the fire they had taken from the singing mountain creating the fire they had continued to use until that day, Chekilli said.

At they mouth of Red River, according to a later version of the migration story (see below) they

found four herbs or roots, which sang and disclosed their virtues: First, *Pasaw* pasa, the rattle-snake root; second, *Micoweanochaw* mico hoyanidja, red root; third, *Sowatchko* sowatcko, which grows like wild fennel; and fourth, *Eschalapootchke* hitci laputcki, little tobacco. These herbs, especially the first and third, they use as the best medicine to purify themselves at their Busk. At this Busk, which is held yearly, they fast, and make offerings of the first fruits. Since they have learned the virtues of these herbs, their women, at certain times, have a separate fire, and remain apart from the men five, six, or seven days, for the sake of purification. If they neglected this, the power of the herbs would depart; and the women would not be healthy.

These are the Yuchi medicines which Chief Samuel Brown, Jr. said his people gave to the Cussetas and never gave to anyone else.

In Chekilli's narration there follows a traditional account of the manner in which the Cussetas won the dispute with the Chickasaws, Alabamas, and Abihkas over which tribe was the oldest and should rule.

It was decided:

They would then go to war; and which ever Nation should first cover its pole, from top to bottom, with the scalps of their enemies, should be the oldest.

They all tried, but the Cussitaws covered their pole first, and so thickly that it was hidden from sight. Therefore, they were looked upon, by the whole Nation, as the oldest. The Chickasaws covered their pole next; then the *Atilamas* [Alabamas]; but the *Obikaws* [Abihkas] did not cover their pole higher than to the knee.

The story continues with an account of how a huge bird who once came regularly and ate their people was killed when his offspring, a red rat, ate his bow string and made him vulnerable. It also tells of how the eagle came to be the king of birds which the Cussetas still venerate in all of their ceremonies, carrying his feathers painted red in time of war and white in peacetime. Referring to the place where they had received the medicines, Chekilli continued:

After this they left that place, and came to a white footpath. The grass and everything around was white; and they plainly perceived that people had been there. Afterward they turned back to see what sort of path it was, and who had been there, in the belief that it might be better for them to follow that path. They went along it to a creek called *Coloose-hutchi*, that is, Coloose-creek, because it was rocky there and smoked.

They crossed it, going to the sunrise, and came to a people and a town named Coosaw. Here they remained four years. The Coosaws complained that they were preyed upon by a wild beast, which they called man-eater or lion, which lived in a rock.

The Cussitaws said they would try to kill the beast. They digged a pit and stretched over it a net made of hickory-bark. They then laid a number of branches, crosswise, so that the lion could not follow them, and going to the place where he lay, they threw a rattle into his den. The lion rushed forth in great anger, and pursued them through the branches. Then they thought it better that one should die rather than all; so they took a motherless child, and threw it before the lion as he came near the pit. The lion rushed at it, and fell in the pit, over which they threw the net, and killed him with the blazing pine-wood. His bones, however, they keep to this day; on one side, they are red, on the other, blue.

The lion used to come every seventh day to kill the people; therefore, they remained there seven days after they had killed him. In remembrance of him, when they prepare for War, they fast six days and start on the seventh. If they take his bones with them, they have good fortune.

After four years they left the Coosaws, and came to a river which they called *Nowphawpe*, now *Tallasi-hutche*. There they tarried two years; as they had no corn, they lived on roots and fishes, and made bows, pointing the arrows with beaver teeth and flint-stones, and for knives they used split canes.

They left this place, and came to a creek, called *Wattoola-hawka-hutche*, Whooping creek, so called from the whooping of cranes, a great many being there; they slept there one night. They next came to a river, in which there was a waterfall; this they named the *Owatunka-river*. The next day they reached another river, which they called the *Aphoosa pheeskaw*.

The following day they crossed it, and came to a high mountain, where were people who, they believed, were the same who made the white path. They, therefore, made white arrows and shot at them, to see if they were good people. But the people took their white arrows, painted them red, and shot them back. When they showed these to their chief, he said it was not a good sign; if the arrows returned had been white, they could have gone there and bought food for their children, but as they were red they must not go. Nevertheless, some of them went to see what sort of people they were; and found their houses deserted. They also saw a trail which led into the river; and, as they could not see the trail on the opposite bank, they believed that the people had gone into the river, and would not again come forth.

At that place is a mountain, called *Motrell*, which makes a noise like beating on a drum; and they think this people live there. They hear this noise on all sides when they go to war.

They went along the river [identified later as the Chattahoochee], till they came to a waterfall, where they saw great rocks, and on the rocks were bows lying; and they believed the people who made the white path had been there.

This is the Coweta Falls on the Chattahoochee River between Columbus, Georgia and Phenix City, Alabama. The great rocks described here are now under water behind a dam across the river just below the falls. The Chekilli account continues:

They always have, on their journeys, two scouts who go before the main body. These scouts ascended a high mountain and saw a town. They shot white arrows into the town; but the people of the town shot back red arrows. Then the Cussitaws became very angry, and determined to attack the town, and each one have a house when it was captured.

They threw stones into the river until they could cross it, and took the town (the people had flattened heads), and killed all but two persons. In pursuing these they found a white dog, which they slew. They followed the two who escaped, until they came again to the white path, and saw the smoke of a town, and thought that this must be the people they had so long been seeking. This is the place where now the tribe of Pallacolas live, from whom Tomochichi is descended.

Samuel Williams Brown was known to possess these qualities. He had the claim to the ancient kingship through his mother, *Suttah*, or "Polly." As explained above, Suttah was the sister of the most recent Yuchi chief, *Fushudgee*, and of *Tisoso*, who had been hanged in Girard, Alabama in 1836. Brown, in addition to his eligible heritage, also had attained mature adulthood and had demonstrated his ability as leader of his fellow tribesmen during the recent war.

Brown was born near Van Buren, Arkansas on June 20, 1833. His mother had migrated there from Alabama with her two sisters, Margaret and Harriet Barnard.[1] His father was Sam Houston, famed for his later role in the history of Texas.[2] Apparently the identity of his father was not a source of pride to Brown or to his son neither of whom are known to have spoken of it publicly.[3]

It is clear that the male parent was not always a matter of concern in the selecting of the sun kings. The younger Chief Brown brought a photograph to the Columbus Museum of a man bearing a striking resemblance to himself. He explained that this was a half-brother of his father who had disappeared as a child sometime in the 1840's. He said that after his father's death some of the Osages had brought the picture to him and explained that the man shown in it was a brother of the elder Brown and had been "adopted" by them to be reared as a chief. The Oklahoma historian, Carolyn Thomas Foreman, recorded this episode, giving additional details:

> Chief S. W. Brown's mother Polly had two sons other than he. One was named William F. Gordon, and the other was kidnapped by an Osage while a small boy, adopted into the tribe and enrolled as an Osage. After the death of Chief S. W. Brown, Sr., the Osage chief Paul Red Eagle sent for Chief S. W. Brown, Jr. (father of Dorothy Jean Brown) and told the story of this adopted Osage boy. His Osage name was *Tsa-pah-ke-ah* (also spelled *Sah-pe-ke-ah*), and he became a prominent member of the Osage, serving on delegations representing the tribe. He died, never knowing his brothers, in 1910. His Osage roll number was 511, Allotment No 485. His son's name was *Kah-shin-kah*, or James Black, now deceased.[4]

His tribesmen had chosen well in selecting S. W. Brown to be their leader for the remainder of his life. He held the chieftainship 49 years until 1916 when he assembled the council and, explaining to them that symptoms of age had convinced him he must find a successor, suggested that they name his son "Willie," in his place. This was done by general agreement and transfer of the chieftainship was effected.[5]

---

[1] Carolyn Thomas Foreman, "Samuel W. Brown, Sr., Chief of the Yuchi Tribe," *The Chronicles of Oklahoma*, vol. XXVII, no. 4 (Winter 1959–60), pp. 485–92.

[2] Information on his death certificate in Bureau of Vital Statistics, Sapulpa, provided by his son, Samuel W. Brown, Jr.

[3] In a letter to the author dated March 28, 1990, Mrs. Juanita Brown Tiger, the eldest daughter of the younger Chief Brown sent a copy of her grandfather's death certificate she had recently discovered and commented concerning it: "Working on geneology in regards to my grandfather, I knew I couldn't obtain a birth certificate so I sent for a death certificate. When it came, much to my surprise, information was verified that he had told me about. That General Sam Houston was his father, that he was born where Van Buren, Arkansas was. His mother was a Yuchi. I said, 'Grandpa, history says the Cherokees was where Sam Houston lived and his eyes twinkled and he said,'The Yuchis were there too.' He continued, 'my father, Sam Houston, made two crops and I rode on the horse's back.'

[4] Foreman, "S. W. Brown, Sr.," 485–86.

[5] Samuel W. Brown, III, in an interview with this author in 1963, told of having been present at the meeting his grandfather called for this purpose. Explaining that as a nine year-old boy he had been allowed to sit unnoticed in the room where his grandfather assembled the Yuchi Council. He listened as the old man announced his decision to find a successor. "He explained that he had served the Yuchi people for almost fifty years and had now grown too old to continue effectively," the grandson remembered. "There were protests from the council members that this was not true as they urged him to reconsider his decision. He told them firmly that his mind was made up and that they must find someone to take his place." Remembering what had occurred almost fifty years earlier, Brown said that a discussion followed as to who might be suitable to assume this responsibility. Several persons were considered because of their birthright, but each in turn was disallowed as unsuitable for one reason or another. "Finally, the chief mentioned his son,'Willie,'" he recalled, "and there was general agreement that he was the one. 'I declare that he is my son,' my grandfather said." This was apparently to establish the hereditary right, about which there was no doubt in the case of the normal matriarchal practice of choosing the son of an eligible woman.

S. W. Brown, Sr. soon after returning from the Civil War, 1866. (Courtesy Columbus Museum)

Tsa-pah-ki-ah, Chief Brown's half-brother who was reared as an Osage and became an important leader of that tribe. (Courtesy Columbus Museum)

S. W. Brown seated in front of home at Wealaka, Oklahoma with Mrs. Brown and members of his family about 1900. (Courtesy Columbus Museum).

Chief Brown, the younger, described to me the formal transfer of the chieftainship from his father to himself. He said that he had not been informed of the council's decision even when his father called for all the Yuchis to assemble on the old ceremonial ground about one mile east of the present one at Kellyville. He said the people gathered on the ground with the men sitting in their designated places beneath the three arbors. The old chief took his position beside the center pole in the west arbor. He spoke to the people telling them that the time had come when he should no longer expect them to rely on his enfeebled leadership and that he had asked the council to select someone in his place and that they had done so. With this, he turned and placed his buck skin jacket, replete with beaded Yuchi artwork, on the seat he had just vacated. He then went to his son, led him to the seat and handed him the jacket. The transfer had been completed.

Almost twenty years passed during which the elder chief lived and continued to work with his son on behalf of their tribe. He was a 32nd Degree Mason, the last surviving Union Army officer in Oklahoma, and, among many other achievements, had been an original member of the Creek House of Kings and served a term as treasurer of the Creek Nation. At two funerals several of the organizations of which he had been a member accorded him traditional honors. These included the Masonic Order and the Sons of the Grand Army of the Republic in addition to the Creek National Council and the Yuchi Tribe.

Newspapers reported erroneously that he was ninety-two years old and that his father had been S. W. Williams, a lieutenant in the United States Army. It is now known that when he died his son, who had always been notably reticent about the identification of his paternal grandfather, went to the State Department of Health and supplied accurate information about the time and place of his father's death and birth and recorded the true identity of his male parent, one "Gen. Sam Houston."

According to one report the elder Brown adopted his name from a prominent Indian, S. C. Brown, a trustee of the school he attended who had taken an interest in him.[6] After attending this school for a while, the youth went to the Presbyterian-supported Tallahassee Mission school in the Creek Nation and remained there for about seven years. This provided him with the rudiments of an English education and the basis for a lifelong conviction that all young people should have the opportunity to attend school.

Brown was instrumental in establishing and operating the Wealaka Mission school in 1881 to replace the Tallahassee Mission which had burned the previous year. The Creek National Council paid for the construction of the three-story building for this school. Chief Brown was one of its principal supporters and set up a store on property he bought nearby. The community came to be known as Wealaka and this was the name given the post office established there in 1880. Chief Brown was the first postmaster. He served several years as trustee of the nearby Wealaka Boarding School.

Two Caucasian visitors from the east motivated to record their observations of native customs and living conditions left interesting glimpses of Brown's home, his family, and of life generally in the Indian Territory of this era. One of these was W. O. Tuggle, an attorney from LaGrange, Georgia, who had been sent by the War Department to settle claims dating from the time of the removal from Georgia and Alabama. The other was Jeremiah Curtin, a linguist or philologist from the Bureau of Ethnology, Smithsonian Institution. The Yuchi chief was hospitable to both and invited them as his guests, although his house was only partially completed.

Tuggle, who arrived there in 1889, described the Brown homestead and its owner:

On a rocky timbered ridge, surrounded by a prairie on which grazed fine Durham cattle and a few sheep, was situated the home of Sam Brown, the Uchee Indian, superintendent of public schools and public blacksmith shops. Rather a peculiar combination, but why not sharpen agricultural as well as mental tools at national expense? A small wiry man with Roman nose & blue eyes came to the gate followed by several dogs. . . . We stopped at the well and took a deep

---

[6] Foreman, "S. W. Brown, Sr.," 486.

draught from the bucket, doubly appreciated on account of a long ride over a dusty trail. We sat on the little porch in front of his house and talked till dark, when his wife, a small black-eyed woman invited us into a shed room to supper saying, in an apologetic manner that the coal-oil was out. We groped in the dark room to the table, having but one lamp to guide us & that was the lamp of experience, which answered very well on the route to our mouths. On that occasion it did not cast any light, nor did it illuminate the countenances of our companions, nor local surroundings.[7]

Curtin arrived at the Brown home in 1883. He later wrote concerning his efforts to find a boarding place for himself and his wife:

The only possible one was at an unfinished house in a clump of trees, the home of Sam Brown, a half breed Yuchi. Both Brown and his wife had been educated at the mission; they spoke English, and were willing to assist me in learning Yuchi. The Yuchi tribe live about six miles from Wealaka. Mr. Brown sent for an old man reputed to be wise, and before the evening I had the creation story of the Yuchis, the children of the Sun. As the house was unfinished, the rooms were cold and untidy. At times as many as a dozen Indians sat huddled around the little stove in my room an unkempt crowd.[8]

Both Tuggle and Curtin wished ethnographic information from their host and his tribe. Brown and his wife cooperated in the recording of certain data. Much of this information found its way in to various Bureau of Ethnology publications, especially works of John R. Swanton and Frank G. Speck, the latter devoted entirely to the study of Yuchi culture history. Tuggle made rough sketches of a pottery drum, a medicine pot, the ceremonial scratcher, and Mrs. Brown's ingenious cradle in which the later chief Samuel Brown, Jr., was probably being rocked at the time.

Tuggle recorded superficial details relating to the ceremonial ground and the annual Green Corn ceremony. He also learned enough to give a fairly full description of the stick-ball game. One statement he attributes to Chief Brown, "Tradition among my tribe says that when William Penn made his treaty, the Yuchis lived in that part of the country," will be considered in another association below.

Although he was prominent in the affairs of the Creek nation and was a consistent supporter of the Creek national school at Wealaka, Chief Brown wanted the Yuchis to have their own school. He said later that he fought three years in the Creek National Council for the founding of this school, called the "Euchee Boarding School." The facility opened in 1894 east of the town of Sapulpa and was open to both boys and girls. He continued to work for the good of the school for the remainder of this life, serving at one time as its superintendent. In his latter years, the old chief referred to it as a "monument to his life work."

A description of the school as it appeared in 1929 and a short history of the school published in the Tulsa *Daily World* that year indicate that Brown was justified in his pride. Excerpts follow:

The school is approached today through an avenue of beautiful flowering catalpa trees. The buildings are in excellent repair, all snowy white. The grounds are well landscaped with nicely trimmed hedges and brilliant flower beds. Through the grounds, where the grass is cut just as it should be, run graveled driveways. The native blackjacks have been supplemented with other trees that flourish in this climate.

A herd of thoroughbred Holstein cows graze in a pasture adjoining these grounds, while in the garden, the orchard and vineyards may be seen in the rear. . . .

---

[7] Eugene Current-Garcia and Dorothy B. Hatfield, ed., *Shem, Ham & Japheth, the Papers of W. O. Tuggle, Comprising his Indian Diary, Sketches & Observations, Myths and Washington Journal in the Territory and at the Capital, 1879–1882* (Athens: University of Georgia Press, 1973).
[8] *Ibid.*, 489.

Views of Euchee Schoool, 1932.

Home # 2

General View

Starting the garden

(National Archives, Courtesy of W. Keith Overstreet).

Supt. O. A. Wright came to the school this year (1929) from the southern part of the state. Many buildings have been added and great improvement made since Mr. Wright was in Sapulpa 23 years ago. Even then, there had been changes since Noah Gregory, first superintendent, took charge when the school was opened 10 years before.

This was when the woodland surrounding the school looked like an Indian village toward opening in September and again at closing around the first of June. Parents came, drove their ponies for miles and camped for several days before starting back.

Mr. Brown rode all over the nation persuading parents to send their children for education, and carry away a little boy behind him on his horse to the school. . . . It is as a horseman that old-timers always think of him. For many years he was a familiar figure throughout the Creek Nation on his white pony. He continued to ride his pony until 1920 when he suffered a dislocated hip from helping to push an auto out of the mud, since he has had to depend upon an automobile to carry him around, and uses crutches in walking.[9]

The story in the Tulsa newspaper continued with additional information concerning the interest the then aged chief had always maintained in the welfare of children. This included the fact that, while he served on the Board of Education in the Creek Nation, two orphan homes were established. One of these was for Indian children near Okmulgee and the other was for Negro children on Pecan Creek.

Brown did not limit his efforts on behalf of the Creek and Yuchi people to developing schools and orphanages. In the same year he became chief of the Yuchi (1867) he was elected to represent his home "town" in the House of Kings in the Creek National Council, a position to which he was re-elected until after 1890. He served one term of two years in the House of Warriors, the lower house of the Creek National Council. During 1880–1882, he was one of the two superintendents of the Creek national schools. Prior to this he had served three years as district judge in the Nation. He served as treasurer of the Creek nation 1883 to 1887.

The Yuchi chief owned a cattle ranch near his store at Wealaka. In 1890 he owned 700 head of cattle, 60 stock horses and mules; about 200 acres of land under fence, and a comfortable home with garden and orchard. Although he and his wife were members of the Baptist Church, he continued to participate in the traditional tribal religious and social ceremonies. His support of the Green Corn ceremony each July was unfailing and his contributions and participation helped to preserve this ancient religion.

Many of his contemporaries, even some of his relatives, did not share Chief Brown's sympathy for their native religion. A cousin, the Rev. Noah G. Gregory, was one of the least sympathetic. In 1890 he compiled information for a sketch on the "Euchees" for a dictionary of leaders in the Indian Territory. Concerning religion Gregory wrote:

The Euchees are among the most superstitious of the Indian tribes, and to the present day [1890] the majority believe implicitly in witchcraft. The witch, in their imagination, most frequently takes the shape or form of the night-owl or night-hawk, and in the silence of the night plucks the heart from its victim which dies the next day.

Originally, the Euchees. ...were sun worshipers. At the present they have no religious observances. Their town chief, Copaychunnie, is a predestinarian, and is strongly prejudiced against the Bible and the Christian doctrine. He believes that a tree without fruit is useless, and as such he looks upon Christianity, whose followers set such a wicked example to the unlettered sons of the forest.[10]

---

[9] Tulsa Daily *World*, July 21, 1929 (Quoted in Foreman, "S. W. Brown, Sr.," 490–91.

[10] H. F. and E. S. O'Beirne, *The Indian Territory: Its Chiefs, Legislators and Leading Men* (St. Louis: n.p., 1892), p.25.

Right: View of mound covering earthlodge at Ochmulgee National Monument, Macon, Ga. (National Park Service photo).

Below: Interior of earthlodge reconstructed on original floor and walls. The dais in the form of an eagle with forked eye design contains seats for the King and his "left hand tiger" and "right hand bear." (National Park Service photo).

other things. They would go into this lodge that was three to four feet deep and, also, had a fire in there that was in the shape of an anchor, that had slats of small trees trimmed down that made an anchor.

And there they would sit and carry on their discussion of what's to be, maybe a war, maybe some other kind of conflict. They would make a decision that they pick one man and this man had no choice. He was instructed to go straight away to meet the people who they hoped kind words may subdue and save blood. This man would have an elm bark made for that purpose around his waist. That would hang down about four inches.

The purpose of that was when he arrived there to see the headmen, he would tell them he was the mouth of the Yuchi people come to see them and he had no answers; he had no decisions to make. '' However /he said/ you see me in person. I'm friendly, I have no weapons but I have the elm bark that's placed around me; that if you bite it off, then I will return to my people and report to them that everything seemed friendly.''

Chief Brown continued the account of the peace envoy, leading directly from that into comments on the general culture of the Yuchis. These comments convey something of the attitudes that can be detected many times in the historical sources, notably in references to the ''refuge'' or ''peace towns'' of the eighteenth century. The implication of the chief's remarks were that the missions sent under the circumstances he described were usually successful, for without further explanation he proceeded to refer to the former trouble-makers as ''neighbors.''

Then they would invite these neighbors and they would talk and discuss and make their boundary lines as to be peaceful with one another. The Yuchi people were very aggressive people and self-supporting. They raised food of all kinds to eat, but no matter how humble, they would break their bread with anybody.

And so, when they had these meetings, the king would say, ''I have sent the broken days out and you have come a long ways on a rugged path. I know you are hungry and thirsty and we receive you in our house, the oldest house of all the houses, welcome to part of it. Here, therefore, we are happy that our Master who gave us all the wisdom from these sacred places that it may continue in peace forever and ever. And then the elm bark was stripped from the man and it was folded and dried, and placed away for other summers to pass.

They never used the words ''weeks'' and ''months,'' but ''summers.'' And when the dark lines of winter came, they knew how to prepare for that when Mother Earth was sleeping and germinating for the new year to appear with everything green and the edibles growing so they could prosper from the four elements that the Great Master of all Masters created all. That is the Con-queror of all Conquerors.

Chief Brown paused for a while as if in deep thought and then resumed his narration. On the tape there is a pace in his speaking which suggests that he is simultaneously thinking in his native language and speaking in English and that he is giving, at least partially, a formal memorized speech. The same pace is frequently apparent in his recorded recitations of Yuchi customs and religious philosophy. He was clearly thinking of the stories he had heard of the earthlodges as he spoke these words:

First, the meeting was called and there they entered as the sun came. They say we come as the sun came. And there they sat with the thoughts that might be given to them that they have more wisdom. This selected man, no one touched these fires but he. They kept them going so the white smoke would ascend to the heavens that the Master said would break the clouds and therein the people would follow each other to the spiritual world and to the great world for all people who followed the dictation of the Creator.

Miss Brown asked her father, ''. . . . they selected this man to carry the elm bark to another group of people—that was an enemy?''

"That was supposed to be an enemy," was the reply. "That was [done] to try to head off bloodshed—to make brothers."

In another recorded narration, the elderly chief, anticipating the last Green Corn ceremony he was ever to attend, captured the true spirit of the old Yuchi religion as he said:

And, as I have said before, the sacred ground is still being carried on by my little tribe that's left and [they] try to be happy and forget and live the way of other people's lives, not their own, as they were taught. And on the thirteenth of this month (July 1957), there will be an Arbor Dance, they will prepare for the sacred dances, they're called. We don't call them dances, but that's what they're called. Many fine singers and songs, everybody happy. Any man can come with a Bible under each arm, he's welcome. They'll divide with him; they won't make fun of him. They will say he's a good man. Let him participate because he's tired and has come a long ways. We'll break our bread with him.

Although the main emphasis of Brown's education, indeed his life's work, seems to have been upon learning and teaching his Indian heritage, this did not prevent his pursuing his mother's suggestion that he could "learn what little the white man knows" as well. He learned by active participation in several of the white man's activities including cattle raising, the oil industry, and politics.

January 1954, Chief Brown joined members of the Chisholm Trail Association to point out the route of the Sampson Chisholm Trail. At that time he was believed to be the last person living who had driven cattle along this famous path.

Brown grew to manhood surrounded by the cattle industry. When he was born in 1879, his father owned the cattle ranch and the herd already mentioned in chapter six. In his later years, the chief wrote sometimes of his memories of the days of his youth. Some of this was at the urging of Oklahoma historians. In one such narrative he wrote of some of his experiences in the frontier society of an earlier time.. He mentioned the family ranch and the need to get the cattle to market in Missouri and recorded his memories of one such trip in these words:

Before statehood there was a time that I went with a train load of cattle to St. Louis. Then a man had his choice, riding with the cattle or on the passenger car. Well I preferred the passenger car, and since they were my cattle that was going riding, I bought a ticket on the same train. The ticket cost the same, didn't make any difference where they rode, but some way it did to the conductor. It was on the way back from St. Louis that this conductor came in and called for tickets. I had on the newest thing in fashion, a brown derby, and wrapped around my arm was a nice little wicker basket, full of Black berry wine, and apple jack. It was so pretty. And it tasted good too. But then the conductor called for my ticket, and when I reached for it I got the top of it, and there it fell reeling like a ribbon.

"This man doesn't like me, I am an Indian." He said to me, "You go get in a cattle car." I said nothing, but then when he shook my arm, after punching my ticket, and told me to get the hell out into the cattle car, that was when I said for him to "Please put me there." If he liked it so good, then maybe we would both ride out there, providing of course he put me there. That was sort of funny you know because he didn't try to put me there. I just sat where I was with my little wicker basket, and rode home to Sapulpa. That was on the Frisco Railroad.[1]

In 1951 Chief Brown, (c) rides in a Christmas Parade in Harlingen, Texas wearing his prized bear claw necklace and the buckskin jacket he inherited from his father. (ISAC Research Center).

---

[1] Samuel W. Brown, Jr. to Muriel H. Wright, August 24,1948. Copy in Brown Collection, Manuscript Division, Oklahoma Historical Society.

1797. At about the same time, the newly-arrived agent noted concerning Tukabatchee, "The ancient name of this town is *Ispocogee*."[1] It has already been stated in Chapter 3 that the Ispogogee were one division of the Shawano to whom the king line belonged. In 1957 Chief Samuel Brown, Jr. referred to himself as Ispogogee Mico It is known from Chekilli's narration of their history, quoted above in chapter five, that the Cowetas were adopted by the Tukabatchee when they arrived in the East. The Tukabatchee queen could also have been the Coweta queen.[2] If so, she was the mother of Little Prince. .

Thus she was the person to whom Hawkins referred when he visited the Lower Creeks for the first time. On January 23, 1797 Hawkins wrote in his diary: "Dined with the old queen, the prince's mother. She had sent for me. She received me and treated me with much attention."[3] This reference to her son as prince means, of course, that he was of the regal Zoya family. An affirmation of this is found in a statement by Timothy Barnard implying that Little Prince was acting on behalf of an elderly uncle: "The Prince said he would have sent a horse for goods, but had none able to go. His uncle that you wrote to, says, he hopes you will think on him when you come up, as he is an old man and your friend; he is the man you wrote the other letter to."[4] This uncle of Tustenuggee Hopoi (Little Prince) could well have been the young emperor *Togulgee*, the grandson of Emperor Brim. The young man had recently succeeded his father, Malatchee, when he came to Savannah in 1759. The time span of thirty-four years is suggestive of this as Togulgee would have been at least in his mid fifties in 1793 old enough to have his nephew act for him. His sister was then the "old queen" who had Benjamin Hawkins to dinner in 1797.

The identity of Fushudgee whom Trumbull sketched in New York in 1790 as *Micco Thlucco* on other occasions is proved in the record of the conference the Lower Creek chiefs had with Governor David Mitchell of Georgia in July 1811. There is this statement in the record of the conference: "The principal speakers were Tustenuggee Hopoi, or Little Prince, Micco Thlucco of Cusseta, (Known in the treaty at New York by Birdtail King.")[5] He was the same man Benjamin Hawkins wrote a few years earlier was "called by the white people the birdtail king."

"Fosache Mico" was one of eight chiefs who met at Tukabatchee Town, March 6, 1835 and petitioned the Secretary of War to help them stop the "fraud being practiced upon our people" in the dishonest schemes by Euro-Americans to obtain individual land allotments. Among the chiefs were also the "Young King" and the "Old King." I propose that this Fushudgee Mico was the young man who went to Indian Territory and lived until 1862. His uncle was Micco Thlucco, the "Old King," who had already passed the title on to his successor. The "Young King" may have been Tisoco who died the following year on the gallows at Girard.

Although these partially conjectural identities and relationships are based on the best evidence available, some of the details are not certain. When the exact identity or kinship of individual kings and queens of this hereditary line can not be determined otherwise, it is useful to study their names as indications of societal roles. In the case of men at least, their titles are usually given as names, the meaning of which are sometimes recorded in two or more languages, In order to make positive identifications, it is necessary to know the literal meaning of the title in question and something of the ceremonial organization of the socio-religious system these leaders represented.

---

[1] Benjamin Hawkins, "Sketch of the Creek Country," "*Georgia Historical Society Collections*, Part 1, Volume III, ed. William B. Hodgson (Savannah: Georgia Historical Society, 1848), p.

[2] It should be noted here that only the more recently arrived Muskogeans were thus adopted. They took the name of the "Man-Tobacco" division of the Tukabatchee from whom they received the Red Fire. The other division of the immigrants were adopted by the Apalachicola and were given the Yuchi medicines and the "White Fire" of those people. They were the Cussetas.

[3] "Letters of Benjamin Hawkins," *Collections of the Georgia Historical Society*, Vol. IX, ed. William B. Hodgson (Savannah: Georgia Historical Society, 1916). Cited hereinafter as Hawkins *Letters* or by date.

[4] Timothy Barnard to James Seagrove, March 26, 1793. (All Barnard letters quoted are from "Unpublished Letters of Timothy Barnard" (Microfilm), including a biography by Lousie Frederick Hays (Atlanta: Department of Archives and History, 1968, 1939).

[5] Barnard Letters, 1811.

To learn this one must understand the interactions of what was basically a confederation of the sun and the moon, whose underlying organization we may infer from the pre-scribed formal seating order in the arbors on the ceremonial Square Ground. This same order prevailed in the seating arrangement in the town square when the men gathered there for formal deliberations or informal discussions. This earliest record of this arrangement is that Benjamin Hawkins included in this *Sketch of the Creek Country* in which he compiled information to send to the government in Washington. In a section he headed "Government of the Towns," is this:

The towns, separately, have a government and customs, which they derive from a high source. They have their public buildings, as well for business as pleasure; every town has a chief who presides over the whole; he is their *Mic-co* called by the white people, "King." The grades from him are regular and uniform, throughout all the towns. In the description of the publics buildings, these grades will be explained.

Choo-co-thluc-co, (big house), the town house or public square, consists of four square buildings of one story, facing each other, forty by sixteen feet, eight feet pitch; the entrance at each corner. Each building is a wooden frame, supported on posts set in the ground, covered with slabs, open in front like a piazza, divided into three rooms, the back and ends clayed, up to the plates. Each division is divided lengthwise, into two seats; the front, two feet high, extending back half way, covered with reed-mats or slabs; then a rise of one foot, and it extends back, covered in like manner, to the side of the building. On these seats, they lie or sit at pleasure.

The rank of the Buildings which form the Square.

1st. Mic-ul-gee in-too-pau, the Mic-co's cabin. This fronts the east, and is occupied by those of the highest rank; the centre of the building is always occupied by the Mic-co of the town; by the Mic-cos of other towns, and by respectable white people.

The division to the right is occupied by the Mic-ul-gee, (Miccos, there being several so-called in every town, from custom, the origin of which is unknown), and the counsellors. These two classes give their advice, in relation to war, and are in fact the principal coun-sellors.

The division to the left, is occupied by the E-ne-hau Ul-gee, (people second in command, the head of whom is called by the traders, second man). These have the direction of the public works appertaining to the town, such as the public buildings, building houses in town for new settlers, or working in the fields. They are particularly charged with the ceremony of the a-ce, (a decoction of the cassine yupon, called by the traders black drink), under the direction of the Mic-co.

The Mic-co of the town superintends all public and domestic concerns; receives all public characters; hears their talks; lays them before the town, and delivers the talks of his town. The Mic-co of a town is always chosen from some one family. The Mic-co of Tuck-au-bat-che is of the eagle tribe, (Lum-ul-gee). After he is chosen and put on his seat, he remains for life. On his death, if his nephews are fit for the office, one of them takes his place as his successor; if they are unfit, one is chosen of the next of kin, the descent being always in the female line. They have, in this town, a Mic-co of another family, the Is-po-co-gee Mic-co, the ancient name of the town.

When a Mic-co, from age, infirmity, or any other cause wants an assistant, he selects a man who appears to him the best qualified, and proposes him to the counsellors and great men of the town, and if he is approved of by them, they appoint him as an assistant in public affairs, and he takes his seat on this cabin accordingly.

The Micco of a town generally bears the name of the town, as *Cussetuh Mic-co*. He is what is called by the traders the Cussetuh King.

2nd. Tus-tun-nug-ul-gee in-to-pau, the warrior's cabin. This fronts the south; the head warrior sits at the west end of his cabin, and in his division the great warriors sit beside each other. The

Because Little Prince outranked the younger war chief from Tukabatchee, he became the recognized head of the Creek Confederation following the death of Big Warrior and remained so until his death in 1831. If he were succeeded, as I believe he was, by the young man who had the same name (Tisoso) as Emperor Brim, this means that the young man's father, Casenney Barnard, would have been a close relative of Little Prince and a descendant of Brim. This conclusion seems inescapable as the Fushudgee line is clearly linked to the Cussetas and the descendants of the emperor are considered as belonging to the Coweta town.

There are two circumstances which suggest that the mother of both Timpoochee Barnard and Casseney Barnard belonged to the king line and was from Coweta. One of these is the fact that Timpoochee was widely recognized as a "chief" of the Cowetas, and the other is that the only reasonable explanation for the name "Casenney" seems to be that it is an abbreviated form of Sakasenney or "Little Bear." This indicates his descent from a Chechi or "Bear King."

Although his name appears only rarely in extant documents of the period, it is clear that there was a Fushudgee or "Birdtail King" more or less contemporaneous with Little Prince. He was the Cusseta king already mentioned as Fushudgee and Micco Thlucco in the 1790's. It seems he was the uncle of Fudhudgee who attended a council at Tuskegee in 1835 and signed a document protesting the continuing seizure of Creek lands. There were also an "old king" and a "young king" who attended this council. This "old king" must have been a brother of Little Prince and the "young king" his great nephew, *Tisoso*, to whom he had already relinquished his kingship to an acceptable heir as the older Chief Brown did in 1916.

Another facet of the kingship requires explaining. This is the title *Tisoso*, more properly, I believe, *Tizoco*, which the younger Chief Brown, as quoted in the first paragraph of this chapter, said was the name of the Emperor Brim and means "flint." In the form I have suggested, the word breaks down: *Ti* (divine essence)-*zo* (sun)-*co* (man). Thus it denotes a combination of man and divinity. There is further significance when it is known that the fire is kindled on the sacred ceremonial ground from a spark produced by striking a piece of flint with a metal object. The flint is said in Yuchi tradition to be the only stone which "contains the sun's blood." As mentioned above, the "sun people," the *Zoya*, according to their tradition, came into existence when a drop of blood from the sun mixed with earth creating the first of their people. It was thus appropriate for their ranking king to be named "Flint."

If the "old queen" who entertained Benjamin Hawkins in 1797 were only forty years old, she would have been born in 1757, a mere thirty years after the death of the renowned Emperor Brim about 1727. Even if she were younger than that, it is highly likely that she was born less than twenty years after 1739 when General James Edward Oglethorpe, the founder of the colony of Georgia, journeyed to the same Coweta Town in which she resided to make a treaty with the immediate successors of the late emperor. She was the right age to be Emperor Malatchee's granddaughter and the daughter or niece of his son Togulgi.

One of the leaders with whom Oglethorpe signed the treaty was Brim's brother, *Chekilli*, who was acting for the Emperor's son, *Malatchee*, until the young man became an age to act for himself. Another of Brim's sons was *Seepycoffee* who was formally recognized as commander-in-chief of all the Creeks by Tobias Fitch, acting as agent for the colony of South Carolina in 1726. A third son was *Hollata* who wholeheartedly joined the English cause and died fighting the Yamassees in 1715. Seepycoffee may have been Hollata's twin. He was not living, however, in 1740 when Oglethorpe visited Coweta. Malatchee was one of the youngest of Brim's sons born about 1712. *Skimporaffee*, another son, perhaps the youngest, was acting as guardian for Malatchee's son, *Togulgi*, on a visit to Savannah in 1759.

In April 1742 Malatchee visited Oglethorpe at Fort Frederica and offered his help in fighting the Spanish who were attacking the Georgia settlements on the coastal islands. On his way to meet with the General he stopped at Savannah and talked with William Stevens, the person in charge there. Stevens wrote in his Journal:

It seems old Chigellie, their chief mico at present, had of late shown an unusual coldness towards meddling in the Wars that we are engaged in against Spain, telling some of his People, that they had no business to interpose themselves among the white Men's Quarrels: Which Behavior of his, it is suspected arose from some French and Spanish Emissaries among them; but the main party of his people were eagerly bent upon joining the General, and his nephew, Malatchie, who was the son of Old Bream, their former mico, stuck close to them and put himself at their Head,[7].

On May 3, Stevens wrote that Mrs. Matthews (Mary Musgrove), the interpreter had arrived from the south, by whom came several letters and orders from General Oglethorpe. Accompanying her were Malatchee and three or four head men and noted warriors of the Coweta Nation returning from their talk with the General. According to Stevens:

(Malatchee) was so well pleased, that he was now making the like speed home, resolved to put his Purpose in Execution; and if Chigellie opposed him, to cut off his Head: For the farther Explanation whereof, it should be observed, that when the old Bream, the father of Malatchee, died, his Son was a Youth; and therefore Chigellie had the Power put in his Hands by the old men, till Malatchee came to the Age of Maturity: During which time, the young Man has signalized himself to be a great Warrior, and behaved so well, that he is now looked on as the greatest man of that, or most other Nations: which makes him highly esteemed among them: Nevertheless (he says) he never intended to take the Government out of old Chigellie's Hands, but let him die possessed of it, had he ruled for the Good of his Country; but now, if he shews no longer Regard to the pleasing his People, it is Time to put an End to his Power; and he thinks himself of Age sufficiently to take his own Right, being near Thirty: And as to his Ability, as well as his Good-will to the English, is not questioned: so his Person is very engaging: His stature but a little short of six Foot, his Make clean, and perfectly well shaped from Head to Foot, as he appears when naked to his Skin; and when he puts on a Coat and Hat, his Behaviour is such, that one would rather imagine from his complaisance, he had been bred in some European Court, than among Barbarians: At the same Time, though the Features of his Face were inviting, and shew Tokens of Good-Nature; yet there is something in his Aspect which demands Awe.[8]

Malatchee assumed power, but apparently without having to take so drastic a measure as cutting off his uncle's head. Chekilli was active in the Battle of Bloody Marsh two years later sharing leadership with Matlachee over some 1500 warriors who arrived in time to turn the tide of battle in favor of the Georgia colonials.

There are occasional references to Malatchee through the following several years until his death some time prior to October 1759. That month Georgia Governor Henry Ellis has a long conference with a party of Creek Indians headed by *Togulgi*, the young Emperor and his Uncle, *Skimporaffeee*. Details of the meeting were recorded in the Council *Journal*:

The young Emperor's Uncle Speaker. Indian: "This young man (pointing to Togulgi) is the Head of Our Nation, you see he is young and unexperienced in Public Affairs: I being his Uncle am deputed to speak for him and all of the rest present who are the head men of two of the principal Towns in our Nation."[9]

Brim's descendants retained a leadership role in the confederation Emperor Brim had years earlier brought to the attention of England, Spain, and France, the three great European nations with colonial ambitions in the American Southeast. He successfully thwarted these ambitions and played the foreign powers against each other in a manner that would bring acclaim to any professional diplomat. His tenure in this powerful role continued for about thirty years, and possibly longer. More will be said of him below in the next chapter.

---

[7] *Colonial Records of Georgia*, Vol. IV, ed. Allen D. Chandler (Atlanta: Franklin Printing and Publishing Company, 1906), p. 565.

[8] *Ibid.*, 566.

[9] *The Colonial Records of the State of Georgia, Volume VIII, Journal of the Proceedings of the Governor and Council, March 8, 1755–December 31, 1762*, inclusive. comp. and ed. Allen D. Chandler (Atlanta: The Franklin-Turner Company, 1907) p.161.

with him, in the effort to represent the Indian sound of that name by English letters, spells it in seven different ways ranging from "Brmns" through "Brimins" to "Brunin."[1]

Brim's biographer believed that he was mentioned in Spanish documents as early as 1682 when Cabrera, the Governor at St. Augustine, wrote to the King of Spain concerning the *Gran Cazique* who exercised jurisdiction over eleven tribes: "He is the chief most feared in all those lands that border on the Chucumecos and other provinces and give their allegiance to the English settled in the province of San Jorge."

The allegiance to the English the Spanish governor mentioned in 1682 began in 1666 when Robert Sandford, whom the Lord Proprietors of the Colony of Carolina commissioned to explore the land they had recently been granted by Charles II, sailed along the coast of the future South Carolina and visited the Audusta King in Port Royal Sound.

The English explored the region and took on wood and water during the several days the ship was moored near the town of this king. When they were ready to sail the king came on board with a young man, the son of his sister, who he proposed should go with Sandford and learn the ways of their prospective future neighbors. In return the captain proposed that he leave an Englishman with the king for the same purpose. To make the agreement more secure, Sandford went ashore and put the proposal before the assembled people. They signified their assent unanimously.

After a day's sojourn in the town, Sandford sailed away leaving a willing young "surgeon," Henry Woodward, in the care of the native king. He was to learn the language and customs of his people and to maintain possession of the land in the name of the King of England's grantees.

Woodward was then only twenty years old, although he had come as the surgeon of the expedition. He was young indeed to have this position and the additional responsibility he had assumed of holding as tenant at will the vast, poorly defined territory the English claimed between their colony at Cape Fear and Spanish Florida.

The king assured Sandford that the sojourner among his people would be well treated and have all his needs supplied. He gave Woodward his niece, the sister of the young man who went away with Sandford, "to dress his victuals and be careful of him." He was also given the best field of maize as his own. Apparently his residence of some two years accomplished its purpose. Woodward learned the language of his hosts and their customs. He also won their lasting friendship, a fact that would prove of the greatest value when a permanent settlement was established among the neighboring Kiawa four years later.

In the intervening years, however, all did not go as planned either for Robert Sandford or Henry Woodward. Instead of returning in ten months as he planned and promised the Edisto king, Sandford did not return at all. Almost four years later, after an incredible series of adventures, Henry Woodward was with the English when they finally returned to establish the proposed colony. Sandford was not.[2]

Sandford made his promise in good faith, but he did not take into consideration the time that would be required for the Lords Proprietors to devise plans and make arrangements to assure that they would be adequately repaid for any money they invested in the Carolina venture. They had John Locke, who was later widely renowned as a constitutional authority, prepare a set of "Fundamental Constitutions for the Government of Carolina." This instrument, in addition to a scheme for a political and social organization that was more theoretical than workable, contained very practical provisions to insure the Lords Proprietors an income in perpetuity from every acre of land they granted.

It was not until April 1669 that the proprietors eventually worked out details for governing a colony, obtained colonists, and agreed that they should each deposit five hundred pounds in a fund

---

[1] Walter A. Harris, *Here the Creeks Sat Down*, Macon, Ga.: Printed by the J. W. Burk Company, 1958, p. 45.
[2] *Ibid.*, 190.

for purchasing the arms, ammunition, tools, and provisions "for the settlement of Port Royall within the Province of Carolina." It was March 21 of the following year before the 200-ton frigate *Carolina* with 92 passengers finally reached Port Royal. Henry Woodward was aboard to serve as interpreter in the negotiations with the Natives he had come to know during his residency with them.[3]

Meanwhile, Woodward had managed to become acquainted with the Spanish in St Augustine as well, an achievement that would greatly benefit the new colony. Leaving his hospitable friends at Fort Royal, he made his way alone to this Spanish garrison and mission center. By one account he went deliberately in order to ingratiate himself there for his own purposes. By his account when he joined the English again, he fled there from soldiers the Spanish sent to seize him to prevent his gaining further influence with the Indians whose tolerance of the Spanish was minimal at best.

However motivated, Woodward appeared one morning at the door of Father Francisco de Soto in St Augustine a penitent young man, confessing the error of his heresy and begging that he be baptized into the faith of the Holy Catholic Church. He had already sent the Governor, Don Francisco de la Guerra, a letter written in Latin begging that the writer, one Henry Woodward, be allowed to be baptized in the Church and be welcomed by the governor as a good citizen.[4] It appears that the arrival of the letter was so timed that the good father had already received the penitent into the church before the governor received the letter or knew that Woodward was in St. Augustine.

La Guerra, the governor, who was not noted for decisive actions, allowed the presumed new convert to remain in the town unrestrained, although he had earlier sent a band of soldiers and Indians from St. Catherine to capture the interloping Englishman and bring him to St. Augustine. He failed in this effort. The Indians who were his hosts denied any knowledge of Woodward's whereabouts and the mission failed. Evidently the governor was unwilling to risk trouble with the English king by harming one of his subjects in a time of peace, especially since this subject was now under surveillance and could be watched.

Needing someone with the unusual ability Woodward had of translating both the English correspondence that came to the governor and communicating with the infidel Indians, La Guerra made the newly converted Englishman his official interpreter.[5] Apparently the arrangement was effective for a while. Eventually, however, Woodward learned all he needed to know about the weakened state of the Spanish government and garrison at St. Augustine and was ready to return to England as soon as there was an opportunity.

The opportunity soon came in the form of a raid by a band of buccaneers who seized St. Augustine in March 1669 without a shot being fired. The pirate vessel which came in by night under the guns of the Spanish fort guarding the approaches to the city was the *Cagway* commanded by one Robert Searle. The crew of seventy men sacked the town taking what little they could find of value from the combined population of approximately 500 soldiers and civilians. They sailed away with their booty and Henry Woodward on board.[6]

Writing of the episode, Walter Harris doubted that the raid was motivated simply by the prospect for plunder. In his biographical sketch of Woodward there is this comment:

> The sudden onslaught of the Buccaneers on so unimportant a town as St. Augustine was so meaningless, so out of character for them, that some effort was made to account for it. The story went about that a French doctor who had been a prisoner at St Augustine, incensed at his treatment by the Spaniards there, had communicated with the Buccaneers and induced Captain Searle to sack the town. No records prove it, but it is not too great a stretch of the imagination to believe that the Doctor Pedro Pequez was English, not French, and that his real name was Henry

---

[3] *Ibid.*, 137.

[4] *Ibid.*, 80.

[5] *Archivo General de Indias Audencia de Santo Domingo y Mexico*, copies in the Hargett Library, University of Georgia, Leg. 56. (Cited hereinafter *AGI*).

[6] Paul Quattlebaum, *The Land Called Chicora: The Carolinas Under Spanish Rule with French Intrusions, 1520–1670* (Gainesville: University of Florida Press, 1956) p, 91; Harris, *Here the Creeks Sat Down*, 83–84.

one although he had heard that three had formerly been there. Tying a noose to a pine tree and then to his neck, the Indian was suspended from the ground to frighten him. When he saw himself exhausted he said in a loud voice that on that day he was dying for the English.

The heroism of the captive appealed to Matheos, so he cut him down and then tried to get information through another approach, namely kindness. This did not work either. The Indian lied and his captor knew it was a lie and did not take the information he was offered.

For five more days Matheos drove his column of four hundred Indians and one hundred Caucasian soldiers through the unmapped swamps and forest bordering the west bank of the Chattahoochee. Such houses as they found were all deserted. Finally they reached Coweta.

In this town where the emperor was said to reside there was Woodward's little warehouse from which the Spanish took 605 deerskins, eight pairs of heavy socks and a yard and a half of heavy cloth, and an ornament of imitation gold. The town was completely deserted. The emperor and all of the residents had simply disappeared into the woods, taking their personal belongs and household effects with them.

Messengers were sent out to all the chiefs of the confederated towns ordering them to come in or face the consequences of the Spanish vengeance. The only people to come were the old king of Apalachicola and a chief of one small village. They would not tell where the Englishmen were hiding although Matheos offered them certain inducements and threatened to destroy their towns and supplies without leaving one house or grain of corn if they did not reveal the location of Woodward and his men.

The threats were all in vain. Finally on January 30, 1686, the Spanish made good on their threats and burned the towns of Tuskegee, Cusseta, Colone, and Coweta. Only a few exceptions were made in the destruction. At Cusseta there were two old women who could not leave. He spared them their household utensils. At Coweta he did not burn two houses from which the owners had not fled, saying: "In this way those absent could see their error and those that followed them would also."

As all of his exertions proved fruitless and thirty of his soldiers became ill, Matheos withdrew within a few days after the futile destruction of the towns. He sent the sick men down the river in canoes and marched with the remainder overland along the east bank of the river to Sabacola where they had left their horses.

Soon afterwards Woodward also became ill and ordered his four English associates back to Carolina. The emperor placed his friend on a litter and sent more than 100 loyal Cowetas to transport him and protect him on his way home.[17] It appears from extant records that the Indian escort delivered Woodward and his friends safely across the vast reaches of the confederation and into the presumed safety of the Carolina colony where they left their charges to make their way the short distance that remained to reach their homes.

Harris pieced together details of what appears to have been the tragic termination of this journey. He narrated the fact that Cabrera, realizing that the venture to prevent the English from getting control of the Chattahoochee River had failed, took the more drastic course of a direct attack to destroy the main British colonies at Port Royal and Charleston.

He took the garrisons from the missions of the coastal islands and incorporated them with the soldiers from the fort at St. Augustine. He placed these regular soldiers and a number of loyal Indians from the missions under the command of Captain Alexandro Thomas de Leon. The force embarked on two pirogues and a schooner and sailed to attack the Scottish colony at Port Royal. They were able to surprise the Scots and plunder and destroy the colony thoroughly. They then sailed up the North Edisto River and burned a settlement at Bears Bluff where they took as prisoner a brother of Governor Morton.

---

[17] Harris, *Here the Creeks Sat Down*, 137–139. This is the most complete account of the climactic episodes just recounted with full citation of original sources. However, there are some additional details in Fretwell, *Remote Frontier*, 82–92.

After these successes the Spanish force set sail for Charleston. A hurricane struck them and two of de Leon's ships were driven ashore and wrecked. One of these the Spanish burned and in it Governor Morton's brother perished in chains. De Leon's own vessel, the *Rosario*, was a complete wreck and he perished in it. Charleston was spared a potentially devastating attack.

Harris narrated the ironic by-product of the ill-fated Spanish campaign.

Five Indians from Guale had been with de Leon on his galleon. They survived the wreck, and in a strange and hostile country made themselves a little canoe and sought to sail back to Guale. When they came to the mouth of an unnamed river they encountered five Englishmen and two Indians on a little barge. The simple Guale Indians told the English that they were Christians. This was sufficient information to let the English understand that they were allies of Spain. The English promptly bound them, but did not search them thoroughly. One of the prisoners had a little knife made of a shell with which in the night time he cut his own bonds and then released his fellows. Silently they crept upon the Englishmen. Four sleeping together were killed instantly. One was sleeping apart with his two Indian friends. Though one of his Indian companions was killed and the other captured and he himself had two great blows from which an ordinary man would have died instantly, the lone Englishman escaped into the brush. All night long the Spanish Indians hunted him in the darkness. At their bidding the other Indians called out to him that they were Christians and would not kill him. There was no response. Somewhere in those shades the Englishman lay sleeping, and none ever waked him.[18]

The leader of the Apalachicola river towns who protected Woodward was a much younger man than the elderly emperor who had traveled to Charleston in 1671. He was almost certainly his successor, however, and, according to the normal order of succession, his nephew. He was, then, himself a *chechi* of the Fish people, who were the dominant element of the Pala*chu*colas or Apalachicola, some of whom resided on the Savannah and were relatives of the Edisto. The Yamasee and Yamacraw were divisions of these coastal Apalachicola. That they were the same people as the Apalachicola on the Chattahoochee was made clear by Chekilli, who explained that the Apalachicola, the people who adopted the Cussetas, were Tamachechi's people.

It is less certain that the emperor who held forth on the Chattahoochee in the 1680's was the same man as Emperor Brim who dominated the affairs of the entire region after 1700. This latter personage may have been the successor of the man who befriended Henry Woodward or he may actually have been that man. Walter Harris, who researched the subject over a long period and as thoroughly as extant sources permitted, believed both indeed were the same man he called the "greatest American Indian."

With the English gone from the Chattahoochee and the offending Apalachicolas humbled by the destruction of their towns and the bellicose colony at Port Royal destroyed by the ill-fated raid under de Leon, Cabrera was relieved of the British threat from the north, at least temporarily. In 1687 he was replaced as Governor of Florida by Don Diego de Quiroga y Lasada, a nobleman with considerable military expertise. He brought to St. Augustine the experience, courage, and resourcefulness needed to meet the treats to his domain which existed from the sea as well as from land.

The immediate threat was from English and French pirate raids along the Atlantic coast and from the Gulf of Mexico along the rivers into West Florida. Already the missions and outposts on the coastal islands had been destroyed and St. Augustine had been severely threatened the previous year. Raids from the Gulf had destroyed the new Apalachee fort and a plantation on the Suwannee River.

Quiroga was forced to halt work on the stone fortress, Castillo de San Marcos, at St. Augustine for lack of funds although it had been under construction for fifteen years and was nearing completion.

These disturbing occurrences augmented by continuing rumors that the French were planning a settlement somewhere along the Gulf coast caused the new governor to attempt to maintain the

---

[18] Harris, *Here the Creeks Sat Down*, 142–143.

existing acquiescence to the Spanish by the people of the Apalachicola towns. In order to observe for himself the situation in regard to these people as well the situation in Apalachee. He made the long trip to San Luis and thence to Alapache, the Spanish mission settlement nearest the troublesome province.

He met with the disgruntled people from the towns Matheos burned, assured them of good treatment in the future and urged them to resume trade with the Spanish at Apalachee. He hoped, he said, to make the river once again a friendly pathway between the two provinces. He, in fact, envisioned an even closer cooperation between the northern province and the Spanish. In a report to the king, dated April 1, 1688, he presented the plan he had in mind:

The untilled lands of these provinces (Apalachee and Apalachicola) are so fertile that if Your Majesty were pleased to settle them with a hundred families of Galicians from Tuy and Orense, because they are strong and laboring people, a beautiful town could be formed, a rich kingdom would result.[19]

Quiroga awaited in vain for a reply to his letter from the governmental bureaucracy in Madrid. More than a year passed. Meanwhile, news arrived regularly of visits by Carolina traders to the river towns. The governor became convinced that the Apalachicola people were not going to respond agreeably to his efforts to keep them loyal to Spanish interests by offering kindness and compassion. He determined to take another course.

The Spanish fort among the Apalachicolas, a diorama formerly in the Columbus Museum.

On June 8, 1690 he again wrote the king with the information that he had constructed a blockhouse at the main Apalachicola town in which there were stationed twenty infantrymen and a lieutenant. He enclosed a carefully drawn plan of the installation.[20]

Again there was delay while the letter made its way through the Council for the Indies, but this time a positive action resulted. On September 6, 1691 the Council recommended to the King that Quiroga be reprimanded for building a fort without authorization and that he "should avail himself of missionaries and use this gentle and sure method and not that of military arms and force."

[19] Fretwell, *Remote Frontier*, 97.
[20] *Ibid.*, 99.

Any action by the Council or the King was of no consequence in this instance. On September 18, a few days after the Council's opinion was recorded, a meeting of the colonial officials was held in the Governor's house in St. Augustine to determine what they could do to defend the town against a French corsair with many men and powerful guns, which they had just learned was on the way to attack the town. It was decided that the garrison at Apalachicola would be ordered to return at once to assist in the defense. The fort was ordered demolished to prevent it from falling into enemy hands.[21]

During the months that the Spanish occupied the little fort in their midst many of the inhabitants of the river towns moved to resettle on the river the English called Ochese Creek, later the Ocmulgee. There some English traders built a small fortified trading house and resumed the bartering Woodward had begun of manufactured goods and numerous other commodities for deerskins, beaver and other pelts, horses, and slaves captured in war with other tribes. The threat to Spanish Florida posed by the English in this new location was no less than it had been from the towns on the Chattahoochee.[22]

Finally in 1702 Governor Zuniga at St. Augustine decided that this influence had grown so great that it was time to crush the confederacy of tribes which now centered on the Ocmulgee and expel the Charleston traders. To accomplish this he sent a force of 900 Apalachees led by the lieutenant from San Luis up the Flint River. Zuniga expected this campaign to be decisive and to establish Spanish authority throughout the vast area between the mountains and the territory he already controlled.

When he learned of the Spanish invasion, Brim resorted to strategy rather than awaiting an attack on his warriors or his towns. He placed 500 men under the command of one Captain Antonio and other Carolinians from the English trading post. This force marched to meet the invaders at a point on the Flint river where the Spanish raiders would be expected to leave it for the overland march to the Ocmulgee.

Brim's men arrived at nightfall and prepared camp making sure that the fires marked their position clearly. Knowing well the Indian custom of attacking at dawn, they expected the Apalachees to act in accordance with it. Just before the break of day they withdrew leaving a blanket by each fire arranged so that it appeared to have a man sleeping under it.

The Apalachees attacked as they were expected to firing their single-shot muzzle loading rifles into the dummy blankets. Before they could reload the defending force sprang from the shadows and killed or captured nearly the entire force. Only a small remnant fled back to San Luis and the villages from which they came.[23]

This success apparently convinced Brim that his old enemies, the Spanish and their Apalachee henchmen, were not invincible. James Moore, recently governor of the Carolina colony, came to the same realization. Moore, one of the few colonists eligible to style himself "Gentleman," came to Charleston in 1674 from Barbados. He soon linked himself with a group of adventurers known as the "Goose Creek men" and set about building a political base which resulted in his virtually dominating the affairs of the colony. He espoused the cause of the Established Church of England and of strict construction of the colony's Fundamental Constitutions.

Moore was able to consolidate his following into a sufficiently powerful group to win the support of the Lords Proprietors and bring about the arrest and trial of Woodward in 1680 for conspiring with the Westoes to kill certain leaders of the colony. He was found guilty and ordered to give bond of 1,000 pounds that he would not trade or communicate with the offending Indians in any way.[24]

[21] *Ibid.*, 100–104.

[22] Bolton, *Spain's Title to Georgia*, 58.

[23] Fretwell, *Remote Frontier*, 114–115.

[24] *Journal of the Grand Council of South Carolina, Aug. 25, 1671, June 24, 1680,* ed., A. S. Salley, (Charleston: Historical Commission of South Carolina, 1907) p.85.

eager to join the effort as were the Shawnee. No information seems to have reached the English, either in the Carolinas or Virginia, concerning the widespread scheme to effect their annihilation. The South Carolina traders continued their trade replete with its objectionable practices and political intrigues. Their counterparts from Virginia, although forewarned of potential consequences by the bloody uprising of the Tuscaroras in 1711, extended their similarly demoralizing activities among the smaller tribes of their hinterlands and even among the Cherokees beyond the Blue Ridge mountains.

Because of their obvious benefit to his overall strategy, Brim encouraged the French in effecting their alliance with the Choctaws and sanctioned their establishing, in 1714, Fort Toulouse among the Alabamas at the junction of the Alabama and Tallapoosa rivers. He thus eliminated the chances of trouble from his rear when he diverted his attention and war parties elsewhere.

That diversion came quickly and without warning. On April 15, 1715 the erstwhile cooperative Yamassees suddenly attacked the trading establishment at Pocotaligo and massacred all the English there. All the outlying settlements in the South Carolina colony were simultaneously captured and destroyed. The only survivors among the settlers were those who managed to escape and flee to Charleston. Brim's forces moved on Charleston itself but were stopped by the heroic effort of the militia forces.

News of the South Carolina disaster spread to the other colonies along with the fear of Indian attacks from their own borders. The English traders among the Creeks and Choctaws were all slain, but the Cherokees failed to abide by their promise to cooperate in the uprising and, in so doing, destroyed its chance of total success. Brim sent a party of his warriors to join in their promised attack on the Carolinians. Suddenly, instead of putting the joint venture into effect the Cherokees slew all the Creeks in their towns and joined with the English in the effort to destroy Brim's main war-party.

The South Carolina colony was saved by the appearance of a voluntary army from North Carolina led by Maurice Moore, son of James Moore. Facing this seasoned unit of backwoodsmen and the large group of Cherokees who joined the English, the Creeks were forced to retreat to their principal towns, Coweta and Ocmulgee on the river now known by the latter name. There is no mention in the South Carolina records of the retaliation the South Carolinians and their allied inflicted on vanquished enemy in this the heart of their home territory.

All that is known of the vengeance that was taken is the fact that these towns were abandoned at that time and never occupied by them again. An incidental statement by James Adair written more than fifty years after the episode confirms the destruction:

> They will all affirm that they have seen, and distinctly, most surprising apparitions, and heard horrid shrieking noises. They pretend, it was impossible for all their senses to be delyubed at the same time; especially at *Okmulge*, the old waste town, belonging to the *Muskoge*, 150 miles S.W. of Augusta in Georgia, which the South-Carolinians destroyed about the year 1715. They strenuously aver, that when necessity forces them to encamp there, they always hear, at the dawn of the morning, the usual noise of Indians singing their joyful religious notes, and dancing as if going to the river to purify themselves, and then returning to the old town house: with a great deal more to the same effect.[32]

From the new Coweta, now his principal town on the Chattahoochee River, Brim sent emissaries to Governor Johnson, who wrote on February 7, 1718: "Several of the Heads of the Creek Indians have been with me to offer peace and have been kindly received and sent back."[33] In July 1721 Colonel George Chicken recorded in his journal that "Auletta", eldest son of "Breem Emperor of the Creek Indians," came to Charleston to hold a talk with Governor Nicholson and make up their differences. Another son, Seepycoffee, was recognized as commander-in-chief of the Creeks in the place of his father by Tobias Fitch on a mission for the South Carolina government in 1725.

---

[32] Williams, *Adair's History*, 39.
[33] *Records in the British Public Records Office* 7 Vols., (Atlanta: Historical Commission of South Carolina, 1930. vol. 7) p. 120.

Walter Harris thus evaluated the condition and attitude of the great Coweta leader in his final years:

> The failure of his great design does not crush Brim. He will go no more to war against the white man. In such wars as the law of retaliation requires him to wage against other Indians, Chekilli, his faithful headman, will lead his warriors. Henceforth, he will sit in his town on the river and devote himself to maintaining the independence of his Confederacy by peaceful application of his doctrine of the balance of power. He will not join one of the white nations in war against another white nation but always when one of the three seeks to encroach upon the rights of his people, he will hold over it the threat that he will take the field on the side of one of its rivals.

> He accepts the presents of the French, the entertainment of the Spanish, and the favors of the English.

> From his policy his people reap commercial advantages as well as security from invasion. When the Governor of South Carolina contemplates sending troops against him, the English envoy at Coweta writes to protest against it saying, "It is the trade governs these people. If there comes any army they will fly to the French."

> To keep the white men in suspense, Brim does not object to the Upper Creeks' favoring one side while the Lower Creeks favor the other. He even encourages a division of allegiance between his two sons. Seepycoffee becomes the favorite and honored guest first of the Spanish and then of the French. His other son Hollata throws himself wholeheartedly into the English cause and dies fighting with the English against the Yamassees.

> When the white men accuse him of double-dealing, he feels no shame, for he knows that it does not lie in their mouths to make such a charge. Quietly he reminds Tobias Fitch that he has heard that Colonel Chicken and his South Carolinians are among the Cherokees giving them encouragement against the Creeks, while Fitch is at Coweta trying to induce Brim to make peace with those same Cherokees. Again, he suggests to Fitch that his people cannot understand the presence of Englishmen among the Yamassees, though, of course, he professes his own complete satisfaction with Fitch's explanation.

> The delicate intimations that he has fathomed the secret of their forest diplomacy are not very reassuring to the South Carolinians; for since 1717 their hope of accomplishing the ultimate purpose of all their negotiations with the Creeks and Cherokees has depended on keeping both in ignorance of the design starkly outlined by Joseph Boone to the proprietors in these words, "It is a matter of great weight to us how to hold both as our friends for some time and assist them in cutting one another's throats without offending either. If we cannot destroy one nation of Indians by another our country must be lost".

> Hollata's death makes a change in the plans of Brim. The law of retaliation requires that it be avenged upon the Yamassees. But they are now allies of Spain and enemies of the English, so Seepycoffee must leave his friends the French and join the English in order to avenge his brother's death.

> Brim turns this necessity to account by securing the support of the English for Seepycoffee as his successor. He tells Fitch that he is now too old for the charge he has. Since Hollata is dead there is none of his family but Seepycoffee who is fit to take that charge upon him and it is the general opinion of his people that Seepycoffee should succeed him.

> And so on December 15, 1725, in the last council of his people over which we see him preside, he hears Fitch confer the King of England's commission upon Seepycoffee "to be commander-in-chief of this nation under his father Emperor Brim's direction."

> The pathos of his appeal for English recognition of Seepycoffee and the pomp and ceremony with which that recognition is received, convince the South Carolinians that, in his old

Above: Verilst portrait of Tamachechi and Toonahowi. (Courtesy the Georgia Historical Commission, Savannah, Georgia).

Above: Coconut shell rattle of the sort Tamachechi's attendants shook in their ceremony welcoming General Oglethorpe and the Georgia colonists in 1733. This is one of four of these ritual items the Yuchis took to Oklahoma in 1836. Chief Samuel W. Brown, Jr. used it in the 1957 peace ceremony in Columbus and afterward deposited it in the city museum. (Columbus Museum photo).

provide insight into his own religious philosophy but reveal something of the moral calibre of the colonists. The statements by Tamachechi are from the copious diaries of John Wesley.

After he had been introduced to the missionaries, the old man remarked to Wesley: "I am glad you are come. When I was in England I desired that some would speak the great word to me. I will go up and speak to the wise men of our nation, and I hope they will hear. But we would not be made Christians as the Spaniards make Christians; we would be taught before we are baptized."

A short while later the old man's feelings regarding the Christians had cooled notably. Jones took notice of this change and commented:

It is a common error to estimate the character of a religion by the conduct of its professed believers. By this standard Tomo-chi-chi weighed the religion of the colonists, and as he became more intimately acquainted with the white race, as he observed that in their daily conduct his more intelligent neighbors were subject to passions, animosities, excesses and frauds very like those which characterized his own people, he was naturally led to distrust the wonderful influence and the restraining graces of that religion which they professed.[6]

Tamachechi told John Wesley:

When I was in England I desired that some one would speak the great word to me; and our people then desired to hear it; but now we are all in confusion. The French on one side, and the Spanish on the other, and the traders in our midst have caused us much perplexity, and made our people unwilling. Their ears are shut. Their tongues are divided, and some say one thing and some another. But I will call our chiefs together and speak to the wise men of our nation, and I hope they will hear.

Wesley's reply was not of the sort to inspire confidence or enlist the special interest of the strong-minded old Mico. He said: "There is but one,—He that sitteth in the heaven,—who is able to teach man wisdom. Though we are come so far, we know not whether He will please to teach you by us or no. If He teaches you, you will learn wisdom; but we can do nothing."

At a later interview, when Wesley urged Tamachechi to adhere to the doctrines of Christianity and become a convert, the old man scornfully responded: "Why these are Christians at Savannah! Those are Christians at Frederica! Christians drunk! Christians beat men! Christians tell lies! Me no Christian."[7]

The good relations that began when Chekilli made his first visit to Savannah in 1736 were further improved when Oglethorpe traveled to Coweta in the summer of 1739 to attend a conference the Creeks were holding with the Choctaws to restore relations that had not been good since the joint English-Creek war against this tribe some twenty-five years before.

Oglethorpe traveled with a small contingent of soldiers and traders along the old trading path from Augusta through the then abandoned Ocmulgee town to Coweta, along probably the same route Woodward had followed more than half a century earlier. While he was in the capital of the Creek Confederacy, Oglethorpe signed a firmer treaty of peace with the Nation, crossing the river to the "white town," Cusseta, to do so.

Becoming ill with a fever, Oglethorpe was in bed for several days and did not return to Augusta until the end of September. When he arrived there, he was confronted with two unwelcome pieces of news: England had gone to war against Spain assuring immediate hostilities between his colonials and the Spanish in Florida, and Tamachechi had died. He left immediately by boat down the river and reached Savannah in three days in time to attend the funeral ceremonies there for his Indian friend. He then proceeded directly to Fort Frederica to prepare for war with the Spanish.

Tamachechi was interred in Percival Square (now Wright Square) in a traditional ceremony including the burying with him of certain possessions and offerings to facilitate his journey to the spirit world. Oglethorpe ordered that the ceremony include full military honors accorded by the colonial troops. He ordered also that a pyramid of stone be constructed over the old king's grave. If this were ever done the stones were removed long ago and the exact location of the grave was forgotten. A huge stone boulder was placed in the square and inscribed in his memory a century ago to mark the approximate site of the grave.

---

[6] Jones, *Tomo-chi-chi*, 58–76.
[7] *Ibid.*, 103

Chapter 11

Offspring of Sky and Earth

The Shawanos were the cohesive force which held together the diverse peoples of the North American continent east of the Great Plains in the epoch the archaeologists call the Woodland period. They served the same function when the peoples bearing the culture known as Mississippian made their way outward from the banks of their namesake river spreading their distinctive customs, notably their flat-top temple mounds and sophisticated symbolic art, along the Ohio River and its tributaries and southward into what is now the Gulf states, Georgia and the western portion of the Carolinas. At the beginning of the Mississippian epoch it was the resident Shawano who met the intruding newcomers and undertook the task of fitting them into the existing societal pattern of the region, peaceably if possible or by force if necessary.

In the younger chief Samuel Brown's carefully composed statement quoted in chapter three the original people were the *Zoyaha* or *Yustafawano* who he said are "better known today as Yuchis." Following this was the statement: "And their original name was *Zoyaha-wano*, which was the governing word, as it is of today, from their starting point."

It is necessary to translate these names before the meaning of Brown's statement can be determined. *Zoyaha* is "sun-fused" (*zoya*) plus the first personal ending (*ha*) meaning "we are." *Yustafa* means "first" or "top ranking." Its components translate thus: *fa* "place" and *Yusta*, an ancient ceremonial name for the moon. *Wano* is sometimes translated as "people," but a more accurate rendering is "alien beings." I believe this is what the Chief said precisely translated into English: These people were the sun beings or Moon beings. Their original name was sun beings, which it is of today, from their starting point.

Brown continued with his explanation of the names: "And their leader had many nations. Spiritually they inherited instilled in them their lineage for generations to come. They had a tribal town, a big one, at *Coshafa*. That is a Yuchi word." The name contains the elements *co* "man," *sha* "falconidae" or "serpent," and *fa* "place." This name provides another evidence of the union of earth and sky. Brown said further: "And it was said by the old people that was what they called *Shalala Wano* "Waterfowl beings" or *Sha Wano* "Falconidae-serpent beings," that they called themselves *Shawanogee*. That is not a Yuchi word." It is the name *Shawano* plus *gee*, "earth" in the old ceremonial or "Red Man's language."

Brown continued his exposition: "They traveled and branched off in different branches and from *Shawanogee* became known to the public and to the world as Shawnees. There was a big tribe of them (Shawano) and one bunch called itself *Ispogogee*, another *Kispogogee*, and another *Iste Muscogulgee*, and the last *Muscovee*."

The foregoing explanation identifies the Shawanos and the Yuchis as the same people, one division of whom are associated with the sun and another with the moon. They are both children of the sky and the earth. The *Zoya* were created when a drop of the sun's blood fell to earth; the other was shaped from clay in the image of *Cohantoney*, the Breath Master. Elsewhere I have shown that these names for divisions of the Shawano contain distinguishing elements by which they can be identified in various historical contexts.[1]

James Adair was a Scotchman who came to Charleston in 1735. He soon went as a trader to live among the Overhill Cherokees and within a few years moved to the Chickasaw towns in northern Mississippi. He had an intimate association with these tribes for forty years and frequently passed

---

[1] Mahan, *The Secret*, 133.

through, and sometimes visited, the Upper Creek towns in northeastern Alabama. During these years he secretly compiled the most comprehensive ethnographic study that was ever done of any eastern North American Indian tribe while native cultural patterns were still virtually in their aboriginal form. In 1775, at the beginning of the American Revolution Adair's *History* was published in London. Because of the war and the consequent disruption of communications, the book was never widely circulated in the United States.

By the time some American scholars were aware of Adair's work the main thesis it espoused had fallen into disfavor with a new generation of savants. This thesis held that the Indian tribes Adair knew were the descendants of the Lost Ten Tribes of Israel. As a consequence of this "unscientific" viewpoint no new edition of the work was published until the 1930's. Only a few erudite studies devoted to proving Adair's hypothesis had appeared in the intervening century and a half. Most notable of these were Elias Boudinot's *A Star in the West* (1815) and Edward King's (Viscount Kingsborogh) *Antiquities of Mexico. . . .* (9 volumes) (1830–1848). Neither of these exhaustively researched studies has ever been given credence, or even mention, by professional students of the Native Americans.

Regardless of Adair's undeniable determination to prove his point concerning the Israelite ancestry of the tribes he knew, there is much information in his twenty-three Arguments for the Semitic relationship that gives valuable insights to data gathered elsewhere. One bit of information which contributes significantly to determining cultural relationship of the priestly order is his description of the manner in which the name of Divinity is invoked in the annual ceremonies of renewal:

The eldest of the priests leads the sacred dance, ahead of the innermost row, which is next to the holy fire. He begins the dance around the supposed holy fire, by invoking Yah, after their usual manner, on a bass key, and with a short accent; then he sings YO YO, which is repeated by the rest of the religious possession; and he continues his sacred invocations and praises, repeating the divine word, or notes, till they return to the same point of the circular course, where they began: then HE HE in like manner, and WAH WAH. While dancing they never fail to repeat those notes; and frequently the holy train strike up *Halelu, Halelu*; then *Haleluiah, Halelu-Yah,* and Aleluiah and Alelu-Yah,. . .[2]

One example of his detailed observation found in the old trader's discussion of the role of the intertribal priesthood, which he calls the *Magi*:

The title of the old beloved men, or archimagi, is still hereditary in the panther, or tyger families:. . .[3]

Istohollo (*Iste Yoholo*) is the name of all their priestly order, and their order, and their pontifical office descends by inheritance to the eldest: those friend towns, which are firmly confederated in their exercise and plays, never have more than one *Archi-magus* at a time . . . . Notwithstanding the Cherake are now a nest of apostate hornets, pay little respect to grey hairs, and have been degenerating fast from their primitive religious principles, for about thirty years past—yet before the last war. Old Hop, who was helpless and lame, presided over the whole nation as *Archi-magus*, and lived in Choate, their only town of refuge. It was entirely owning to the wisdom of those who then presided in South Carolina, that his dangerous pontifical, and regal-like power was impaired, by their setting up *Atta Kulla Kulla*, and supporting him so well, as to prevent the then easy transition of an Indian high-priesthood into a French American bloody chair. . . .[4]

Adair's History contains many firsthand observations that attest to his long and close association with the people he described. Although his observations are selective because of his wish to convince his readers of the Hebrew ancestry of his subjects, no reason has been found to believe he

---

[2] Williams, *Adair's History*, 101–103.
[3] *Ibid.*, 33.
[4] *Ibid.*, 85–86.

deliberately misrepresented what he saw. He had further information to report concerning the special class of priests he called *Magi*:

> Before the Indian *Archi-magus* officiates in making the supposed holy fire, for the yearly atonement of sin, the Sagan clothes him with a white ephod, which is a waistcoat without sleeves. When he enters on that solemn duty, a beloved attendant spreads a white-drest buck-skin on the white seat, which stands close to the supposed holiest, and then puts some white beads on it, that are given him by the people. Then the *Archi-magus* wraps around his shoulders a consecrated skin of the same sort, which reaching across under his arms, he ties behind his back, with two knots on the legs, in the form of a figure of eight. Another custom he observes on this solemn occasion, is, instead of going barefoot, he wears a new pair of buck skin white moccasenes made by himself, and stitched with the sinews of the same animal. The upper leather across the toes, he paints, for the space of three inches, with a few streaks of red—not with vermillion for that is their continual war-emblem, but with a certain red root, its leaves and stalk resembling the ipecacuanha, which is their fixed red symbol of holy things. They have one (tribe) they call *sphane*, the meaning of which they have lost; perhaps it might have signified the *man*.[5]

The archimagi were associated with special towns of refuge in which they provided protection for persons accused of crime until their guilt or innocence could be determined. Adair wrote at length of these havens of mercy, which are well known from other contemporary historical sources.[6] Because of his belief in the Hebrew kinship of his subject peoples, Adair emphases that the Israelites had a similar institution:

> The Israelites had Cities of Refuge, or places of safety, for those who killed a person unawares, and without design; to shelter them from the blood-thirsty relations of the deceased, or the revenger of blood, who always pursued or watched the unfortunate person, like a ravenous wolf: but after the death of the high-priest the man-slayer could safely return home, and nobody durst molest him.

> According to the same particular divine law of mercy, each of these Indian nations have either a house or town of refuge, which is a sure asylum to protect a man-slayer, or the unfortunate captive, if he can once enter into it. The Cheerake, though now exceedingly corrupt, still observe that law so inviolably, as to allow their beloved town the privilege of protecting a wilfull murtherer: but they seldom allow him to return home afterwards in safety—they will redeem blood for blood, unless in some very particular case when the eldest can redeem. However, if he should accept the price of blood to wipe away its stains, and dry up the tears of the rest of the nearest kindred of the deceased, it is generally productive of future ills; either when they are drinking spirituous liquors, or dancing their enthusiastic war dances, a tomohawk is likely to be sunk into the head of one of his relations.

> Formerly, when one of the Cheerake murdered an English trader he immediately ran off for the town of refuge: but as soon as he got in view of it, the inhabitants discovered him by the close pursuit of the shrill war-whoo-whoop: and for fear of irritating the English, they instantly answered the war cry, ran to arms, intercepted, and drove him off into the Tenase river (where he escaped, though mortally wounded) lest he should have entered the reputed holy ground; and then had it stained with the blood of their friend; or he had obtained sanctuary to the danger of the community, and the foreign contempt of their sacred altars.

> This town of refuge called Choate, is situated on a large stream of the Mississippi, five miles above the late unfortunate Fort *Loudon*,—where some years ago, a brave Englishman was protected after killing an Indian warrior in defense of this property. The gentleman told me, that as his trading house was near to that town of refuge, he had resolved with himself, after some months stay in it, to return home; but the head-man assured him, that though he was then safe,

---

[5] *Ibid.*, 87–88.
[6] Mahan, The *Secret*, 27–28.

it would prove fatal if he removed thence; so he continued in his asylum still longer, till the affair was by time obliterated, and he had wiped off all their tears with various presents. In the upper or most western part of the country of the Muskohge, there was an old beloved town, now reduced to a small ruinous village, called *Koosah*, which is still a place of safety for those who kill undesignedly. It stands on a commanding ground, over-looking a bold river, which after running about forty leagues, sweeps close by the late mischievous French garrison *Alebamah*, and down to Mobille-Sound, 200 leagues distant, and so into the gulph of Florida.

In almost every Indian nation, there are several peaceable towns, which are called "old-beloved," "ancient, holy, or white towns." (White is their fixt emblem of peace, friendship, happiness, prosperity, purity, holiness, &c. as with the Israelites.): they seem to have been formerly "towns of refuge," for it is not in the memory of their oldest people, that ever human blood was shed in them; although they often force persons from thence, and put them to death elsewhere.

The "white towns" were moon towns and were apparently deliberately situated in close proximity with "red towns," usually known as "war" towns. The latter were sun towns of which Tukabatchee is the best known example. This is the Upper Creek town with which James Adair was most familiar. His description of this ancient people includes information on the sacred metal plates associated with them:

In the Tuccabatchees on the Tallapoose river, thirty miles above the Allabahamah garrison, are two brazen tables, and five of copper. They esteem them so sacred as to keep them constantly in their holy of holies, without touching them in the least, only in the time of their compounded first-fruit-offering, and annual expiration of sins; at which season, their magus carries one under his arm, ahead of the people, dancing around the sacred arbour; next to him their head-warrior carries another; and those warriors who chuse it, carry the rest after the manner of the high-priest; all the others carry white canes with swan-feathers at the top.

Following an explanation of his sources of information on which this account was based, the author presented two outline drawings of the brazen "tables," one of these done in copper. Concerning them he wrote:

Old Bracket, an Indian of perhaps 100 years old, lives in that old beloved town, who gave the following description of them: He said—he was told by his forefathers that those plates were given to them by the man we call God; that there had been many more of other shapes, some as long as he could stretch with both his arms, and some had writing upon them which were buried with particular men and that they had instructions given with them, viz., they must only be handled by particular people, and those fasting; and no unclean woman must be suffered to come near them or the place where they were deposited. He said, none but this town's people had any such plates given them, and that they were a different people from the Creeks. He only remembered three more, which were buried with three of his family, and he was the only man of the family now left. He said, there were two copper plates under the king's cabbin, which had lain there from the first settling of the town.

It is important to note here that Tukabatchee was the source of the red fire given the town of Coweta upon their arrival in the east. See chapter five. The close relationship of Tomachechi's Yamassee people to the Tuckabatchee will be pointed out elsewhere.

There is another substantiation of the often-repeated statement by Upper Creeks that Tukabahchee was their head war-town and that its fire was the "grandfather" of the fire which burned at Coweta, the war-town of the Lower Creeks. This fire and its attendant rituals were brought to the Tukabatchee by people from the sky, some of whom remained to assure its preservation, according to an ancient story sometimes recorded by visitors to the town. One of the most complete versions of that story was told to General Ethan Allen Hitchcock about 1840 by an old man known as "Ispocogee Micco:"

John R. Swanton in his "Social Organization and Religious Usages of the Creek Indians," rephrased the story:

> According to the story as obtained from this source, seven persons of both sexes were sent down from heaven in very old times; later they attempted to return, but one of them, thought to have been a man, died, whereupon the others came back. They then sat down in a square and performed some ceremonies which the Indians wished to learn. At first they were unsuccessful, but at last they discovered something about it, and the strangers then taught them how to make a fire and how to worship the great spirit. They also brought certain plates from heaven which they gave to the Creek chiefs. . . . The new comers told them to make a new fire once a year by friction, having extinguished the existing fire, and to thank the Great Spirit for his blessing; at that season they were to exhibit the plates. When this happened the Indians were using bows and arrows and lived entirely by hunting, but after a time they found some white people and from them obtained knives and other useful articles. At a similar early period the Tukabahchee met the Coweta. They smoked the pipe of peace together and agreed to an eternal friendship which they have ever since maintained, and all the other Indians are obliged to look up to them.

Swanton stated that this aged mico was the last person to preserve knowledge of the identity of the Ispogogee, adding: "Theoretically there always is such a chief, but since the death of Tukabahchee mico the knowledge of him has become lost. This knowledge was anciently preserved by means of a certain council formed about the sacred fire in the busk ground."[7] Swanton was clearly mistaken, as proved by details that are related in this chapter and elsewhere.

As Tukabatchee was the head war-town of the Upper Creeks, it is to be expected that a peace-town was located close by. There was. This town was Abihka a few miles away on the same river, the Tallapoosa. Swanton, gave a brief history of this town including the close relationship of the members to the Shawano:

> A second body of Shawnee lived for a time among the Abihka Indians. This band originally at least, seems to have belonged to the Piqua division. It moved into Pennsylvania in 1692 along with a Frenchman named Martin Charier, who died there in 1718. It moved into Pennsylvania in 1692 along with a Frenchman named Martin Chartier, who died there in 1718. Peter Shabonee, or Pierre Chartier, his son by a Shawnee woman, also married a Shawnee and settled among Indians of his tribe at Allegheny on the right bank of the Allegheny River below the mouth of the Kiskiminetas or Conemaugh. In April 1745, in consequence of a reprimand given him by Governor Gordon of Pennsylvania, he instigated 400 Shawnee to leave the government of Pennsylvania. A French document represents them as having come down from Sandusky, moved to a spot high up the Wabash, and then descended to the junction of the Wabash and Ohio, where they lived two years and passed on to the Abihka country.[8]

There are several bits of information, in addition to the sources Swanton used, to verify details of the historical sketch just quoted. One such verification was supplied by the Tennessee historian John Haywood, who wrote in 1823:

On the 21st of July, 1821, Mr. Earl proceeded to the mound near Nashville on the field of David McGavock, Esquire, with workmen furnished with spades and pickaxes to cut into it. This is the mound upon which Monsieur Charleville, a French trader, had his store in the year 1714, when the Shawanese were driven from Cumberland by the Cherokees and Chickasaws. It stands on the west side of the river and on the north side of French Lick Creek, and about 70 yards from each.[9]

This M. Charleville was not Chartier, but was still living in 1779 and reported that as a boy he had worked for the French trader whose store was in a fort on this mound and that he (Charleville) had

[7] Swanton, "Social Organization," 66.

[8] *Ibid.*

[9] John Haywood, *Natural and Aboriginal History of Tennessee up to the Settlements Therein by the White People in the Year 1768*, Ed. Mary U. Rothrock (Jackson, Tenn.: McCowart-Mercer Press, Inc., 1959),p. 127.

been away when the Chickasaw and Cherokee attacked and killed the trader and many of the Sawano, the others fleeing to join their kinsmen in Pennsylvania.[10] Descendants of these people were most likely among the people Pierre Chartier led from the mouth of the Conemaugh to Abihka in 1745–47. Other people with Chartier were descendants of the Abihka people who had fled from their trading town on the Savannah River and gone north to join Chartier and his group after the Yammassee War of 1715.

James Adair saw the Chartier group in 1747 as they came south to join the upper Creeks. Not so much interested in their history as their skin color, he wrote:

I took particular notice of the Shawano Indians as they were passing from the northward, within fifty miles of the Chikkasah country, to that of the Creeks; and by comparing them with the Indians which I accompanied to their camp, I observed the Shawano to be much fairer than the Chikkasah; though I am satisfied, their endeavours to cultivate the copper color, were alike.[11]

The Shawano, whose forced migrations to settle among strangers albeit their ethnic kinsmen, were mere remnants of the great people the French Jesuits called the *Chauvanans* a century earlier as they told how their large defenseless towns along the Ohio River drainage were decimated by the Senecas and other Iroquois using firearms they had obtained from the Dutch and Swedes of New Amsterdam. The surviving refugees were the *Kispogogee*.

The Kispogogee took their name from the eagle just as their kinsmen Shawano, the Ispogogee took theirs from *Man*. They were in fact the same people who spoke the same language, sometimes called *Sawanese* and sometimes *Yuchi*. The significance of the eagle as a ceremonial rank was the subject of a taped interview in 1957 between Dorothy J. Brown and her father, Samuel W. Brown, Jr. Miss Brown asked her father: "Which was the highest clan of all?" This led to the following exchange:

The chief answered: "The ranking one was the bear, and the Tiger, and the eagle was the superior."

"And the eagle was the 'number one' clan?"

"It was the lookout clan."

"Didn't they have a caste system like rank, more or less?"

"The eagle was the fellow that flew up and made his warning by cries."

"Was the eagle clan considered the top one, the first one, that is the upper class?"

"Yes, and most of the women are birds."

"And what was next?"

"The Bear."

"And then the Tiger?"

"The Tiger—well, the Wolf was the third one."

"And what was next?"

"The Fox."

---

[10] *Ibid.*,207–208.
[11] Adair, *History*, 21.

In Chief Brown's hesitancy and then decision not to include the Tiger among the Shawano clans there is verification that this high-ranking clan was of separate origin. This supposition is strengthened by the fact that Chief Brown frequently referred to the tiger as the king's immediate subordinate in the ceremonial hierarchy in at least an equal rank with the Bear. The reasonable conclusion, based on this and other accumulated evidence, is that the Tiger is the head of the Zoya or Sun division of the sun-moon union and the bear has the same relationship to the moon division. They are thus respectively the heads of the "red" and "white" towns.

One of Dorothy Brown's questions on the identity of the clans remained unanswered, although she did not realize this at the time. She assumed her father to imply that the bird clan was synonymous with the Eagle. Actually, he did not. He only agreed that the Eagle was a bird and that "most of the women are birds." The Eagle has a deeper, esoteric meaning.

This meaning is symbolized in the title, *Fushudgee*, the "Birdtail" king of the Apalachicolas and Cussetas. The feathers of the Eagle's tail were emblems of accomplishment, which Chief Brown explained in his account of the meetings held by a special council in certain underground lodges. He spoke of a "medicine," *pardeh*, used at that time and said that:

> First they washed in it and the more they—you might say—prayed or asked their Master to guide them, they will follow the eagle until he is stripped of his twelve feathers in his tail. This is a symbol that they go by and they go by it until this day. The eagle is the mighty monarch of the air that flies high up into the skies; and he hatches his young and there he defends with his wings and no one can hardly ever get to one of these eagles and, therefore, he is the sacred bird of all birds.

All of this tradition had enormous meaning to the aging chief. He realized the need for some of the knowledge he possessed to be preserved and used to help restore for his people their proper position in the world's history. Nevertheless, he found it difficult to impart information in a manner completely unprecedented among his forefathers. He explained this reluctance to me and said he could only give me certain guidance in the directions in which I should pursue research. He voiced this reluctance more forcefully in a recorded statement to his daughter and the Yuchi people which is quoted in chapter three.

If the eagle was thus highly symbolic and sacred, why was it not the alter ego of the Yuchi-Shawano women, who after all, in a matriarchial system such as theirs must have had very high rank? The answer is simple; there is another totemic bird held in equally sacred regard by the sky people and this bird exclusively symbolizes peace. The feathers of this bird also have symbolic meaning. This bird is the crane whose feathers adorn the cane staffs borne on occasion by two men each from the north and south arbors in the annual Green Corn ceremonies. These were also the white feathers and bird wings which accompanied Tamachechi on the occasion of his formal welcoming of Oglethorpe and the Georgia colonists.

It is of further interest to note here that the carved wooden birds the French observer Du Pratz described and pictured atop the Natchez temple, which description is quoted herein, looked more like a waterfowl than an eagle.

It is reasonable to assume from Brown's use of the word, from use by the Yuchis of symbolic crane feathers on the "King's Ground" at Kellyville, Oklahoma and from the seemingly aquatic nature of the Natchez temple bird effigies that there was a waterfowl associated with the sun kings. *Shalala* (goose) is the name for the specific bird that is totemic to the Yuchis and was mentioned in Chief Brown's formal identifying statement as one of their names, *Shalalawano* or Shawano. This identification is reinforced in the traditional reference by the Zoya division of the Yuchis to their bluish gray eyes as "goose eyes."

I learned from diverse sources that the Great Goose represents the Earth Mother and so, of course, the Shalala-wano are her children. One day halfway around the world from the American Southeast where I knew this identification was pertinent I learned that it applied to the Asian Yuchis as well. One day in the city museum at Pershawar, Pakistan I saw a relic casket from a nearby

Buddhist *stupa* which was made to contain some of the physical remains of *Kaniska*, a famous Indian emperor (c. 120 − 162 A.D.), who was a descendant of the *Yueh-chih*, the Asian Yuchis.

Earlier I had read a letter from a monk who was invited by Kaniska to discuss Buddhist doctrines with him. As he was too old to travel, the monk put his advice into the form of a poetic epistle. He urged the king to give up hunting of wild beasts, exhorting him to live an exemplary Buddhist life: "Train yourself," he wrote, "in the way of your own people born in the *Kusa* race, do not impair the household law of your ancestors, the sun of the Arya." He further urged Kaniska to refrain from any killing, to be compassionate, and "Since we can not look upon the hurtful sun, act, O Moon of Kings, like the Moon."[12] After I studied the casket I described in *The Secret* what I discovered:

It is an urn less than a foot tall and is beautifully carved from the hard gray schist of that region. On the lid in the place of a handle stands a three-inch-high figure representing the emperor. He is flanked by figures of the Sun and Moon.

This seemed appropriate as I studied these figures. Here were the symbols representing the great Sky-God in the two aspects the old monk had mentioned in his letter of advice to his king. The implication was that Kanishka was descended from both. This would have told the story of the Kushan emperor's identity even if I had not looked at a frieze in low relief which circles the rim of the vessel. When I found that it consisted of a row of geese with their necks stretched as though they were asleep or dead, I knew that Kaniska, although a mighty king, a son of the Sun and a follower of Sha, also belonged to his mother the Earth, represented here by the goose. His people were the *Shalalawano* (Goose people), just as Chief Brown said the Yuchis were.[13]

The name *Shalalawano* may also apply to the crane, the bird of peace. The role of the eagle, as has just been demonstrated, is that of protection, specifically for the people of the moon. There is another bird, the hawk or falcon, who has this relationship to the sun people and is an even more powerful protector. He is thus associated with the red fire and is related to the Tiger in the same way the eagle is with the Bear.

The Sun people, or Zoya, had a direct relationship to Shawnee. Their name identifies them as the "little" *Sha* (falconae-serpent) people. They are also the descendants of the Shawano. This being true, there should be historical evidence indicating a close relationship between the Yuchi and the Shawnee since the earliest period they are known to history.

There is such evidence in abundance from the sixteenth century to the present. Further indications of this close relationship is found in the continued uncertainty of ethnologists and historians concerning the true identification of the Indians of Savannah, the eighteenth century trading town on their namesake river. This town was abandoned in 1715 during the Yamassee war. Verner W. Crane, the foremost student of the subject, without any hesitation identifies them, at the time of their helping to defeat the Westos in 1680, as a "migrating group of Shawnee, recent comers, apparently from west of the mountains.[14] Crane cited English colonial sources.

From the same period, Swanton found Spanish documents to show that these same people were Chisca (and therefore Yuchi) to support his contention that the latter were late migrants from the north, although by the same argument, they were shown to be the Westo.[15] Except in the case of the Westo, they were both correct; the Chisca, who were the same as the Savannah, and the Savannah people themselves consisted of both Yuchi and Shawnee.[16]

[12]   John Rosenfield, *The Dynastic Arts of the Kushanas* (Berkley and Los Angeles: University of California Press, 1967), p. 34.
[13]   Mahan, *The Secret*, 187.
[14]   Crane, *Southern Frontier*, 19−20.
[15]   Swanton, "Early History."
[16]   Thomas Woodward, *Woodward's Reminiscences of the Creek, of Muscogee Indians, Contained in Letters to Friends in Georgia and Alabama, With a Foreword by Peter Brannon* (Tuscaloosa: Alabama Book Store, 1939) pp. 40−42.

Ironically, later scholarly investigation of the question resulted in a denial of Swanton's identification of the Chisca as Yuchi. Apparently on the basis of sound documentation, notably seventeenth century maps, J. Joseph Bauxer, in his study of Yuchi ethnology, wrote:

> There is no area on the map identified specifically as Shawnee; and of the labeled villages only Mequatchaiki can be identified with any degree of certainty as Shawnee. However, the trade route legend clearly indicates that the trail originates in the Shawnee country; on the 1684 map it specifically originates at the Cisca village. Thus, the logical conclusion is that the Chisca and the Caskepe, together with the Mequatchaiki, were in the province of the Shawnee—and that the Chisca were indeed a band of Shawnees.[17]

The possibility of the Yuchi and Shawnee both being called, in many instances, by the same name eluded the most exacting researchers until Brown's statement of their relationship was available. This relationship was simply that both were integrated with the Zoya to form a confederation known as the Shawanos, the "people of the sky and earth."

---

[17] J. Joseph Bauxer, "Yuchi Ethnohistory, Part I: Some Yuchi Identifications Reconsidered," *Ethnohistory*, IV,(Summer, 1957) pp. 292–93.

Chapter 12

The Sun-Moon-Fire Spirit

In order to understand the powerful influence the Shawano exerted among the numerous and diverse peoples of eastern North America it is necessary to understand the nature of the peculiar knowledge they perpetuated through the select class of learned individuals Adair called the Magi and whom the peoples of the Muskogean confederation called the Miccos. This class of savants included as their central unifying element a secret-guarding organization already introduced in chapter two as the Order of the Four Roads. It has also been known since the sixteenth century as the Great Medicine Society.

The earliest known mention of the inter-tribal organization to Europeans resulted from their first encounter with the people of the Carolina coast. In 1525 a young native was captured there in a slave raid led by one Vasquez D'Ayllon and taken to Santo Domingo. His apparent intelligence and seeming adaptability led his captor to teach the youth the Spanish language and take him to Spain where he remained for three years. There he told intriguing stories of his homeland and a powerful kingdom nearby which he called *Chicora*. Chicora, he said was very rich and ruled over by a king and queen.

The Spanish named the youth Francisco of Chicora, although he belonged to another people, probably one of the coastal Siouan tribes. It appears the name the youth used is the same as *chicola* in the name of the Apala*chicola*, the peopl e of lower South Carolina and Georgia who have been introduced in chapters nine and eleven. In the Siouan languages the sound of R is rendered L which would explain the disparity of the final syllable in the two names.

Of interest here, however, is the mention of a special class of people Francisco called the *Tihe*. This name has the sound *tee eh* and translates in Yuchi as *ti*, "medicine," and *eh*, "big." He told the Spanish that these people wore a distinctive style of clothing peculiar to themselves and cared for the sick, even going to battlegrounds and treating the wounded without regard to their being friend or foe.

Although they did not mention the religious organization, members of the DeSoto expedition who crossed southern and central Georgia and northwestern South Carolina in 1540 recognized the uniformity of religious beliefs and practices among the peoples they encountered. Writing more than thirty years later from interviews with at least one man who had been on that ill-fated effort at exploration, Garcilaso de la Vega wrote that the various peoples of the region "differ little or nothing from each other, even in their idols and their rites and ceremonies of paganism (of which there are but few)."[1]

Garcilaso, who was himself the son of an Incan princess and a Spanish father, devoted much attention to the ceremonialism surrounding the kings who resided in the mound towns. He did not realize, or did not mention, that the identical form of the ceremonies conducted by the attendants to these widely dispersed kings, which he described, indicated that they learned the ceremonies from a common source.

It is probable that the Spanish observers did not record all they saw of overt religious and ceremonial activities. The likelihood is, however, they saw only a few of these because of the disruptive nature of their brutal practices and the resulting distrust and hatred of them on the part of the native people.

---

[1] Garcilaso de la Vega. *The Florida of the Inca* (Translated and edited by John Grier Varner and Jeannette Johnson Varner. Austin: University of Texas Press, 1951), p 170.

Certain artifacts which served as parts of ceremonial costume were in themselves symbols of the same significance and were frequently represented in graphic form on copper plates and carved shell gorgets, and on painted or engraved pottery vessels. One of these symbolic objects is an arrow with two kidney-shaped lobes flanking the shaft just below the point. The lobes are connected by a bar traversing the shaft, thus forming a cross, and by a "string: which frequently connects the tips of the lobes to complete a circle. An additional feature is present in that the lobes are frequently shown scalloped or rayed in a manner identical to the stylization accorded the sun circle. In some instances the lobes are actually shown merged to complete this circle. The conclusion that these bi-lobed arrows symbolize power from the deity of the fire and sun appears obvious. Knowing that the arrow represents the human spirit and traditionally returned to the sun upon the death of the Zoya, the sun's children, has given further significance to the symbol.

This being true, it follows that the obvious resemblance of the symbol to male genitalia was intended and further states that the person wearing it is an offspring of the sun, albeit a male sun. Here appears a significant difference of sun relationship as the Zoya were children of the female sun (Zo), the Breath Master, and the Earth.[11]

Another symbolic object known both from the recovery of an original example and from its graphic representation on other items is the so-called "baton" shown on certain cult items as a separate motif or carried in the hand of anthropomorphic beings who are part falconidae and part man. The baton is shown as a flat, violin-shaped form supported by raised central and traverse bars which form a cross motif. The edges are usually smooth with a tassel attached to each of the two bulging sections. However, examples containing stepped or terraced edges are known from all the major Cult sites. This treatment is most probably a stylized representation of clouds or the sky.[12]

Non-utilitarian axes comprise another type of symbolic ceremonial item common to all the cult centers. These axes are basically of a flaring blade, ungrooved "celt" or wedge-shaped type. They are made of polished stone, sometimes copper covered, or of thin laminated copper. Hafting was commonly of wood, but occasionally both haft and bit were carved from a single piece of stone. Examples of these "monolithic axes" have been found at all the major Cult centers and elsewhere through out the entire temple mound area. Axes of this type are sometimes found with other less common axe forms, i.e. the elongated "spud" and the flat, broadened perforated blade. The frequency with which all these types were placed in the burials of Cult leaders suggests that a sacred significance appertained to the axe. In context with other Cult symbolism, the axe appears to represent one of the multiple aspects or powers of the deity.

The zoomorphic beings just described above as "part falconidae and part man" are depicted on copper plates and circular shell discs or "gorgets." Examples of the former were first found at the Etowah site during the Smithsonian excavations conducted there by John P. Rogan in 1885.[13] Several similar examples of both types have been recovered elsewhere in the century since they were first seen. The shell gorgets appear to have had a more limited distribution than did the copper plates, however, being almost exclusively limited to the Tennessee and North Georgia area.[14]

The "eagle-men" are shown in a naturalistic, somewhat stylized manner as eagles or hawks possessing human characteristics in varying degrees, ranging from figures with no human features to others in which these features are dominant. The two prime examples from Etowah depict perhaps the classic prototype of these beings. Of these specimens the complete human figure appears poised in a dancing position, torso and arms shown from a frontal view with head and legs shown turned toward the subject's right and in profile. Wings appear to sprout from the rear of the shoulders and to extend downward to the figure's heals. The wings are drawn in the same stylized manner as that used in all representations of these beings, a series of scallops representing spots or individual feathers along longitudinal lines which terminate in points resembling one half of a feather tip.

---

[11] Mahan, *The Secret*, 187.

[12] Williams, *Waring Papers*, 87–88.

[13] Cyrus Thomas. "Report on the Mound Explorations of the Bureau of Ethnology," *Twelfth Annual Report of the Bureau of American Ethnology, 1890–91* (Washington, D.C.: Government Printing Office, 1894),pp. 302–303, 305.

[14] Williams, *Waring Papers*, 41.

The figures wear multiple rows of beads on the ankles, below the knee, on the wrist, and over the biceps. They have necklaces of large oval beads with a pendant made from the central spiral column of the conch or whelk shell. Rows of large beads appear in the form of a waist band beneath which is a pointed apron-like item. From the rear there appears a flaring pendant shape which curves on the bottom in line with the tips of the wings. This apparently represents the tail.

The humanoid face of these beings has a curved, beak-like nose and a forked design which extends around the mouth and across the cheek. A similar figure from Missouri has this circumoral design shown as a hand. On most of the figures of this type there is a design surrounding the eye which is commonly called the "forked eye." It terminates at the temple in two or three points. More rarely this design is comma-shaped having only one point or extending downward in a jagged form suggestive of lightning. The two Etowah figures lack this circumocular marking, rather the forked eye is present on the face of what appears to be a mask which each of the beings holds in his left hand.[15] All of the figures of this general type wear large circular earspools in their extended ear lobes, usually with short strands of beads descending from a central perforation.

The Etowah eagle-men and their counterparts elsewhere carry the baton described above held erect in their right hands and wear the bi-lobbed arrow as the crowning piece of their headdresses.

In his evaluation of the esoteric meaning of these anthropomorphic beings Antonio Waring wrote:

> While Willoughby and others have persisted in referring to these plates as eagle "dancers," or have spoken glamorously of "Eagle Warriors," it is obvious . . . that we are not dealing with representations of people dressed as eagles, but rather of beings with eagle attributes. There is certainly no evidence of a mask shown in the drafting of the face, and the nose is drawn in a curved, beak-like manner. The wings and tail are naturalistic and certainly do not seem to be parts of a costume. While there is some evidence that this being was impersonated at Etowah, and the Bi-lobed Arrow hair emblem and Fringed Apron may be based on actual costume, there can be little doubt that the object of the person who made these plates was to represent a supernatural winged being rather than a man dressed up as an eagle.[16]

In 1956 Lewis H. Larson uncovered in the core of Mound C at Etowah several burials of adult males wearing various of the items represented in the drawings of "eagle-men." One of these was wearing examples of most of the items depicted on the copper plates from the same mound. In addition he was in possession of a monolithic axe.[17]

Based on his knowledge of historic and ethnological data from other cultures and time periods, Waring reached the conclusion that the eagle-men composites represented mythological cult-bringers who taught esoteric knowledge of the fire-sun-deity religion to the worshipers in the Southeast. A reader of the present work should suspect at this point that these were the Shawanos. It was Warren's belief that the copper plates were regarded as sacred items which had come as special gifts from the deity as the Tukabatchees said their copper and brass axes and sun discs had come to their ancestors. Regarding this belief Waring wrote:

> It seems possible that these copper plates were originally spread by small proselyting groups impelled by a new doctrine and not over anxious to deny a semi-divine origin, if such were assumed; time passed, the pure air spirits, who were figured on the plates and who probably functioned in the original conceptual framework as intercessors with the supreme Sky Being, gradually merged with the original accounts of the cult-bringers, finally resulting in the confused and fragmentary picture which comes down to us in historical accounts.[18]

---

[15] S.W. Brown, Jr. stated to me categorically in June 1957 that these were indeed masks representing another personality the beings could assume at will.; Mahan, *The Secret*, 18–23.

[16] Williams, *Waring Papers*, 41.

[17] A. R. Kelly and Lewis H. Larson, "Explorations at Etowah, Georgia 1954–1956," *Archaeology*, X (Spring, 1957), 39–48.

[18] Williams, *Waring Papers*, 50–51.

the twelve giants "carved in wood" which the same author described as banishing various weapons in the posture of guards of the temple doorway.[12]

The human image which, in the eighteenth century, James Adair wrote was preserved in the Creek Town of Tukabatchee apparently had somewhat the same significance as the temple effigies. This figure seemed to Adair "to have been originally designed to perpetuate the memory of some distinguished hero, . . ." English traders who had seen it asserted "that the carving is modest, and very neatly finished, not unworthy of a modern civilized artist."[13]

From these several pieces of evidence it may be assumed that the practice of revering either stone or wooden statues representing important ancestors was a feature of the Southern Cult and of the Fire-Sun-Deity religion of later centuries as well.

As details of their temples were common to them all, the peoples of the lower Mississippi Valley shared as well the sacred fire which burned continuously within the buildings. Charlevoix observed that all the nations of Louisiana were obliged to rekindle their sacred fires at the temple of the Mobilians. DuPratz quoted the National account that The who first gave them the fire instructed that two temples be constructed on opposite sides of their territory as a safeguard against losing their sacred fire. In this way, if the fire should go out in one of the temples they could relight it from the other, Father Poisson, another French observer, added additional information on this point, saying: "They know by tradition that if it happens to be extinguished, they must go to the Tunicas to relight it.[14]

Du Pratz, having information from the chief of the guardians of the temple and from the Great Sun himself, was able to write with a high degree of authority concerning Natchez religious beliefs and the origin of their religion. On these points the other writers are silent. The meaning of the Natchez sacred fire as Du Pratz explained it would seem to apply equally well to other such fires, not only in the Louisiana area but throughout the Southeast generally. From the privileged information he had, Du Pratz wrote:

They all agree that there is a supreme being, author of all things, whom they call *Coyocop-Chill*. The word *Coyocop* signifies in general a spirit, but that of Chill can not be well rendered in our language. To enable it to be understood I will make use of a comparison. Fire, for example, is called *aua* by the savages, and the sun *Aua-Chill*; that is to say, fire *par excellence*, the most excellent of all fires, or, if one wishes, the supreme fire. Also they say that this great spirit has created all things by his goodness alone, even the angels which they call *Coyocop-Thecou*, that is ministering spirits.[15]

The French writer was told "that all nature has been formed by the order and the will of the supreme spirit except man who alone has been formed by this same spirit from a little earth and water kneaded together." On the circumstances of man's creation Du Pratz was told that when the Supreme Spirit "had been made, formed, completed, and rounded him and found him good, he placed him on the earth and breathed upon him,[16] that immediately this little figure put itself in motion, had life, and began to grow."[17]

Upon being asked who had taught the Natchez to build a temple and whence came the eternal fire, the chief of the guardians related traditional history which answered these questions. Saying that it was his duty to know these things, the chief continued:

A very great number of years ago there appeared among us a man and his wife who had descended from the Sun. It is not that we thought that he was the son of the sun or that the Sun had

---

[12] Garcilaso, *Florida*, 317, 319.

[13] Adair, *History*, 25.

[14] John R. Swanton, "The Indians of the Southeastern United States," *Bureau of Ethnology Bulletin 137* (Washington: United States Government Printing Office, 1946), p. 29.

[15] Swanton, "Indian Tribes," 167–68.

[16] *Ibid.*,

[17] In taped narrations and correspondence with me, S. W. Brown, Jr. made repeated references to the Creator's having blown the breath of life into man's nostrils at the time of creation. Cohantoney, the name the Yuchis commonly use for the Creator, has the same implication in that its literal translation is "Breath Master."

Stone images from Etowah Mound C. Female is 22½ inches high. The male is an inch and one half taller. Both are of Georgia marble. They were found by Lewis H. Larson, state archaeologist, in 1954 during final exploration of the mound in preparation for its restoration after earlier excavations by himself, Warren K. Moorehead, and the Smithsonian crew under Cyrus Thomas in 1886. The statues are now in the Etowah Mounds Museum.

a wife by whom he begot children, but when both of them were seen they were still so brilliant that it was not difficult to believe that they had come from the Sun. This man told us that having seen from above that we did not govern ourselves well, that we did not have a master, that each one of us believed that he had sufficient intelligence to govern others while he was not able to guide himself, he had taken the determination to descend in order to teach us how to live better.[18]

There were basic moral principals in the teaching which the awesome alien gave the Natchez in order for them to live a better life. These principals may be presumed to have been cardinal to the precepts of the Fire-Sun-Diety religion wherever it was practiced in relatively uncorrupted from. This would be true among whomever the people may have been who were the fountainhead of this religion, as well as among converts like the Natchez, at least at the time of its introduction among the latter. It was true of the sky people who brought their medicines and religion to the Tukabat-chees.

So authoritative and complete a statement of these essential tenets as the one presently under discussion is never known to have been given to any other European except Du Pratz. Nevertheless, the existence of these precepts can be recognized as governing the culture patterns of various peoples who comprise the confederations governed by the sun kings throughout eastern North America. Indeed evidence of these patterns is so abundant in the existing descriptions of these people and of their individual and societal behavior and attitudes that it provides one of the surest means of recognizing them even when they appear under unaccustomed names and in unexpected localities.

---

[18] Swanton, "Indian Tribes," 169–70.

The statement by the Natchez chief guardian of the fire was as follows:

He [*The*] then told us that in order to be in a condition to govern others it was necessary to know how to guide one's self, and that in order to live in peace among ourselves and please the Supreme Spirit it was necessary to observe these points: to kill no one except in defense of one's own life, never to know another woman than one's own, to take nothing that belongs to another, never to lie or become drunk, and not to be avaricious, but to give freely and with joy that which one has and to share food generously with those who lack it.[19]

The manner in which the Natchez accepted the teacher of this moralistic doctrine as their own ruler was undoubtedly approximated many times through several millennia and among many peoples as other teachers of the same doctrine spread it far and wide. The Natchez religious functionary further told Du Pratz that:

This man impressed us by these words because he said them with authority, and he obtained the respect of the old men themselves, although he did not spare them more than the others. The old men assembled then and resolved among themselves that since this man had so much intelligence to teach them what it was good to do he must be recognized as sovereign, so much the more as in governing them himself he could make them remember better than any other what he had taught them. So they went in the early morning to the cabin where they had him sleep with his wife and proposed to him to be our sovereign. He refused at first, saying that he would not be obeyed and the disobedient would not fail to die. But finally he accepted the offer that was made him.[20]

There were conditions stipulated in this acceptance, however, with which the Natchez complied. The most basic of those conditions are also clearly these which prevailed in all societies governed by sun kings. These include hereditary rule by offspring of the man and woman who came from the divine source—the Sun, the descent of the rulers to follow a matriarchal pattern. Under this system a son inherits the position of sovereign from his mother, and it descents from him to the son of his sister or her daughter if this sister has no son. In this way actual descent of the reigning sovereigns from the semi-divine originators of the position is assured. Another condition imposed by the Natchez cult-bringer is also typical. This was that "in order not to forget the good words which he had brought to us a temple should be built into which only princes and princesses (male and female suns) should have a right to enter to speak to the Spirit."

Although basic elements of teachings and instructions *The* imparted to the Natchez was duplicated in the religion the *Ispogogees* brought to the Tukabatchees, there are apparent differences between the two systems. One of these is in fact that the descendants of the Natchez suns were required to marry "stinkards," the common subjects, thus providing for the thorough physical integration of the ruling group with the general population. Another was the custom the Natchez observed of strangling wives, friends, and retainers incident to the burial of deceased Natchez Suns in order for their spirits to accompany and serve him in the afterlife. This was a practice which had survived from earlier Woodland times, but is not known to have existed among the Shawanos or the people over whom they exercised control.

There is one other recorded segment of Natchez ceremonialism which differs to such a degree from that known to have been followed by other Southeastern peoples that it warrants notice. This is the series of ceremonies they observed at the ripening of the new corn. Du Pratz described the festival that had been described to him:

This feast in incontestably the most solemn of all. Essentially it consists in eating in common and in a religious rite new corn which has been sown with this intention with suitable ceremonies.[21]

---

[19] *Ibid.,* 170.
[20] *Ibid.*
[21] Swanton, "Indian Tribes," 113.

The French author is thorough in his account, describing all the obvious features of the feast held in the month of "maize or Great Corn." His description is substantiated in its major details in a narrative by Dumond dealing with the same annual event. Briefer and somewhat earlier references in the writings of Gravier and Charlevoix add to the information supplied by Du Pratz and Dumond. All of these writers present versions differing from each other in describing the circumstances and nature of the events they witnessed or about which they were told. There is sufficient agreement among them, however, to justify the following general description of the manner in which the Natchez observed each year the ripening of the new maize crop.

The feast making occasion was held some time in July within a specially prepared area said to be a half a league from the principal Natchez town. Special structures for temporary occupancy by the participating families were constructed around an open space in the center of this area. These structures, which the French called "cabins," included those in which the great war chief and the Great Sun himself would reside for the three-day period of special activities. The cabin of the Sun, however, was reported to be "more ornate" and to be constructed on an elevation of earth about two feet high. All of these structures were built of branches covered with leaves and grass or mats and were erected by the warriors a few days prior to the beginning of the festivities.

The warriors also constructed a large circular bin of canes taller than its diameter, lined with mats and raised on poles two feet above the ground. This tower-like structure, which the French called "the tun" because of its shape, was designed to provide temporary storage for the newly ripened maize which would furnish both the purpose of and substance for the feast. Du Pratz described at length the rigidly regulated procedure followed by these warriors in clearing by fire previously untilled ground in which this sacrificial corn was planted. He further asserted:

> All that concerns the working of this field and the culture of this grain is done only by the warriors from the time they have begun to cultivate it to the moment of the feast, and the great war chief is always at their head. . . . The smallest operations are not in the least unworthy of their hands. It would be a profanation if any other should touch it, and if it happened that a native other than a warrior put his hand to it, it is believed he would never be able to go away from the field, but would perish there miserably.[22]

Shortly before the feast the warriors gathered corn and placed it in the specially prepared storehouse to be divided among the people on the day the great chief designated for their eating it communally in the ritual which climaxed the feast. Charlevoix, in describing the same festival as he observed it a few years before Du Pratz, lists several commodities, including maize, which he said "every person" contributed. There were "something of his hunting, his fishing, and other provisions, which consist in maize, beans, and melons." Due to the fact that the ceremonies apparently lasted three days and nights, there is not necessarily any conflict between this statement and the preceding one to the effect that the warriors raised the special corn for the feast. There was ample time for the consuming of this foodstuff as well as the ceremonial eating of the sacred maize. There is also the probability that some of the offerings brought by the people were intended for other uses than simply to feed the assemblage during the festival. Gravier had testified to this effect in his brief mention of the two annual festivals of the Natchez described to him a generation earlier than the time of DuPratz' observations. Referring to a second more abundant feast observed in late November, Gravier wrote: "Besides offering their first fruits in the temple in this village, the woman chief had the corn gathered in for the temple, and no one dare refuse what her emissaries chose to take. This harvest is made for the chief and the woman chief, and to furnish food to the spirits of the deceased chiefs.

The later writer wrote in considerable detail describing the manner in which the Great Sun, seated in a covered litter, was transported by groups of eight men each in relays from his house in the village to the site of the feast. The chief was "adorned with the ornaments suitable to the supreme rank," which included an elaborate feather crown. According to Du Pratz, "Those who carry him and those who receive him do it with so much quickness and skill that a good horse would be able to follow them only at a canter." Dumond gave a similar account of the chief's ride on the

---

[22] *Ibid.*

occasion he was present but commented that the potentate was dressed "in the French manner but without shoes." At an earlier time, Gravier reported that the female chief had also ridden to the festival ground in this impressive manner.

After the arrival of the chief and his retinue, time was allowed for making the new fire "from the violent rubbing of wood against wood." This was apparently a long established custom as DuPratz commented that any other fire would be profane. Presumably, this fire continued to burn during the ceremony of eating the new corn, but neither this information nor the location of the fire is given in any of the existing narratives. It is clear, however, from other recorded details that the fire did not have the place of honor in the center of the ritual area, which was reserved for the sacred fire in the green corn ceremonials observed by contemporary Muskogean and other peoples. It is plainly stated that the Natchez' ceremony lasted only three days in contrast to the eight days observed by the Yuchis on their home or "King's Ground."

From the extant descriptions, it appears also that the Natchez ceremonial lacked many of the basic features characteristic of the Green Corn festivals James Adair saw among the Cherokee, Creeks, and Chickasaw and described as the "grand festival of the annual expiration of sin, at the first new moon, in which their corn becomes full eared."[23] The philosophical concept involved in the rites with which Adair was familiar was not precisely as he interpreted it. The rituals are the source of purification, physical healing, and forgiveness of personal transgressions, but not of sins in the sense Adair understood the word.

Elements of personal purification or sacrifice were very likely present in the Natchez religion as well. They would certainly be compatible with the teaching of *The*, who gave them the basic tenets the chief of the temple guardians told to Du Pratz. If any of these elements had overt manifestation in the feast of the new corn, however, this escaped notice by the visiting French. There is good reason to doubt than any such observance would have occurred without being noted, especially by Du Pratz.

Evidence of undeniable relationship to the Middle Mississippian religion was present in the Natchez observance, specifically in the first ritual the Great Sun performed in the ceremony authorizing the eating of the sacred corn. The ceremony seems to have been remarkable for its brevity and simplicity, whatever the style in which it may have been performed in earlier times. Du Pratz, who is the sole authority, described it in this manner:

> When the great war chief see that all the warriors await orders at the doors of the cabins belonging to their families, he goes with 4 warriors previously chosen and named to distribute the grain to the women. He presents himself before the throne and says to the great Sun: "Speak, I await your word."
>
> Then this sovereign rises, comes out of his cabin, and bows toward the four corners of the world, commencing with the south. As soon as the chief and warriors have gone to the granary, he raises his arms and his hands toward heaven, whither he directs his looks, and says: "Give the grain," and at once seats himself. The great war chief thanks him by a single *hou*, long drawn out, and goes on. The princes and princesses whose cabins are near thank him also by three *hous*. Then all the men do the same thing, repeating it nine times, but three at a time with a little time between. The women and all the young people of both sexes keep a profound silence and prepare their baskets to go after the grain. They go to the granary as soon as the thanks of the people have been given.[24]

There was a suggestion of ritual indicated in the running the women did to carry the corn to their respective cabins and in the feigned efforts by the others, who had remained there, to snatch it from them. Except for this conventionalized behavior it appears that the corn was pounded in a wooden mortar and cooked in a pot, in which water was already boiling, without further ceremony.

---

[23] Adair, *History*, 105.
[24] Swanton, "Indian Tribes," 115.

When the corn had cooked, a woman stood in front of each cabin to indicate this fact to the officials around the Great Sun. Upon signal from one of these called the "master of ceremonies," two plates of the newly cooked corn was brought to the great chief, who thereupon rose and received one of the dishes, going outside his cabin where he presented it "to the four quarters of the world." He then sent it to the great war chief, whose cabin was directly across the square from his own, saying in a loud voice, "Eat," at which time everyone ate. Presumably, the Great Sun ate the contents of the other of the two plates which had been brought to him.

The feast continued until all the corn from the storage bin had been eaten, it being mandatory that no grain of the sacred corn should remain after the feast. Toward the end of the observance when most of the lot had been consumed, an official checked each household to determine how much was uneaten. He hung a corn tassel over the door of every cabin where any considerable quantity remained to signify that more corn was available to those who had already exhausted their own supply.

As soon as the warriors had finished eating, they formed two groups along opposite sides of the open space and sang what Du Pratz called "war songs." This singing lasted for about half an hour and terminated when the great war chief struck a blow on the red painted pole which had been erected in the center of the area and proceeded to recite his exploits and the number of enemies he had killed. All the warriors in turn, according to the degree of estimation in which they were held by their fellow warriors, did the same thing as their chief. Finally the young men were allowed to go and strike the post and "say, not what they had done, for they had never been to war, but what they proposed to do when opportunity permitted."

Two games the men played in the course of the three days' activities undoubtedly had Middle Mississippian origins, both in the details of their performance and in the principle of their inclusion as ritualistic games in the context of religious ceremonialism. One of these games, Dumond said, was called *la soule* in Brittany, where it was still popular among the peasants. In this contest two opposing teams, composed of all the men present, were aligned under the respective leadership of the Great Sun and the war chief. The object of the game was to strike one of two goals with a ball which must not touch the ground or be held in the hand. The two goals consisted of the cabins of the two titular team leaders which were on opposite sides of the open area or square. The ball was made of deer skin filled with the hanging moss called "Spanish beard," according to Du Pratz.

The other game the Natchez men played incident to the new corn festival was "chunkey," known from archaeological evidence to have been universal among Middle Mississippian peoples. Specimens of the distinctive polished stone concave discs, or "discoidals," used in this game have been found on all the major Southern Cult sites and on many others of Mississippian affiliation throughout the Southeast. Figures of Chunkey players in action, engraved on shell gorgets from Spiro and elsewhere and carved in the round to form a unique stone pipe found in Muskogee County, Oklahoma, are executed in the distinctive art style characteristic of the Cult.[25] All of the figures are represented wearing costume or paraphernalia associated with the anthropomorphic beings associated with the Southern Cult. The figures engraved on shell have the characteristic forked eye. This bestowing of religious symbolism on chunkey players served to justify inclusion of the game itself among the diagnostic traits of the Cult.[26]

Du Pratz recorded the manner in which the Natchez played the game, giving one of the most concise of the several extant eyewitness descriptions:

The warriors of these nations have invented the game which is called "of the pole," but should rather be named "of the cross," since this pole which is 8 feet long, resembles in shape a letter "F" in Roman characters. Only two play this game, and each has a pole of the same kind. They have a flat stone shaped like a wheel, beveled on the flat sides like the wheel of the game of Siam. But it is only 3 inches in diameter and an inch thick. The first throws his stick and rolls the stone at the same time. The skill of the player consists in managing so that the stone touches

[25] Funderburk, *Sun Circles and Human Hands*, pls. 21, 49, 95.
[26] Waring and Holder, "Southern Cult," 20.

the pole or stops near it. The second player throws his pole the instant the stone begins to roll. The one whose pole is nearest the stone scores a point and has the right to throw the stone.[27]

Authors of all known descriptions of this game agree in stating that wagering of personal effects, sometimes to the great detriment of the bettors, was a prevailing feature and served to stimulate the extreme interest which was attached to playing it. Dumond wrote graphically to the same effect:

The play continues as far as *pocole*, that is to 10, and the savages often ruin themselves, as I have said, wagering on the game their powder, their guns, their skins, their *Limbourg*, in a word all that they may have.[28] The playing of this game continued in some areas until the latter years of the eighteenth century at which time it seems to have fallen into disuse, although the "chunkey yard" remained a prominent feature of the Muskogean towns until much more recently.[29]

At night during the festival, both men and women danced in a rigidly uniform and repetitive manner, according to Du Pratz who commented, "They dance ordinarily until day." This general statement would describe aptly the night dances which for centuries have accompanied the annual ceremonials honoring the green corn wherever they were performed. There were aspects of the Natchez dance as the Frenchman described it, however, which may have been peculiar to themselves or, at least, to their distinctive culture. These features of their dance do not conform to the pattern of the dances of similar purport often described since the eighteenth century among peoples of known Mississippian cultural affinity.

The narrative by DuPratz contains all the information available on the manner in which the Nachez performed this dance. He included several incidental details such as the fact that the area was lighted by numerous large bundles of cane which served as torches and that the dances were always the same, adding, "He who has seen one has seen all." With that observation he became more specific in his description:

In the middle of a vacant space, proportioned to the number of those who are going to dance, a man seats himself on the earth with a pot in which there is a little water, and which is covered with deerskin stretched extremely tight. He holds this pot in one hand and beats time with the other. Around him the women arrange themselves in a circle at some distance from each other and having in their hands very thin disks of feathers which they turn while dancing from left to right. The men inclose the women with another circle, which they form at some distance from them. They never hold each other by the hand, but leave between a space sometimes as wide as 6 feet. Each one has his *chichicois* (rattle) with which he beats time. The *chichicois* is a gourd pierced at the two ends through which a stick is passed, of which the longest end serves as a handle. As the women turn from left to right the men turn from right to left and all keep time with an accuracy which must be considered surprising.[30]

DuPratz' graphic description has special significance to this history of the sun kings as it provides otherwise unavailable ethnological data relating to a people ruled by the sun kings among whom the Southern Cult never extended its influence. Thus it is possible to identify more precisely both the features peculiar to the "mature" Mississippian religion and those which characterized the earlier Woodland or exclusively Sun religion, the Natchez representing the latter.

---

[27] Swanton, "Indian Tribes," 90–91.

[28] *Ibid.*, 90.

[29] Swanton, "Indian Tribes of the Creek Confederacy," 176–77.

[30] The details of the dance described here differ fundamentally from those known to comprise the "Night Dances" of the Yuchi and Muscogee people.

Chapter 14

The Green Corn Dance of the Shawanos

Until the middle 1600's the valleys of the Tennessee and Cumberland across the present states of Tennessee and Kentucky were thickly inhabited by the nation the early French explorers and missionaries called *Chaouanons*, known later to Anglo-Americans as the Shawanos. The French said they were identical to the nation the Huron missionaries called *Erichonons*, or Cats. The Tennessee historian, Joseph Jones wrote regarding Shawano identity:

> We are justified. . . .in supposing the Eries, Chaouanons, Ontougaunha, Shawnees, Uches, and Savanas, to be the same unfortunate nation whose dominion once extended from the waters of the Savannah River, in the present state of Georgia, to the shores of Lake Erie, and who were persistently followed and relently destroyed by the warlike, cruel, and powerful Iroquois.

> The valleys of the Cumberland and Ohio Rivers appear to have been inhabited for a considerable period by the Chaounanons, for in the earliest maps, we find this region called "the country of the Ancient Chaouanons." The earliest French explorers and missionaries described this nation as populous and powerful, and their right to the soil as well as their power was acknowledged in the earliest treaties negotiated with the Algonquin tribes by LaSalle, nearly two centuries ago. From the earliest period of French occupation in the Mississippi valley, the Chaouanons were, with others of the Algonquin tribes to whom they were closely related by origin and language, firm friends of the French, and were instructed in the Catholic religion as early as two centuries ago by the Jesuit missionaries.[1]

Father James Marquette, famed in history as one of the first to explore the Mississippi, referred in 1673 to the Ohio by a name which metaphorized into Wasbash. "This river," he wrote, "comes from the country on the east, inhabited by the people called Chaouanons, in such numbers that they reckon as many as twenty-three villages in one district, and fifteen in another, lying near each other; they are by no means warlike, and are the people the Iroquois go far to seek, in order to wage an unprovoked war on them; and as these poor people cannot defend themselves, they allow themselves to be taken, and carried off like sheep, and innocent as they are, do not fail to experience at times the barbarity of the Iroquois, who burn them cruelly."[2]

Historian John Gilmary Shea translated numerous writings of the early French visitors to the area of the Lakes and Upper Mississippi. It was his opinion regarding the destruction of the Shawano and their allies that:

> It is scarcely creditable that the Iroquois could have utterly exterminated the entire nation. It is more reasonable to suppose that the Eries were a powerful and populous nation, occupying a wide extent of country south of Lake Erie and that only the towns immediately on the lake, or for some distance south, were destroyed by their vindictive and powerful enemies. This view must necessarily be held, if it be true, that the Eries, Chats, Cats, Outougaunha, Savanos, Chaouanons, and Shawnees, were essentially one and the same people, who once occupied the country from the southern border of Lake Erie to the banks of the Tennessee River, and even beyond, to the mouth of the Savannah River.

---

[1] Joseph Jones, "Exploration of the Aboriginal Remains of Tennessee," *Smithsonian Contributions to Knowledge, No. 259* (Washington: Published by the Smithsonian Institution, 1876), pp. 148–52.

[2] James Gilmary Shea, "Account of the Discovery of Some new Countries and Nations in North America, in 1673," *Discovery and Exploration of the Mississippi Valley* (New York, Redfield, 1852) 41–42.

The Chaouanons (Shawnees) [Here Shea is in error in assuming that the Shawanos and Shawnees were the same people and thus spoke the same language. They did not. The Shawanos spoke the same language as the Yuchis] spoke a dialect of the Algonquin language, which was one of the original tongues of the North American Continent; and was spoken by every tribe from the Chesapeake to the Gulf of St. Lawrence, and westward to the Mississippi and Lake Superior: The Anakis, Algonquins proper, Montagnais, Ottawas, Nipissings, Nes Perces, Illinois, Miamis, Sacs, Foxes, Mohegans, Delawares, Shawnees, and Virginia Indians, as well as the minor tribes of New England, all spoke dialects of this wide-spread language.[3]

Daniel Coxe in his "Description of the English Province of Carolina. . .," wrote in reference to the Ohio River: "Formerly, divers nations dwelt on this river, as the Chawanoes (Shanees), a mighty and very populous people, who had about fifty towns, and many other nations, who were totally destroyed or driven out of their country by the Iroquois, this river being their usual road, when they make war upon the nations, who live to the south and west.

The reason the Iroquois were able to overcome and destroy the numerous and powerful Shawanos with such ease was the use of firearms they had obtained in trade from the Dutch and Swedes along the Hudson River. Their victims were defenseless against these weapons and, as the result were almost destroyed. Surviving bands made their way to join kinsmen and allies in the Savannah River Valley. There they were the Savannahs who settled a large town across the river from the present Augusta, Georgia. The refugees also include the Yuchis who, under their king, *Sinchechi*, settled a village jointly with Tamachechi and the Yamacraws and had earlier occupied several sites on the Savannah River. Others of the Shawanos joined with the Abihkas on the Coosa River and the Apalachicola on the Chattahoochee.

James Adair was the nearest English equivalent of LePage Du Pratz in the colonial period. Lacking the Frenchman's objectivity and attention to detail, the veteran Indian trader compensated in his writings for this deficiency with the more comprehensive knowledge he had gained during his long acquaintance with members of several Southeastern tribes. The great mass of his information and his persistence in writing and publishing his narrative as the copious *History of the American Indians* made an invaluable contribution to Native American history.

Adair lived and traded among the Catawbas, Chickasaw, and Cherokees for the major part of a forty-year period, 1735–1775. He observed the customs and religious ceremonies of his Indian neighbors, especially the Chickasaws and Cherokees, and of other Southern tribes with whom he happened to come in occasional contact. From some of his native acquaintances he learned a little of the esoteric meaning of the native religion, which he recognized as very nearly uniform among the tribes with whom he was familiar.

At some period in his career Adair became convinced that the Indians, those he knew and others on both American continents, were, as he phrased it:

> . . .lineally descended from the Israelites, either while they were a maritime power, or soon after the general captivity; the latter however is the most probable. This descent, I shall endeavor to prove from their religious rites, civil and martial customs, their marriages, funeral ceremonies, manners, language, traditions, and a variety of particulars—which will at the same time make the reader thoroughly acquainted with nations, of which it may be said to this day, very little has been known.[4]

This conviction finally became an obsession with Adair and apparently provided the principal motivation for his great effort to understand and explain the history and customs of the Indian tribes. He became conversant in two of the native languages, Chickasaw and Cherokee, and taught himself Hebrew, apparently with only moderate success.[5] The same may well have been true of his knowledge of the Native languages.

---

[3] *Ibid.*

[4] Swanton, "Indian Tribes," 123.

[5] This was the gist of a recent evaluation by Cyrus H. Gordon of Adair's mastery of Hebrew based on evidence in his *History*. It came in response to a question by me in a March 1992 telephone conversation.

Even his imperfect understanding of the languages gave him an advantage over contemporaries who reported on the American Indians. His overriding opinion on the subject of Semitic ancestry of the American tribes and his frequently stated prejudices make it obligatory to weigh his statements cautiously.

Nevertheless, Adair's *History* makes possible the confident assertion that, although the author frequently pointed out, the old religion I have identified as the Mississippian Southern Cult was suffering a great loss of its former rituals and influence among the people, it was still a powerful influence in the lives of the Southeastern peoples in Adair's time and long afterward.

This religion continued vital in the nineteenth century even outside the area of its greatest force. In 1819 John Johnston, United States agent of Indian affairs at Piqua in southern Ohio reported on the current condition of Indian tribes in his area. These included the Delaware and Shawano. In a section of his report dealing with the general customs of the several tribes in his area, perhaps more particularly with the Shawanos, the agent wrote of their "sacrifices and thanksgivings." In this he gave a more discerning interpretation of the religious meanings inherent in the green corn ceremonial than other writers have expressed, Adair included.

Explaining that the Indians observed two sacrifices each year, Johnson elaborated on one of these:

> The principal festival is celebrated in the month of August; the precise time is fixed by the head chief and the counsellors of the town, and takes place sooner or later, as the state of the affairs of the town, or the forwardness of the corn will admit. It is called the green corn dance; or, more properly speaking, "the ceremony of thanksgiving for the first fruits of the earth."—It lasts from four to twelve days, and in some places resembles a large camp meeting. The Indians attend from all quarters with their families, their tents and provisions, encamping around the council or worshiping house. The animals killed for sacrifice are cleaned, the heads, horns, and entrails are suspended on a large white pole, with forked top, which extends over the roof of the house.

> The women having prepared the new corn and provisions for the feast, the men take some of the new corn, rub it between their hands, then on their faces and breasts, and they feast, the great chief having first addressed the crowd, thanking the almighty for the return of the season, and giving such moral instructions to the people as may seem proper for the time. On these occasions, the Indians are dressed in their best manner, and the whole nation attend, from the greatest to the smallest.

The quantity of provisions collected is immense, every one bringing in proportion to his ability. The whole is cast in one pile and distributed during the continuance of the feast among the multitude by leaders appointed for that purpose.

> In former times, the festival was held in the highest veneration, and was a general amnesty, which not only absolved the Indians from all punishments for crimes, murder excepted, but seemed to bury guilt itself in oblivion. There are no people more frequent or fervent in their acknowledgements of gratitude to God. Their belief in him is universal, and their confidence so strong that it is quite astonishing.[6]

In chapter four I described the green corn ceremony as the Yuchis observe it. It is identical in many respects to the one Johnson described. I called attention in the earlier chapter to the remarkable identity to details of the "Festival of Tabernacles or Booths" of thanksgiving and new beginnings Jehovah prescribed for the faithful in Leviticus 23.

It should be clear to anyone who has read this far that the Yuchis and the Shawanos were the same people in the early nineteenth century, speaking the same language and practicing the same

---

[6] John Johnston. "Account of the Present State of the Indian Tribes Inhabiting Ohio," *Archaeologia Americana: Transactions and Collections of the American Antiquarian Society*, I (1820), 285–387.

About the same distance east of this Georgia city there is a similar structure of very nearly the same dimensions and built of the same type of rocks. There are differences between these two figures, however. The latter is enclosed by a geometrically perfect circle of the same stone as the effigy and which originally was about two feet high. The effigy has a plump, almost circular body and a forked tail. These features give it a very decided resemblance to a kite!

Less that a mile westward from the latter figure is the figure of a rattlesnake of similar stone construction some two hundred feet along its undulating length from its triangular head to the three rock piles representing rattles at the end of its tail. Here, I believe, is the totemic emblem of the earth people of the Shawano (Eagle-serpent people) composite.

Constructing large effigy mounds in this early period was not limited to the Southeast. The best known of such constructions is the serpent effigy mound near Locust Grove, Adams County, Ohio. A multitude of others depicting lizards, bears, and even an elephant still survive in the river valleys of Wisconsin. Countless others have been destroyed by the activities of American settlers in the past century and a half.

The most recently reported effigy mounds of similar construction to those in Georgia are on the Island of Bimini in the Bahamas.[1] They, like their mainland counterparts, are made up of piled stones. In their case, however, coral and limestone are the building material. Quartzite was not available.

Based on the presence of these virtually ageless ethnic "signatures," it may be assumed with confidence that people belonging to the eagle, kite, serpent, and bear gens were present in North America in the Archaic Period.

Evidence of the culture in that period is surprisingly uniform throughout the area east of the Mississippi Valley and southward from Eastern Canada to Florida. However, there are products of certain intrusive traits in the Southeast not found elsewhere on this continent. The most notable of these is a form of crude pottery made with a vegetal fiber binder in the shapes of more widely distributed steatite (soapstone) vessels and smoking pipes.

This fiber-tempered pottery was constructed by moulding and decorated with incised lines and indentations from a round-pointed, pencil-size stylus. Its manufacture and use appears to have been introduced along the St. John's and Savannah rivers in Georgia and South Carolina and to have spread as far as the mountains in both states.

Although it functioned at an early time among presumed "hunting and food-gathering peoples," there is evidence that the Archaic was not a "simple" culture. One revealing clue indicates the presence of writing! The evidence of this is inscribed on one of the most characteristic artifacts of this culture, a polished stone in the general shape of a butterfly with a neat half inch hole drilled lengthwise through the center of the body. As they were usually made of steatite, the "problematic" stones were long thought by relic collectors to be "banner stones" that were mounted on a shaft and held aloft on ceremonial occasions or possibly as a general purpose talisman.

For most of this century archaeologists have been convinced that these carefully shaped and polished stone objects were weights for a device called an *atlatl*, intended as an extension to the arm and thus providing greater thrust in throwing the spear. This presumed usage proved accurate when a typical example of one was found recently near Hartwell, Georgia. It contained a series of characters across it which appeared to be letters. A photograph of the suspected inscription was sent to famed epigrapher Barry Fell who identified the letters as belonging to the Punic alphabet. He read the message: For throwing or hurling."[2] Dr. Fell wrote:

---

[1] David D. Zink, "The Poseida Expeditions: A Summary," *The Explorers Journal*, Vol 69, No. 4 (Winter 1991), p. 124.

[2] Barry Fell, "A Punic Inscription on an Atlati-Weight from Georgia," *Epigraphic Society Occasional Papers, (ESOP)* Volume 18 (1989) pp. 321–325.

To the best of my knowledge no atlatl-weight has ever been reported to carry an inscription engraved upon its surface, still less has one been found that carries an inscription in the Punic alphabet of Carthage of ca 2nd century B.C. Yet, to my amazement, this is seen to be the case in the atlatl-weight shown on page 323, upper left illustration. It came to my knowledge through a letter addressed to me by Dr. Carol Norton of Danielsville, Georgia. Her letter, and subsequent correspondence, disclosed the following facts (details of the exact find locality, and the circumstances of the find are here omitted, in order to protect the site from vandals). Dr. Norton refers to the atlatl weight as a •banner-stone", this term having been in use for many years in North America, before it was understood that in reality the mysterious •banner-stones" are actually weights for spear-throwers. Dr.Norton writes:

•In November of 1956 a friend of ours, George Stowe, with his father and brother, chanced to find a banner-stone lying on the surface of the soil at a site near Hartwell, in Hart County, north-east Georgia. A black celt was also found nearby, and in the intervening years some 1,500 points have also been found there.

•On one side of the banner-stone there is an inscription. We lent the stone to a Cherokee linguist, Jerry King, to study, and he subsequently reported that the letters are not Cherokee.

•A few weeks ago my husband and I met Dr. Joseph Mahan at a seminar in the Columbus Museum, Georgia, and we told him of the find. He suggested that we refer the stone to you."

Upon receiving the stone for study I observed that the inscribed letters are extremely weathered and the patina suggests a considerable age. So weathered are the letters that, in order to photograph them and to see them clearly, the stone has to be tilted different ways with respect to the light source, for each individual letter. Thus in the photos on page 324 not all details are apparent, and so the outlines of the letters have been drawn in on a duplicate photograph beneath. The letters are of the rather degenerate style of Punic writing of the Second Century B.C., as tabulated on pages 184-187 of Peckham (1968), **The Development of the Late Phoenician Scripts.**

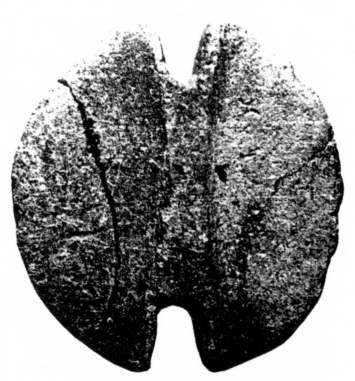

My interpretation of the letters is as shown on page 324, yielding a word that reads, from right to left, M-Sh-L-Kh-T. As no adequate Punic dictionary exists, we are always obliged to deduce the sense from corresponding words in Biblical Hebrew, if such words can be identified. A search through the Langenscheidt Hebrew-English Dictionary, which claims to include every Biblical Hebrew root, discloses a Sh-L-Kh with a nominal sense of •Javelin" and a verbal sense of •casting a javelin", as well as other inapplicable senses. The passages in Langenscheidt that relate are here shown.

שֶׁלַח¹ (šä'läḥ) *m* missile, javelin;

שָׁלַח (šälä'ḥ) *Hi.* הִשְׁלִיךְ, *inf.* הַשְׁלֵךְ, הַשְׁלִיךְ, *imp.* הַשְׁלֵךְ. הַשְׁלִיכוּ, *fut.* יַשְׁלִיךְ. תַּשְׁלֵךְ, *pt.* מַשְׁלִיךְ, *pl. c.* מַשְׁלִיכֵי, to throw, to cast.

Barry Fell's translation of the inscription on the Norton atlatl weight. Reproduced from ESOP Vol. 17 with permission from Dr. Fell.

Woodland. Complicated stamped burial urn from Irene Mound. (Savannah College Museum photo).

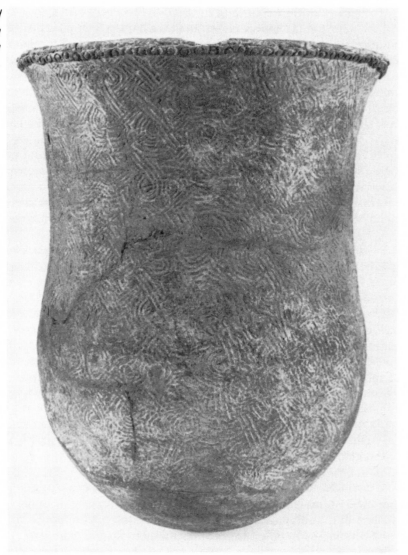

(Tama-chechi's forebears), the *Cana*, the *Sali*, the *Tali*, and the *Chera* in addition to the *Zoyaha* or *Yuchis*.[10]

The *Ku* were another Southeastern people whose name was identical to one of the ancient peoples of India. Their name appears to have meant "bird" or, possibly, "dog" and to have been the stem in the names Coosa and *Cu*tifachechi. This name closely approximates the Yuchean word *Co* in sound and, interestingly, both names may be used for the dwelling place of the same people, depending upon whether their guiding spirit is in his personification of Bird or Man (or Dog) in the experience of the person mentioning him.

The king of *Cosa* was the ruler of a province DeSoto and his cohorts were seeking when they kidnapped the "Lady" of Cutifichechi to lead him there. The Spanish found the king who received them with considerable pomp at a mound town somewhere in northwestern Georgia or neighboring Tennessee. (There is at this time (1992) a sizeable dispute among experts on DeSoto's route concerning this location. There has been no doubt expressed, however, that *Kosa* and *Kusa* are the same place inhabited by ancestors of the later Coosa.).

10 Mahan, *The Secret*, 134—35.

Whether it was the place the Spanish visited in 1540—and there is general agreement that it was not—the great town surrounding the Etowah Mounds was a "bird-man" town. If it were inhabited at that time, it was by a population of Lamar people of Mississippian cultural affinities and not by the Middle Woodland complicated stamp people who abandoned the site at least a century earlier. The great mound there is of such massive proportions as to suggest accretion from an earlier time than merely the beginning of the Mississippian Period. It could well be the large town of the ruler of the Zoyahawano Chief Samuel Brown, Jr. called *Coshafa*, the place of Man-Sha (the falcon-serpent composite).

At a date approximating the eighth century A. D. new culture traits appeared in the Woodland towns of the Mississippi Valley. Most noticeable of these was the building of truncated pyramidal earth mounds as the substructures for temples and the residences of a class of leaders. These have been interpreted by archaeologists to have been sun kings and their coterie of attendant priests and other functionaries. This interpretation is largely based on the various contemporary descriptions of the Natchez "Great Sun," the sun temple there, the Keepers of the Fire, and the privileged relatives of the sun king. It is also based on the description of the temple at Talimeco in the DeSoto chronicles, and on the archaeological evidence for the "Southern Cult."

Whence came these innovative traits has remained a mystery. They seem, primarily, to be associated with "rugged round headed peoples," according to Gordon R. Willey,[11] Harvard archaeologist and pre-eminent authority on the subject. It is Willey's opinion, however, that this physical type did not appear with the new complex of culture traits. He believes that it is "likely that this brachycranic strain [which existed] in the old population simply rose to later dominance and that there was no new immigration into the East from any other area."

Willey further observed concerning the spread of the diagnostic Mississippian traits that:

> It is also quite likely that this rise to dominance was related to the spread and propagation of the vigorous Mississippian tradition with which brachycephalic peoples were associated. This is what seems to have occurred in the expansion of Mississippian culture out of the Mississippi Valley and into marginal subareas. . ., the invading Mississippian populations tended to be more rounded and heavy boned than the earlier Woodland residents.[12]

Willey was even more positive in his conclusion that there was no intrusive language accompanying the cultural changes. He wrote:

> Linguistic data simply suggest that Mississippian culture was developed locally within the East by resident peoples. Muskogean, the language family of the Southeast which has been linked frequently with Mississippian culture, appears to have had an ancient history in the Eastern Woodlands area and to have been remotely related to Algonquin, the language family most generally associated with Woodland cultures. The Siouan people who may have developed the Mississippian tradition form another language family almost certainly long resident in the East.[13]

Assuming Willey accurate in his conclusions, it may be said with confidence that the diagnostic traits of the Mississippian innovations came as ideas or concepts adopted by a predominantly round-headed people already residing in the Mississippi Valley, that there was no new language accompanying the new ideas and practices, and that the innovative patterns of behavior spread outward among populations which already contained an element of round-headed people. It is most likely that these were speakers of either a Muskogean or Siouan language.

Willey's hypotheses appear supported by historical and ethnological evidence presented in foregoing chapters of this book. They add substantially to the details already cleared in the imaginary picture. Certain of those details should now be reviewed.

---

[11] Gordon R. Willey, *An Introduction to American Archaeology*, 2 Vols. (Englewood, N.J.: Prentice-Hall, 1966), I,292.
[12] *Ibid.*, 294.
[13] *Ibid.*

Four Images From Burrows Cave

Photos by Virginia Hourigan

There was another engraved slab which contained a very well executed drawing of a Minotaur holding a serpent in his hand. Here unquestionably were the two principal religous symbols of Ancient Crete reinforcing to an encouraging degree the suspicion I had held for so long that the Minoans were collateral ancestors of many of the precolumbian peoples of the Southeast, especially the Yuchis.

This was a startling turn of events. Other photographs that had come in the same mail with the ones just described were, of similar engraved stones in which were depicted other men, mythological beings, and what were obviously alphabetic inscriptions. There were pictures of other stone artifacts that has been removed from the passageway of a sealed cave found a few years earlier by Russell Burrows somewhere in Illinois. By this time the cave had been named in his honor. The photographs had been made by Virginia Hourigan, a New York musician and cultural historian and a member of the Institute for the Study of American Cultures, of which I was president. They were sent to me and to several other members of ISAC who might be able to offer some suggestion relating to identifying and assigning a date to the items taken from the cave. This book constitutes my contribution toward answering these questions.

THE IMPLAUSIBLE UNION OF ANKH & THUNDERBIRD

But nothing does more to reveal what was in the mind of the ancients than the rites of initiation and the ritual acts that are performed in religious services with symbolical intent.
—Plutarch, "On Calumny," 157.2, *Moralia Frags.* (c.100 A.D.), tr. F.H. Sandbach (Harvard/ Heinemann 1969), XV 287

WHEN (16 Aug. 1991) I showed Joseph Mahan an illustration of 3rd/4th-century-A.D. symbols from Kushan Toprak-Kala murals alongside persisting modern Uzbek matches in door sculptures, a chest painting, & an earring [*Central Asian Review* XIII/1 (1965), 71], Mahan smiled in instant recognition of every one of these motifs as also American-Yuchi. We shall return to them.

Capital of ancient Khorezm (as Persians & Greeks knew the land—*Khawarezm* to Hindus, *Kangha* or *Kanghui* to Chinese), Toprak-Kala flourished in the 200s A.D. among dense towns along the lower Oxus (Amu Dar'ya), which flows north into the Aral Sea; along the lower Jaxartes (Syr Dar'ya), which flows west into the northeastern Aral Sea; & along slave-labor-built canals of a gigantic irrigation system off these rivers—altogether an Uzbekistan region now desert but then verdant as well as urban. It is easy enough to explain a Yuchi connection with Khorezm, which formed part of the Kushan Aral-Sea-to-central-India empire encompassing Afghanistan & also eastern Central Asia. The imperial capital stood at Pushkalavati, West Punjab (in present-day Pakistan), and Kushanas were Yuchi.

Mahan had long realized this Yuchi/Kushan identity. In Pakistan he & his musicologist wife Katherine further verified American-Yuchi correspondences—ethnic type, customs, platformed terraces, toponyms, chant intervals, etc. "To my amazement," Joe wrote [*The Secret* (1983), 168], "I had found that almost all the names of Dravidian-speaking peoples of India are identical to the names of American tribes who lived in close proximity to the Yuchis in what is now the southeastern United States. . . ."

Mahan pondered B.M. Puri's 1965 inference that ready Kushana-Yuchi integration with Indus-valley culture implied prior kinship. That such kinship might have been Aryan rather than Dravidian remained generally contrary to expectation before S.R. Rao's epochal 1982 decipherment of Indus script as proto-Sanskrit (which Sudhansu Kumar Ray & Barry Fell had anticipated), in turn implying that, just as horsey Indo-Europeans invaded pre-horse but already-Indo-European Asia Minor, so Vedic Aryans invaded a not-altogether-horseless already Aryan Indus valley. Dravidian/Aryan confrontation would have occurred with the introduction of Harappa Culture and resumed south of Pakistan in both Vedic & Kushan eras. Yet Yuchi speech in Creek Co., Okla. today sounds pretty Dravidian (sometimes also Akkadian, Tibetan, Chinese, & Polynesian); Mahan has detected Dravidian words & phonemes in the Yuchi language and noted Fell's identification of Dravidian script found in Georgia. We may wonder if in Afghanistan, Sogdiana, & Gandhara the five confederated Great-Yuchi tribes gave up their Indo-Iranian Scythian when they gave up pointed caps & knee-high boots. Although "Moon" people, Yuchis seem not to have given up sun-worship or moundbuilding, even if their mounds shifted from original graves to temple/palace platforms of South, Southwest, & East Asia, comparable to the switch c.850 A.D. in much of what became the U.S., when Mississipian higher, platform-moundbuilding superseded ancient Woodland grave-moundbuilding.

Indo-Europeans penetrated Asia Minor & the Balkans from the north, off Ukrainian steppes. Indo-Iranian Khurrians penetrated Asia Minor from the east through Kilikia, establishing Mitanni in Syria, NW Mesopotamia, & E. Turkey, the chief rival/ally of 18th-Dynasty Egypt. A Khurrian dynasty took over Khatti, under which the Hittite pantheon became Khurrian along with Hittite terms for horsemanship which sound nearly identical to Sanskrit equivalents. The Hittite empire displaced Mitanni as chief rival/ally of 19th-Dynasty Egypt. Respective peace treaties entailed Khurrian and then Hittite queens in Egypt.

Kushan-Uzbek motifs which Mahan recognized as recurrent in American Yuchi symbolism origi-nated long before either Buddhism or Egyptian sun-kings with sky-boats, implying either a Yuchi identity with the universal Neolithic-village cult of the Goddess (of Sky, Creation, mating or separa-tion of Sky & Earth, & fertility) or a post-Bronze identity subsuming pre-Bronze tradition. Her Scythian name, Tabiti, likely originated, with her stairstep motif, in Asia Minor. Yuchi/Navajo stairsteps in space, which we assumed represent clouds (and may but ought, then, occur rounded instead of right-angled), signify at Chatal Huyuk in the Konya Plain c.6000 B.C. the enthroned Goddess profiled, as they also signify at Chatal's later-Neolithic descendant Hajilar (200 miles west), & among heirs in Thessaly & Macedonia. This Neolithic motif persisted in Navajo tradition via Buddhism which car-ried it into Zinjiang (the vast eventual Qara-Khitan empire & Xi-Xia kingdom north of Tibet). At Chatal & Hajilar this motif when mirror-imaged (i.e. ascending & descending) signified the enthroned Goddess viewed frontally, flanked by leopard attendants. This frontal abstraction appears repeti-tiously over parallel coils of a serpentine motif (which in the Neolithic Near East & Greece represents the Cosmic-Waters Snake at Creation) incised on a Yuchi pot excavated from Rood Mounds on the Chattahoochee c.50 miles south of Columbus, Ga. Brown said this motif-pair symbolized the union of Earth & Sky [Mahan, *The Secret*, 22-24].

While the Thunderbird depended on Buddhism for its migration into Central Asia, the Toprak-Kala Kushan symbols common to American-Yuchi had penetrated Central Asia more than a millen-nium before. The basic symbols of the Four Roads Great Medicine Society had taken definitive form in the Mesolithic/Neolithic Ukraine, Asia Minor, Palestine, North Mesopotamia, & West Iran while the Goddess of the Sky reigned supreme in association with the Snake of the Cosmic Waters, thus ambiguously a dove/serpent. But the Society in itself represents highest wisdom at the Bronze transition to a Warrior Weather or Storm God who took command of the sky and subjugated the Goddess into the Earth. A Thunderbird beyond Sun & Moon arose in the *Bronze* mind alongside the dove class of bird. In Egypt, on the other hand, a Sun-King was Horus the Falcon, originally lording at Nekhen (Hierakonpolis, modern village Muisaat) in the conquering South. Egypt also had a Vulture Goddess Nekhbit; the black-banded red-billed Jabiru stork was sacred to the Goddess of the Night Sky, Hat'hor; Thoth the Moon-God had an ibis head; but a Thunderbird remained unknown on the nearly-rainless Egyptian Nile (south of its Delta) where, although pigeons became the chief source of meat, neither Pigeon nor Dove totemized a deity. Gerzean-predynastic falcon & flamingo did persist as Yuchi eagle & crane. The dogwood blossom substituted in Yuchi America for the lotus that was centrally sacred to both Egypt & Buddhism, which in turn displaced the Neolithic-Khalaf "daisy" symbolizing the Goddess, specifically Inanna on Bahrain.

The international eclectic Four Roads retained its coherence into the Iron Age as if "modernity" never came and as if everyone lived at the moment of Creation, the ever-returning same time [see Mircea Eliade, *Cosmos & History*, tr. Willard Trask (Pantheon 1954)]. We cannot say that if we could date the genesis of the Great Medicine Society that that would date its devotees very precisely but, on analogy to coin, pottery, or bone caches, the latest specimen would most accurately date the assemblage.

Kushan-&-modern Uzbek & American-Yuchi symbol assemblages do contain a preponderance of indefinitely pre-Shumerian character. Rows of diamond-framed diamonds, e.g., had run common in art of Asia Minor & Upper Mesopotamia since the 6th & 5th millennia B.C. Patterns of stylized ibexes characteristic of Neolithic/Bronze Iran had antecedents back to Mesolithic Beldibi in Pamphylia. Ambiguously bird-head hooking sea-waves appear on Neolithic Anatolian & Aegean pots. At Hajilar in Asia Minor they stylized leopard *attendants* of the enthroned Leopard Goddess—more & more abstractly until unrecognizable as their forgotten models. Scalloped waves began far west of Uzbek in the Paleolithic. Tasseled pendants show up as a pot design at Samarran Baghuz on the middle Euphrates before middle-Tigris Samarran pioneering of Eridu in Lower Mesopotamia. Stylized bukrania framed in or associated with flower petals go back to Chatal, where both designs signified the Goddess, as they still signified in 5th-millennium Khalaf art, which specially emphasized flower & bukranium motifs. Besides these, Yuchi art threw back to such other Neolithic motifs as triangles, checkerboards, hands, swastikas, & equilateral crosses.

Mahan has rightly emphasized these crosses as logs of the sacred fire partaking of the sun. They had an analogous Early Neolithic meaning, verified by frequent sun-circling or swastika elaboration, as in Yuchi art. Originally, to judge by association of pubic triangles, vaginal diamonds, & schematized goddess figurines, the equilateral cross abstracted the intersection of Goddess pubis & thighs, sometimes explicitly, connoting generative life-force. Pre-agricultural Paleolithic & Mesolithic Eurasiatics already show female-fecundity obsession in relation to heavenly bodies. Primeval peoples seem instinctively platonic, convinced of life as a ritual drama adumbrated in the controlling sky. By living ritualistically always at Creation, Eliade intuited, they avoided experience & also the unbearable present—or, we might amend, made past & present endurable. Eliade may have underestimated tribal effort to remember, as well as memory-erasure in national calamity. Neil Steede interpreted surely-non-Christian equilateral crosses of Maya Comalcalco in Tabasco as probably Christian, notwithstanding the absence of any Christian indication otherwise in symbols, shadow-clock buildings, or multilingual inscribed bricks, which tend to celebrate Quetzalcoatl. Steede found brick size closest to Roman & Carthaginian. The latter, along with Punic among the brick scripts, tallies with Carthaginian influences in Burrows Cave, where Latin also does not occur. An equilateral cross in Egypt signified "town"—another divergence of Nile from Near-Eastern Neolithics/borderline Bronzes beyond. In Mesopotamia a cross diverged as "sheep." So did Indus/Bahrain/Phoenician script diverge from cuneiform.

Anatolian & Upper-Mesopotamian symbols passed with religious cults into Bronze Greece, Shumer/Akkad, Iran, Turkmenistan, Afghanistan, & Indus Valley. Versions of the Goddess cult carried them east & west along trade routes into the patriarchializing Bronze & Iron. Diamonds continued to signify the Goddess. Interlocking block meanders, all the way to China, Mesoamerica, & Peru continued to symbolize the Cosmic-Waters Snake or Dragon of Creation, in association with Goddess birth-giving. (A flying snake did not acquire dragon teeth before Iron Hindu imagination.) The Goddess ruled the sky before her subjugation as Earth Mother; so a bird or butterfly symbolized Her. The Royston, Ga. vertically-drilled stone butterfly had Near-Eastern precedents as beads or amulets such as A.M.T. Moore found at PPNB Abu Hureyra on the middle Euphrates. Numidian script surely postdates atlatls.

TO YUCHIS the sun was preclassically female. Yuchi Scythian ancestors worshipped the sun but, like Minoans, Hittites, Hittites' northern Gashgean ("Moon/Earth"!) enemies, & evidently coastal Asia-Minor Mycenaean Arzauwans (capital Ephesos until Murshilish II destroyed it with the state), Yuchis identified themselves as Moon people, subjects of "*sun*-infused" kings. (Amazons, i.e. Moon Women, designated Hittite warriors possibly because Classical Greeks mistook kilted, shaved soldiers in Hittite sculptures as female but probably because Greeks, to whom the Moon was female, confused Hittite Moon-deity gender by their own Aphrodite.) The male Luvian Moon-god must have gone by the name *Ara/Arma/Ama*. Even Yuchi shooting of an arrow at the sun seems depicted at Beldibi—supposedly preceding Mesolithic invention of bow & arrow. Among oldest Chinese legends, the hero I shot nine suns as ravens. China's "first poet" Chu Yuan (latter 4th-century A.D.) reflected on the 3rd-millennium-B.C. *Shan hai jing* in a famous poem, "Encountering Sorrow," especially on Bk. IX about the bottomless Great Luminous Ravine (Grand Canyon) of the Far East, which another poem, "Heavenly Questions," in the same song anthology, regards the burial-place of the shot suns. As *Zoya* means "sun-infused," Mahan does not miss, *Maya* would mean "moon-infused." Maya civilization also presents (in a distinctly different way) the Yuchi paradox of Egyptian/Semitic/Buddhist hybridization.

IF MUSCOGEEAN proves Numidian, as the inscribed gorget at Etowah suggests, that would account for Muscogeean distant relationship to Algonquin, as Numidian to Egyptian, but would also indicate Mississippi culture as that of a different people. Gordon Willey repeats for Mississippians the argument of comparably eminent scholars for Ubaidians & Shumerians that they were people already residing in the country although untraceable. Without rehearsing the old argument, I assert: these decisive style-changes mean new populations (merging with old). We have probably misjudged the long continuity of a people in the same region in some cases but usually have misjudged discontinuity in apparent *hope* of peaceful or evolutionary change. Mahan has made clear that different peoples of different languages formed confederacies. They may have done so in a different era from former denizens who left Shumerian, Aegean, or Mongolian artifacts. Religious uniformity at different times over vast areas of America gives pause along with the fusion of disparate traditions. Constantly in Neolithic Near-Eastern artifacts one is struck by a "Peruvian" character. Which is to say, what typified the Near East & Aegean in the Neolithic tended to typify the farther Orient &

out and did not thereafter typify Egyptian practice. Yet Narmer himself chose burial back at his former capital, Abydos, where graves of massacred attendants surrounded his double-chambered tomb. A previous king of Abydos (unrecorded except in the fact of supersession) would have conquered Nekhen, home of Horus in association with Hat'hor, which previously dominated Upper Egypt. Nekhen in turn had conquered the earlier dominator Nubet (Hellenistic Ombos, modern village Naqada), seat of the god Set. The grisly mythic battle of Horus & Set may memorialize this conquest. At both Nubet & Nekhen, great twin piles of rocks that looked incongruously like Indo-European tumuli mystified Egyptologists. The largest of these four piles, in the Nekhen countryside, contains intermixed human & ox bones, also potsherds but no located burial beneath. An explanation that did not occur to the distinguished probers is a funeral for a king which included the massacre of his family, attendants, & oxen to accompany him to the spirit-world in the sky. If so, the oxen would not have been sacrificed to propitiate gods and likely provied the funeral feast. Later predynastic kings had tombs in royal cemeteries at both Nubet & Nekhen with remains of a funeral feast but without detectible massacre, which Abydos kings, who appropriated Horus prestige of Nekhen, revived, perhaps in imitation of Mesopotamia, the model for artistocratic Upper Egypt in the whole Late Predynastic. Family/attendant massacre has been observable in a royal tomb at Shumerian Ur, at Shang Anyang, in late-ancient Nubia, & (as of 1987) Moche Sipan, Peru. The Burrows-Cave royal massacre may not be an isolated instance in Mississippian America and might resume an Asiatic as well as an African custom. Archaeologists like Michael Hoffman believe it represents merely a stage in state-formation wherever it occurs but, even if so, seems an interconnected phenomenon along with other cultural traits. It verifies Burrow Cave a cemetery of kings, ruling, as in the other cases, an already-formed kingdom. If, as Mahan astutely contends, Yuchi sun-kings ruled at that southern-Illinois hub which commanded river-highway access in all directions, they may have taken over a longstanding Algonquin-Egyptian tradition and amended it in the cemetery's later centuries, as in Asia they had taken over a longstanding Sky-Goddess/Zoroastrian/Hindu tradition in Afghanistan, Uzbekistan, & Pakistan and amended it within Buddhism. With all the civilizing "medicine" (Buddhism?) Yuchis brought to Archaic tribes in America, they did not apparently bring the Egyptian elements of Burrows Cave including its *ankh*, or Carthaginian including horse-head gold coins & Tanit. Instead of regarding Yuchis Archaic, we could regard them late-arriving cosmpolites retaining non-Egyptian Neolithic/Bronze sun/moon symbolism which proved wholly compatible with Egyptian sun-religion. In precolumbian Peru we find a different perplexing hybrid of Egyptian & Far Eastern, but who in the end can doubt that the former submerged in the latter, that, e.g. the compartmented Peruvian city Chan Chan bore a relation to Tarim-Basin Shanshan (on the model of Sui-rebuilt Chang-an & Shan-shan) superseding Atlantic-borne traditions?

While such speculation remains unsatisfactory, no conventional theory accommodates the Egyptian substrate that astoundingly pervades the Americas in repeated "isolates," partly because hybridized with other strains beyond immediate recognition. Bobbie Smith painfully deciphered a quaint ancient California prescription for determining the summer solstice as Egyptian, although it looks equally Chinese. She reports a party of Hmong people from Laos who said they could read it. Moon-infused (Maya) sun-king dynasties of Mexico & Guatemala, obsessed with sun/royal blood, relied on a dragon-toothed plumed serpent as mediator between this world & the supernatural and built pagoda-topped Bahrain/Cambodian-type ziggurats. (Chinese pagodas originated in India; upturned eaves disguise derivation.) Chichen Itza had an observatory but not early enough for observations of paired constellations at opposite horizons to originate their zodiacal lunar calendar, which they inherited from Olmecs, who had to have brought or acquired it from the ancient Orient, possibly a Hellenistic kingdom (less probably Egypt than Mesopotamia or Bactria). Moran & Kelley detected Hindu, Greek, & Semitic elements in this lunar calendar, explicable if Hellenistic or Kushan transmitted. David Deal has detected a massive Semitic component in Mayan. We recall that Egyptian already contained a massive Semitic component, but Phoenicians, Carthaginians, possibly Chaldeans, certainly Arabs & Jews subjected the ancient & medieval New World to further Semiticization. Yuchis could have acquired the Israelite Festival of Booths directly from Jews, who reached the Southeast U.S. as well as Southwest at different times. But Pakistanis acquired it; Yuchis could have brought it to America with the Kushan-Indus tradition. The American Ku tribe associated with Yuchis may have had a Kushan association, especially in that Mahan identified a Ku people in ancient India. *Shan* is Chinese for "mountain." It would be funny if the Great Yuchis had meant "Bird Effigy"—funnier still if the northwest-wind/fire disaster of Yuchi legend had been cannon of Columbus's circling ships in the Bahamas.

The Canos Mahan identifies as Yuchi poses quite a complication. Canaan underwent long Egyptianization before Egypt annexed it. Phoenician cities occupied North Canaan. Commonality of Egypt & Palestine would help explain Yuchi/Algonquin affinity, should Yuchis have been Canaanite. Jewish colonizations to America took place, as when Jews had great numbers & means in every Aegean & Mediterranean seaport at the failed Bar Kokhba rebellion, but they would not have called themselves Canaanities after c.1230 B.C., rather Israelites or, after c.925, Jews, if natives of the southern kingdom following the division in Rehoboam's Year 5 (Sheshonq's 21). Third-millennium-B.C. Canaanites might have so called themselves but traversing both Mediterranean & Atlantic before even the 12th Dynasty during Minoan/Cypriot domination of sea lanes west made their situation very different from Bahrain, Ceylon, Indo-China, or West Africa. Phoenicians, who occupied North Canaan (and prots of India), conceivably called themselves Canaanites but more likely Tyrians, Sidonians, etc. after their cities. Could *Canos* relate to Kanishka? The *kan* stem meant "youthful." If by chance not identical with Yuchis, "Canaanites" must early have merged with them as they with Shawano, should we have three different ethnic groups.

Much that was Jewish was also Minoan & Egyptian, including circumcision. Moses on Sin (Moon) Mt. seems to relate to the Atlantis (Minoan) custom of baptizing tablets of the law in bull's blood. Jews before the Diaspora were voyaging & caravanning to Indo-China & China respectively. Yuchis would not have to go to or from Judah/Judea to pick up Jewish customs. With the subsuming of Judah in the Hellenistic world, Jews participated in a cultural unity stretching from Libya to the Indus & Sogdiana. Not only in Pakistan & Central Asia, Yuchis would have found Jewish colonies in South India & Ceylon, as, for that matter, on Cyprus, in Alexandria, France, Morocco, or Spain had they taken a Mediterranean route, supposing migration in early centuries A.D. Much of family resemblance to Yuchis in Olmec Mexico looks as Mediterranean as Far-Eastern.

WHAT IF WE TOOK a serious look at the boast "Ruler of the Four Quarters [of the World]" by "Kings of Shumer & Akkad," and at the also-3rd-millennium-B.C. courtier/emperor Yu's despatch of explorers to the four corners of the world? Distant movement had characterized tribal bands from australopithecine times who were following prey, and continued after flock domestication in semiannual or continuous transhumance. Especially before domestication of pack animals, rivers & seas offered the best transportation option. Anatolian colonists who introduced agriculture & animal domestication (with their Goddess religion) to Thessaly chose sea-freighting instead of cattle-driving overland; the Anatolian first settlers of Crete who founded Knossos also took cattle among many other animals on boats; the probably-Palestinian first settlers of Cyprus, at Khirokitia, voyaged with fallow deer as well as sheep, goats, & pigs—each of these colonizations before 6000 B.C., when full-fledged cities existed at Chatal & Abu Hureyra 32 & 28 acres resp. which were in turn conquering/colonizing vastly. We can trace the extensive obsidian network in the Near-Eastern Neolithic (in most cases) to individual source volcanoes by chemical profiling, and the yet more incredibly extensive Neolithic/Protodynastic lapis lazuli trade as far as South Egypt to a single source-region, Badakhshan. We can document a regular Early-Bronze sea-trade between Ur & the Indus via Bahrain—even an Indus trading colony at Lagash. Ships kept sailing east from the Persian Gulf even after Indus ships ceased to sally. A rising water-table and river-silting stranded Lothal (whose dock was a dock as Rao demonstrated and not an irrigation-tank as a pupil of his disputed) in the general degeneration of Harappa Culture which malaria abetted (skeletons showing effects of anemia). Dreadful civil wars among Shumerian cities temporarily cut the Indus trade while it was flourishing and inevitably dislocated dense population like the civil war of White vs. Red in the comparably populous Nile Delta. No surviving narrative tells us what severe repercussions continued in the Delta or the Gulf from swift Archaic-Egyptian/Shumerian-Akkadian & Ur3 Shumerian-reasserting totalitarian progress. Winners holding the field kept silence on their repression. Losers who fled left no record. Pictographic rock inscriptions discovered recently in China & Southwest Japan which are readable as Shumerian jolt our assumptions about voyaging past India from the Persian Gulf as early as the Urukian/Jamdat Nazr Protodynastic.

Hendon Harris's epochal discovery of a quaint map that evidently accompanied the original *Shan hai jing* lends the latter's age & purported extensiveness new credibility. Deal & Donald Cyr have transposed its quaint designations onto a modern world map very convincingly. We formerly supposed the West, e.g., could reach only into Central Asia; Chinese savants from the Han until 1968 (Wei Chu-hsien) supposed the East reached somewhere in the Middle Kingdom itself but could not

Brown, Richar Burnett. "A provisional catalogue of and commentary on Egyptian and Egyptianizing artifacts found on Greek sites." U. Minn. diss. (Xerox U. Microfilms 1975)

Bryson, R.A.; Lamb, H.H.; & Donley, David L. "Drought and decline of Mycenae." Antiquity XLVIII (Mar. 1974), 46–50

Buchholz, Hans-Gunter. "Some observations concerning Thera's contacts overseas during the Bronze Age." TATAW II (1980), 227–40

Burns, A.R. Minoans, Philistines, and Greeks B.C. 1400–900 (Knopf 1930)

Brett, James S. & Cyr, Donald L. "Chinese ancient world mapping." In The diffusion issue, ed. Cyr (Stonehenge Viewpoint 1991), 51–103

Brown, Peter. The world of late antiquity AD 150–750. Hist. Europ. Civ. Lib., ed. Geoffrey Barraclough (Harcourt Brace Jovanovich 1971)

Broyles, William, Jr. "Uncovering a 'history of heroes.'" U.S. News & World Report (2 June 1988), 12

Brunton, Guy. "The predynastic town-site at Hierakonpolis." In Studies presented to F. Ll. Griffith, ed. S.R.K. Glanville (London: EES 1932), 272–76

_____ & Caton-Thompson, Gertrude. The Badarian civilisation and the prehistoric remains near Badari (Quaritch 1928)

Buchanan, Donal B. Report on inscriptions from the Southwest (prepared for Don Rickey, Bur. Land Mgmnt., Dept. Interior) (Vienna, Va.: msc. n.d.)

Budge, E.A. Wallis. Egypt in the Neolithic and Archaic periods. Bks. on Egypt & Chaldea IX (Kegan Paul, Trench, Trubner 1904)

Burkholder, Grace. "'Ubaid sites and pottery in Saudi Arabia." Archaeology XXV/4 (Oct. 1972), 264–69

_____ & Golding, Marny. "A surface survey of the Ubaid sites in the eastern provinces of Saudi Arabia." Aribus Asias XXIII/4 (1971), 294

Burney, Charles. The ancient Near East (Cornell U. 1977)

Burton-Brown, Theodore. Third millennium diffusion (Wootton, Woodstock, Eng.: author 1970) [pottery reassessment]

Bury, J.B. The invasion of Europe by the barbarians (London: Macmillan 1928)

Butzer, Karl W. Comment on Arkell & Ucko, "Review of predynastic development." Curr. Anth. VI/2 (Apr. 1985), 157–58

_____ . "Enviornmental & human ecology in Egypt during predynastic & Early Dynastic times." Bull. de la Societe de Geographie d'Egypte XXXII (1959), 43–87

_____ . Environment and archaeology: an ecological approach to prehistory (Chicago: Aldine 1971)

Cady, John F. Southeast Asia: its historical development (McGraw-Hill 1964)

Campbell, Joseph with Moyers, Bill. The power of myth, ed. Betty Sue Flowers (Doubleday 1988)

Capart, Jean. Primitive art in Egypt, tr. A.S. Griffith (London: H. Grevel 1905)

Cardi, Beatrice de. "The British archaeological expedition to Qatar 1973–1974." Antiquity XLVIII/3 #191 (Sept. 1974), 196–200

_____ . Excavations at Bampur, a third millennium settlement in Persian Baluchistan, 1966. Anthro. Papers An. Mus. Nat. Hist. LI/3 (1970)

Carneiro, Robert L. "A theory of the origin of the state." Science CLXIX/3947 (21 Aug. 1970), 733.-38

Carpenter, Rhys. Beyond the Pillars of Heracles: the classical world as seen through the eyes of its discoverers (N.Y.: Delacorte 1966)

_____ . Discontinuity in Greek civilization (Norton 1968)

Carroll, Thomas D. "The origin, development, and diffusion of musical scales: an index to cultural contacts." Int. Assoc. Historians of Asia, Procs. 2nd biennial conf., Taipei Oct. 1962 (Taiwan Provincial Museum c.1963), 149–78 [U. Washington Library, Seattle]

Carter, George F. "The George Carter letters." In The diffusion issue, ed. Cyr (Stonehenge Viewpoint 1991), 14–20

_____ . "Megalithic man in America?" Ibid., 104–06

_____ . "Pre-Columbian chickens in America." Ch. 9, Man across the sea, ed. C.L. Riley et al. (U. Texas 1971), 178–218

Carus-Wilson, E.M. Medieval merchant venturers: collected studies (London: Methuen 1954/U. Paperbacks 1967)

Cary, M. History of Rome down to the reign of Conmstantine (London: Macmillan 1947)

Casal, Jean Marie. "Excavations at Pirak, West Pakistan." Ch. 12, S. Asian archaeology, ed. Hammond (Cambridge U. 1973), 171–79

_____ . Fouilles de Mundigak. 2 vols. (Paris: C. Klincksieck 1961)

Case, Humphrey & Payne, Joan Crowfoot. "Tomb 100: the Decorated Tomb of Hierakonpolis." JEA XLVIII (1962), 5–18

Caskey, John L. "IVa. Greece and the Aegean islands in the M B Age: III. The people: questions of race, language and chronology." CAH3 II/1 (1973), 135–40

Casson, Lionel. The ancient mariners: seafarers and sea fighters of the Mediterranean in ancient times (N.Y.: Macmillan 1959)

_____ . Ships and seamanship in the ancient world (Princeton U. 1971)

Catling, Hector W. "Archaeology in Greece, 1978–79": "Tiryns" [progress report on Klaus Killian discoveries]. Archaeol. Reports for 1978–79, XXV (1979), 16

_____ . "Cyprus in the Late Bronze Age." CAH3 II/2 (1975), XXIIb, 188–215

Cauvin, Jacques. Les premieres villages du IXeme au VIIeme millenaire avant J-C. Coll. de la Maison de l'Or. Med. Ancien 4, Serie Archeol. 3 (Lyons: Maison de l'Orient 1978)

_____ . "Les fouilles de Mureybat (1971–1974) et leur signification pour les origines de la sedentarisation au Proche-Orient." Ann. Am. Schls. Oriental Res. XLIV (1977), 19–48

_____ . "Nouvelles fouilles a Tell Mureybat (Syrie): 1971–1972. Rapport preliminaire." Annales archeologiques arabas syriennes XXII (1972), 105–15

Chadwick, John. Documents in Mycenaean Greek, 2nd ed. (Cambridge U. 1973)

_____ . The Mycenaean world (Cambridge U. 1976), partic. Ch. 6: "Religion," 64–101

Chakrabarti, Dilip K. "Gujarat Harappan connection with West Asia: a reconstruction of the evidence." Journ. Econ. & Soc. Hist. Orient XVIII/3 (Oct. 1975), 337–42

Chan, Dominic, tr. Shan hai jing, Bk. XIII: Classic of the hinterland east within the seas south of Tun Pei Ju (Hill of Northeast), ed. C. Covey. In Dragon Treasures, ed. Donald L. Cyr (Santa Barbara: Stonehenge Viewpoint 1989), 20–21

Chandler, Wayne B. "Trait-influences in Meso-America: the African-Asian connection." Ch. 12 in African presence in early America (Journ. African Civs. 1987), 274–334

Chapman, Paul H. Discovering Columbus (ISAC 1992)

_____ . The man who led Columbus to America (Atlanta: One Candle 1973)

_____ . The Norse discovery of America (One Candle 1981)

_____ . "Oklahoma runestones." XVI (1987), 91–95

Chard, Chester S. Northeast Asia in prehistory (U. Wisc. 1974)

Charvat, Peter. "The Kish evidence and the emergence of states in Mesopotamia." Curr. Anthropology XXII/6 (Dec. 1981), 686–88

Chavarria-Aguilar, ed. Traditional India. Asian Civ. ser., ed L.A.P. Gosling & W.D. Schorger (Prentice-Hall 1964)

Childs, William A.P. "Lycian relations with Persians and Greeks in the fifth and fourth centuries re-examined." Anatolian Studies XXXI (1981), 55–80

Cho-yun Hsu. Ancient China in transition: an analysis of social mobility, 722–222 B.C. (Stanford U. 1965)

Christensen, Ross T., ed. The Tree of Life in ancient America (Brigham Young U. 1968)

Civil, Miguel. "The Sumerian writing system: some problems." Orientalia n.s. XLII/1-2 (1973), 21–34

Cline, Eric. "Amenophis III and the Aegean." AJA LXXXIX/2 (Apr. 1985), 327–28

_____ . "Hittite objects in the Bronze Age Aegean." Anatolian Studs. XLI (1991), 133–43

Coedes, George. The Indianized states of Southeast Asia, tr. Susan Brown Cowing, ed. Walter F. Vella (Honolulu: East-West Center Press 1968)

Cohane, John Philip. The key (Crown 1969)

Compton, Carl B. "Musical Stones" [from back of gatehouse, Chichen Itza]. Denton, Tx.: The Intermission (c. Oct. 1972), 6

Comrie, Bernard. "The ergative variations on a theme." Lingua XXXII (1973), 239–53

Condominas, G. "Le lithophone prehistorique de Ndut Lieng Krak." Bull. de l'Ecole francaise d'Exttreme-Orient (1951), 359–92 + 5 pgs. plates

Contamine, Philippe. War in the Middle Ages [1980 in Fr.], tr. Michael Jones (Oxford: Basil Blackwell 1984)

Cook, J.M. The Greeks in the East. Ancient Peoples & Places 31 (Praeger 1963)

Coomaraswamy, Ananda K. Hinduism and Buddhism. N.Y.: Wisdom Lib./Philos. Lib. n.d.)

Cooper, Alan M. "Canaanite religion." Ch. 5, Religions of antiquity, ed. R.M. Seltzer (Macmillan 1989), 80−95

Cooper, Jerold S. "Sumerian & Akkadian in Sumer & Akkad." Orientalia XLII/1-2 (1973), 239−46

Couraud, Claude. L'art azilian. Origins, survivance, comparaisons (Paris: Centre national de la recherche scientifique 1985) [incls. 400 pgs. pls.]

Covarrubias, Miguel. The eagle, the jaguar, and the serpent (Knopf 1954)

Covey, Cyclone. Calalus (N.Y.: Vantage 1975)

_____ . "Introduction to the translation of Shan hai Jing, Book XIII." In Dragon Treasures, ed. Donald L. Cyr (Santa Barbara: Stonehenge Viewpoint 1989), 7−19

_____ . Homeric Troy and the Sea Peoples (lakemont, Ga.: Copple House 1987)

_____ . Style as metaphysics. (Columbus, Ga.: Westville Symposium Papers 1975)

Covey, Joan. "African sea kings in America: evidence from early maps." Ch. 5, African presence in early America (Journ. African Civs. 1987), 152−68

_____ . "Egyptians in ancient Russia." La. Mounds Soc. Newsletter 41 (15 Aug. 1991), 7−8

Coxon, P.W. "Script analysis and Mandaean origins." Journ. Semitic Studies XV/1 (Spring 1970), 16−23

Cross, Frank Moore, Jr. "The Phoenician inscription from Brazil. A nineteenth-century forgery." Orientalia XXXVII (1968, 437−60 [Illuminates subject despite erroneous controlling assumption; Cyrus Gordon's "Reply to Professor Cross" follows, p.461 ff.]

Crossland, R.A. "Who were the Luwians?" Proc. Class. Assoc. LXXV (1968), 36−38

_____ & Birchall, Ann, eds. Bronze Age migrations in the Aegean. . . . 1st Int. Colloq. Aegean prehist. Br. Assoc. Myc. Studs. & Depts. Archaeol. & Anc. Hist. U. Sheffield (Noyes 1974)

Crowley, J.L. "More on Mycenaeans at Thera." AJA LXXXVII/1 (Jan. 1983), 83−85

Cyr, Donald L., ed. Exploring rock art (15th annual symposium, Am. Rock Art Res. Assoc.) (Santa Barbara: Stonehenge Viewpoint 1989)

Dabbagh, Takey. [Khalaf pottery designs]. Sumer XXI (1965), 93, & XXII (1966), 23−43

Dabbs, Jack A. History of the discovery and exploration of Chinese Turkestan. Central Asiatic Atudies VIII (Mouton 1963)

Dales, George F. "The decline of the Harappans." Scientific American CCXIV/5 (May 1966), 92−98 [map 94]

_____ . "Harappa outposts on the Makran coast." Antiquity XXVI (1962), 86−92

_____ . "New investigations at Mohenjo-daro." Archaeology XVIII (June 1965), 145−50

_____ . "A suggested chronology for Afghanistan, Baluchistan, & the Indus Valley." In Chronologies of Old World archaeology, ed. R.W. Ehrich (U. Chicago 1965), 257−84

[Damp, Jonathan]. "First pottery in the New World" [Altomayo, Ecuador, c.6000 yrs. old]. Archaeology XLII/6 (Nov./Dec. 1989), 26

Davies, Nigel. Human sacrifice in history and today (Morrow 1981)

_____ . Voyagers to the New World (U.N.M. 1979)

Davies, Norman de Garis. The tomb of Rekh-mi-re at Thebes. 2 vols. in 1. Met. Mus. Egypt. Expl. (N.Y. 1943; Arno 1973)

_____ . "The work of the graphic branch of the expedition: trading with the Land of Punt." In The Egyptian expedition 1934−1935. Bull. Met. Mus. Art (Nov. 1935), Sec. II, 46−49

Davis, Charles T., ed. The eagle, the crescent, and the cross: sources of medieval history I (c.250−c.1000) (Appleton-Century-Crofts 1967)

Deal, David Allen. Discovery of ancient America (Irvine, Calif.: Kherem La Yah Press 1984)

_____ . The nexus: spoken language. The link between the Old and New Worlds (Vista, Calif: author 1987)

_____ . "The Mystic Symbol People" [reply to Don Clifford]. Inst. Archaeol. Res. Newsletter VII/7-8 (July−Aug. 1991), 6−11 [discriminates 4 alphabets] Worlds (Vista, Calif.: author 1987)

Delekat, L. Phonizier in Amerika. Die Echtheit der bekanntgewordenen kanaanaischen (altsidonischen) Inschrift aus Pariaiba in Brasilien nachgewiesen. Bonner Biblische Beitrage XXXII (Bonn: Peter Hanstein 1969)

Dempewolff, Richard F., ed. (int. Isaac Asimov). Lost cities and forgotten tribes (Hearst 1974/Pocket Bks. 1976

Desborough, V.R. d'A. The Greek Dark Ages (London: Ernest Benn 1972)

_____ . The last Mycenaeans and their successors: an archaeological survey c.1200-c.1000 B.C. (Oxford U. 1964)

Dexter, Warren W. Ogam-consaine and Tifinag alphabets: ancient uses (Rutland, Vt.: Academy Bks. 1984)

Dhyansky, Yan Y. "The Indus Valley origin of a Yoga practice." Antibus Asiae XLVIII/1-2 (1987), 89–108

Dietrich, B.C. "Evidence of Minoan religious traditions and their survival in the Mycenaean and Greek world." Historia XXXI/1 (1982), 1–12

Diodoros Sikolos. Library of History (Gr./Eng.), tr, C.H. Oldfather. 10 vols. Loeb Classical Lib. (Heinemann/Putnam's 1933)

Diringer, David. The alphabet . . ., 2nd ed. (Phlios. Lib. 1948)

_____ . "The origins of the alphabet." Antiquity XVII (June 1943), 77–90

Dixon, Robert M.W. "Ergativity." Language LV (1979), 59–138

Dikaios, Porphyrios. Khirokitia: final report on the excavation of a Neolithic settlement in Cyprus on behalf of the Department of Antiquities, 1936–1946 (Oxford U./Gov't. Cyprus 1953)

Donadoni, Sergio. "Remarks about Egyptian connections of the Sahara rock shelter art." In Prehist. art of the western Mediterranean & the Sahara, ed. L. Pericot Garcia & E. Ripoll Parello [Burg-Wartenstein symp. 1980]. Vik. Fund Pubs. Anth. 39 (Wenner-Gren Found. Anth. Res./Curr. Anth. 1964), 185–90

[Donnan, Christopher]. "Archaeologists find tomb of [Moche] 'Peruvian King Tut.'" (UPI Washington) Winston-Salem Journal 14 Sept. 1988), 2

Doran, Edwin, Jr. "The sailing raft as a great tradition." In Man across the sea, ed. C.L. Riley et al. (U.Texas 1971), 115–38

Dothan, M. "A sign of Tanit from Tel 'Akko. Israel Expl. Journ. XXIV/1 (1974), 44–49

Dothan, Trude. The Philistines and their material culture (Yale U./IES 1982)

Doumas, Christos G. "The Minoan eruption of the Santorini volcano." Antiquity XLVIII/190 (June 1974), 110–15

Dupree, Louis. Afghanistan (Princeton U. 1973)

During Caspers, Elisabeth C.L. "Dilmun: international burial ground." Journ. Econ. & Soc. Hist. of the Orient [hence JESHO], XXVII/1 (Jan. 1984), 1–32

_____ . "Harappan trade in the Arabian Gulf in the third millennium B.C." Mesopotamia VII (1972), 167–91

_____ . "Sumer, coastal Arabia and the Indus Valley in Protoliterate Early Dynastic eras. Supporting evidence for cultural linkage." Journ. Ec. & Soc. Hist. Orient XXII/2 (May 1979), 121–35

_____ & Govindankutty, A. "R. Thapar's Dravidian hypothesis for the locations of Meluhha, Dilmun and Makan." JESHO XXI/2 (Mar. 1978), 113–45

Eberhard, Wolfram. A history of China, 2nd ed. (Berkeley & L.A.: U. Calif. 1960)

Eckholm, Gordon F. "The possible Chinese origin of Teotihuacan cylindrical tripod pottery and certain related traits." Cingreso Int. de Americanistas, Actas y Memorias XXXV (1964), I 39–45

_____ . "Wheeled toys in Mexico." Am. Antiquity n.s. XII (1946), 222–28

Edgerton, William F. & Wilson, John A. Historical records of Ramses III: the texts in Medinet Habu I & II. Studs. Anc. Or. Civ. 12 (U. Chicago 1936) [See below, Epigraphic Survey]

Edwards, Emily (photog. Manuel Alvarez Bravo, foreword Jean Charlot). Painted walls of Mexico (U. Texas 1966)

Edwards, I.E.S. "The Early Dynastic period in Egypt." CAH3 I/2 (1971), XI, 1–70

Eissfeldt, O. Review of Delekat's Phoenizier in Amerika. Journ. Semitic Studies XV/1 (Spring 1970), 102–04 [Summarizes the international controversy]

Eliade, Mircea. Birth and rebirth: the religious meanings of initiation in human culture [U. Chicago Haskell Lectures 1956], tr. Willard R. Trask (Harper & Bros. 1958)

_____ . Cosmos and history: the myth of the eternal return [orig. 1949], tr, Trask (Harper & Row 1954/Harper Trchbks.-Bollingen Lib. 1959)

Ellis, Florence Hawley & Dodge, Andrea Ellis. "The spread of Chaco/Mesa Verde/McElmo Black-on-White pottery and the possible simultaneous introduction of irrigation into the Rio Grande drainage." Journ. Anthr. Res. XLV/1 (Spr. 1989), 47–52

Emery, Walter B. Archaic Egypt (Penguin 1961)

_____ . Great tombs of the First Dynasty, II (EES/Oxford U. 1954)

Ensuit, J.F. & Jarrige, J.F. "Chalcolithic pottery from four sites in the Bolan area of Baluchistan, West Pakistan." Ch. 13, S. Asian Archaeol., ed. Hammond (1973), 181–96

Georgiev, Vladimir. "Mycenaean among the other Greek dialects." *In* Mycenaean studies (Procs. 3rd int. colloq. Myc. studs. at 'Wingspread' 4–8 Sept. 1961), ed. Emmett L. Bennett, Jr. (U. Wisc. 1964), 125–39

_____ . "Sur l'origine et la langue des Pelasges, des Philistines, des Danaens et des Acheens." Jahrbuch fur Kleinasiatische Forschung (1951), 136–41

Gibson, McGuire. "Population shift and the rise of Mesopotamian civilization." *In* Old World archaeology. Readings from Sci. Am. (S.F.: Freeman 1972), 165–73

Gimbutas, Marija. "The first wave of Eurasian steppe pastoralists into Copper Age Europe." Journ. Indo-Europ. Studs. V/4 (Winter 1977), 277–338

_____ . The gods and goddesses of Old Europe 7000 to 3500 B.C.: myths, legends and cult images (U. Calif. 1974)

_____ . "The image of women in prehistoric art." Quarterly Review of Archaeology II/4 (Dec. 1981), 1, 6–6

_____ . "Old Europe 7000–3500: the earliest European civilization before the infiltration of the Indo-European peoples." Journ. Indo-Europ. Studs. I/1 (Spr. 1973), 1–20

_____ . The prehistory of eastern Europe, I. Mesolithic, Neolithic and Copper Age culture in Russia and the Baltic area, ed. Hugh Hencken. Am. School Prehist. Research Bull. 20 (Peabody Museum 1956)

_____ . "Proto-Indo-European culture: the Kurgan culture during the fifth, fourth, and third millennium B.C." *In* Indo-European & Indo-Europeans: 3rd Indo-European Conf., ed. Geo. Carons et al. (U. Pa. 1970), 155–97

Girardot, N.J. Myth and meaning in early Taoism: the theme of chaos (*hun-tun*) (Berkeley/L.A./London: U. Calif. 1983)

Giveon, Raphael. "An inscription of Rameses III from Lachish." Tel Aviv X/2 (1983), 176–77

_____ . "Dating the Cape Gelidonya shipwreck." Anat. Studs. XXV (1985), 99–101

Glob, P.V. & Bibby, T.G. "A forgotten civilization of the Persian Gulf" (Oct. 1960). *In* Old World archaeology, int. C.C. Lamberg-Karlovsky. Readings from Sci. Am. (S.F.: Freeman 1972), 165–73

Gnoli, Gherardo. "Iranian religions." Ch. 7, Religions of antiquity, ed. R.M. Seltzer (Macmillan 1989), 122–27

_____ . "Manichaeism." Ch. 16, ibid., 206–300

_____ . "Mithraism." Ch. 17, ibid., 301–04

_____ . "Zoroastrianism." Ch. 8, ibid., 128–47

Goff, Beatrice Laura. Symbols of prehistoric Mesopotamia [Hassuna through Jamdat Nazr] (Yale U. 1963)

Gokhale, Balkrishna Govind. Ancient India in history and culture , 4th ed. (Bombay/N.Y.: Asia Publ. House 19590

_____ . "Buddhism in the Gupta age," Ch. 6 *in* Essays on Gupta culture (Delhi 1983), 129–53

Gophna, Ram. "Egyptian immigration into southern Canaan during the First Dynasty?" Tel Aviv III/1 (1976), 31–37

Gordon, Cyrus H. Before Columbus: links between the Old World and ancient America (Crown 1971)

_____ . Forgotten scripts (N.Y.: Basic Bks. 1968)

_____ . "A Hebrew inscription authenticated." La. Mounds Soc. Newsletter 39 (15 May 1991), 5–6

_____ . "The Metcalf Stone." Manuscripts XXI/3 (Summer 1969), 159

_____ . Riddles in history (Crown 1974)

Grant, Michael. The Etruscans (Scribner's 1981)

Grayson, A.K. ed. II. Mesopotamia. Papyrus and tablet (Prentice-Hall 1973)

Greenberg, Joseph H. "The classification of African languages." Am. Anthropologist L (1948), 24–29

_____ , ed. Universals of human languages. 4 vols. (Stanford U. 1978)

Greenwood, Stuart & Bhussry, "Teotihuacan—an interpretation." Ancient Skies II/6 (Jan.–Feb. 1985), 1–2 [Illuminate alignments on untenable thesis]

Griffiths, J. Gwyn. "Hellenistic religions." Ch. 13, Religions of antiquity, ed. R.M. Seltzer (Macmillan 1989), 237–58

_____ . "The interpretation of the Horus-myth of Edfu." JEA XLIV (Dec. 1958), 75–85

Guha, Amalendu, ed. Central Asia: movement of peoples and ideas from times prehistoric to modern. Int. Conf. on Central Asia New Delhi Feb. 1969 (Barnes & Noble 1971)

Guido, Margaret. Sardinia. Anc. Peoples & Places 35 (Thams & Hudson/Praeger 1963)

_____ . Sicily: archaeological guide (Praeger 1976)

Guidon, Niede. "The first Americans: cliff notes." Nat. Hist. XCVI/8 (Aug. 1989), 6, 8, 10, 12
_____ . "On stratigraphy and chronology at Pedra Furada." Curr. Anth. XXX/3 (Dec. 1989), 641
_____ & Delibries, G. "Carbon-14 dates . . . 32,000 years ago." Nature CCCXXI (19 June 1986),
    769-71 [See above: Bahn 1991]
Gupta, S.P. Archaeology of Soviet Central Asia and the Indian borderlands. 2 vols. (Delhi: B.R. Pub.
    Corp. 1979)
Guterbock, Hans Gustav. "The Hittites and the Aegean world: Part 1. The Ahhiyawa problem
    reconsidered" (Dec. 1981). AJA LXXXVII/2 (Apr. 1983), 133-38
Gurney, O[liver] R[obert]. The Hittites (Penguin 1952; rev.: Allen Lane 1975)

Hackett, Walter. "A Portuguese place in Massachusetts annals" [Dighton Rock]. N.Y. Times (16 July
    1967), p. cropped
Haley, J.B. & Blegen, C.W. "The coming of the Greeks." Am. Journ. Archaeol. XXXII (1928), 141-54
Hall, H.R. "Keftiu." In Essays in Aegean archaeology presented to Sir Arthur Evans in honor of his
    75th birthday, ed. Stanley Casson (Oxford 1927), 31-41
_____ . "Keftiu and the Peoples of the Sea." Ann. Br. School Athens VIII (1902), 157-89
_____ . "The Keftiu-fresco in the tomb of Senmut." ABSA X (1904), 154-57
Hallager, Birgitta Palsson. "Crete and Italy in the Late Bronze Age III period." AJA LXXXIX/2 (Apr.
    1985), 293-305
Hallo, William H. & Simpson, William Kelly. The ancient Near East: a history (Harcourt Brace
    Jovanovich 1971)
Hambis, L. "L'histoire des Mongols avant Gengis-Khan d'apres les sources chinoises et mongoles,
    et la documentation conservee par Rasidu-d-'Din." Central Asiatic Journ. XIV/1-3 (1970), 125-33
Hamilton, Clarence H., ed. Buddhism [selections from Pali, Sanskrit, Chinese, Japanese, & Tibetan
    Buddhist lit.] (N.Y.: Liberal Arts Press 1952)
Hammond, Nicholas G.L. Migrations and invasions in Greece and adjacent areas (Noyes 1976)
_____ . Studies in Greek history (Oxford U. 1973)
_____ . "Tumulus burial in Albania, the grave circles of Mycenae, and the Indo-Europeans."
    Br. Sch. Athens LXII (1967), 77-105
[Hansen, Richard] (AP Los Angeles). "Even older: Mayan civilization traced to 630 B.C." [Nakbe,
    Guatemala]. Winston-Salem Journal 14 Nov. 1989), 2
Harden, D.B. "The Phoenicians on the west coast of Africa." Antiquity (Sept. 1948), 141
Harris, Hendon Mason. The Asiatic fathers of America (n.p., n.d.[Taipei 1973])
_____ . "Treassure maps of Fu-sang," ed. Donald L. Cyr. In Dragon treasures, ed. Cyr
    (Stonehenge Viewpoint 1989), 23-49, 58-68
Hartner, Willy. "The earliest history of the constellations in the Near East and the motif of the
    lion-bull combat." JNES XXIV/1-2 (Jan.-Apr. 1965), 1-16 + 16 plts.
Harvey, Wilfred, tr.-ed. The periplus of the Erythraean Sea, ed. W. Schoff (Longmans 1912)
Hassan, Fekri A. "The beginnings of Egyptian civilization at Hierakonpolis." Qrtly. Review of Archae-
    ology V/1 (Mar. 1984), 13-15
_____ . "The predynastic of Egypt." Journ. World Prehistory II/2 (June 1988), 135-85
_____ . "The roots of Egyptian writing." Qrtly. Rev. Archaeol. IV/9 (Sept. 1983), 1, 7-8
[Hayden, Dorothy L.] "Mystic Symbol artifact from Ohio State Historical Society Museum Collection."
    Mt. Vernon, N.H.: Am. Inst. Archaeol. Res. Newsletter VIII/1-2 (Jan.-Feb. 1992), 24 (Cf. also p. 14:
    ST #5 Henriette Mertz Coll. showing one of many elements comparable to Burrows Stone
    elephants)
Hayes, William C. "Chronology I. Egypt—to the end of the Twentieth Dynasty." CAH3 I/1 (1970). Ch.
    VI, 173-93
_____ . Most ancient Egypt, ed. Keith C. Seale (U. Chicago 1965)
_____ . The scepter of Egypt: a background for. . .study of Egyptian antiquities in the Met.
    Mus. of Art. 2 vols. (Met. Mus./Harvard U. 1953)
Haynes. C. Vance, Jr. "Elephant-hunting in North America." Scientific American (June 1966), 104-12
Hays, T.R. "Predynastic Egypt: recent field research." Curr. Anth. XVII/3 (Sept. 1978), 552-54
Heine-Geldern, Robert. "Traces of India and Southeast Asiatic Hindu-Buddhist influences in Meso-
    america." In XXXV Cong. Int. Americanistas, Actas y memorias (Mexico City 1964), I, 49
Helfritz, Hans. Mexican cities of the gods: an archaeological guide (Praeger 1970)
Heras, H. Studies in Proto-Indo-Mediterranean culture, I (Bombay: India Hist. Res. Inst. 1953)
Hermann, Georgina. "Lapis lazuli: the early phases of its trade." Iraq XXX/1 (Spr. 1968), 21-57

Hermann, Paul. Conquest by man, tr. Michael Bullock (Harper & Bros. 1954)

Hernandez-Pachero, Eduardo. Las pinturas prehistoricas de las Cuevas de la Arana. . . Evol. arteru-prestre de Espana (Madrid: Museo nacional de ciencias naturales 1924)

Herodotos. Histories (Istoriai) (Gr./Eng.), tr. A.D. Godley. Loeb Class. Lib. 4 vols. (Harvard U./ Heinemann 1941). Also: tr. George Rawlinson in The Greek historians (Random House 1942) I, & Great bks. of the Western world, ed. R.M. Hutchins & M.J. Adler (Encyc. Britannica 1952), VI; & tr. Aubrey de Selincourt (Penguin 1954, 1965)

Hijara, Ismail Hussein. "Arpachiyah." Excavations in Iraq, 1978. Iraq XXXIX/2 (Aut. 1977), 302–04

_____ . "Three new graves at Arpachiyah." World Archaeology X/2 (Oct. 1978), 125–28

Hoffman, Michael A. "The City of the Hawk: seat of Egypt's ancient civilization." Expedition XVIII/3 (Spr. 1978), 32–41

_____ . Culture history and cultural ecology at Hierakonpolis from Paleolithic times to the Old Kingdom. U. Wisc. diss. (Xerox Microfilms 1971)

_____ . Egypt before the pharoahs: the prehistoric foundations of Egyptian civilization (Knopf 1978)

_____ . "Excavations at Locality 14." Journ. Am. Res. Center Egypt IX (1972), 49–74

_____ . "A rectangular Amratian house from Hierakonpolis and its significance for predynastic research." JNES XXXIX/2 (Apr. 1980), 119–37

Hoffmann, Curtiss Russell. The lion, the eagle, the man, and the bull in Mesopotamian glyphic, I & II. Yale diss. (Xerox U. Microfilms 1974)

Hoffner, Harry A., Jr. "Hittite religion." Ch. 4, Religions of antiquity, ed. R.M. Seltzer (Macmillan 1989), 69–79

Hogan, Patrick. "Dinetah: a reevaluation of pre-revolt Navajo occupation in northwest New Mexico" [entered by c.1450 A.D.].Journ. Anthr. Res. XLV/1 (Spr. 1989), 53–66

Hohenberger, Johannes. The nominal and verbal afformitives of Nilo-Hamitic and Hamito-Semitic with some phonetic observations and a new vocabulary. Deutsche Morgenlandische Gesell-schaft Abhandlungen fur die Kunde des Morgennlandes XLII/2 (Wiesbaden: Franz Steiner GMBH 1975)

Holmes, Y. Lynn. "The foreign trade of Cyprus during the Late Bronze Age." In The archaeology of Cyprus, ed. Moel Robertson (Noyes 1975), 90–110

Homer. The Iliad (Greek/Eng.), tr. A.T. Murray. 2 vols. Loeb Class. Lib. Heinemann/Harvard U. 1937). Also: tr. Richard Lattimore (U. Chicago 1951) & many other translations

_____ . The Odyssey (Gr./Eng.), tr. A.T. Murray. 2 vols. Loeb Class. Lib. (Heinemann/Putnam's 1919). Also: tr. Richard Lattimore. Harper Colophon (Harper & Row 1967) & several other translations

Honore, Pierre. In quest of the white god (Putnam 1964)

Hood, M.S.F. "The Tartaria tablets." Sci. American CCXVIII (May 1968), 30–37

Hope, Orville L. 6000 years of seafaring (Gastonia, N.C.: author 1983)

Hope Simpson, Richard. Mycenaean Greece (Noyes 1981)

Horn, Siegfried H. "Foreign gods in ancient Egypt." In Studies in honor of John A. Wilson. Oriental Inst. Studs. in Anc. Or. Civ. 35 (U. Chicago 1969), 37–42

Hornell, James. "Naval activity in the days of Solomon and Rameses III." Antiquity XXI/82 (June 1947), 66–111

Houwink ten Cate, Philo H.J. The Luwian population groups of Lycia and Cilicia Aspera during the Hellenistic period. Documenta et Monumenta Orientis antiqui 10 (Leiden: Brill 1961)

_____ . The records of the early Hittite Empire c.1450–1380 B.C.) (Istabul: Nederlands Historisch-Archaeologisch Inst. in Let Nabige Oosten 1970)

Huxley, G.L. Achaeans and Hittites (Belfast: Queen's U. 1960/1968

Hyde, Walter Woodburn. Ancient Greek mariners (Oxford U. 1947)

Ikeda, Daisaku. Buddhism, the first millennium, tr. Burton Watson (Tokyo/N.Y./S.F.: Kodansha Inter-national 1977)

Immerwahr, Sara A. Aegean painting in the Bronze Age (U. Park & London: Pa. St. U. 1990)

_____ . "Mycenaeans at Thera: some reflections on the paintings from the West House." In Greece and the eastern Mediterranean in ancient history and prehistory: studies presented to F. Sschachermeyr, ed. K.H. Kinzl (Berlin: de Gruyter 1977), 173–91

Irwin, Constance. Fair gods and stone faces (St. Martin's Press 1963)

Jacobsen, Thorkild. "Mesopotamian religions." Ch. 1, Religions of antiquity, ed. R.M. Seltzer (Macmillan 1989), 3–33

Jairazbhoy, Rafique A. Ancient Egyptians and Chinese in America (London: Prior 1974)

_____ . Ancient Egyptian in Middle and South America (London: Ra Pubs. 1981)

_____ . "The Egyptian presence *in* South America." Ch. 3 in African presence in early America (Journ. African Civs. 1987), 76–135

Jaritz, Kurt. "Tilmun-Makan-Meluhha." JNES XXVII/3 (July 1968), 209–13

Jaynes, Julian. The origin of consciousness in the breakdown of the bicameral mind (Houghton Mifflin 1977)

Jennings, Francis. The invasion of America: Indians, colonialism, and the cant of conquest (U.N.C. 1975/Norton 1976)

Jett, Stephen C. "The development and distribution of the blowgun." Assoc. Am. Geographers Annals LX/4 (19 0), 622–88

_____ . "Pre-Columbian transoceanic contacts." Ch. 13, Ancient native Americans, ed. Jesse D. Jennings (S.F.: W.H. Freeman 1978), 592–650

_____ . "Precolumbian transoceanic contacts." *In* The diffusion issue, ed. Donaldy L. Cyr (Santa Barbara: Stonehenge Viewpoint 1991), 21–50

Jenkins, Nancy. "The smell of time" [142 +', 40 + tons displacement Khufu solar-boat]. Aramco World Mag. XXXI/1 (Jan.–Feb. 1980), 12–17

Jewell, Elizabeth Ruth. The archaeology and history of western Anatolia during the second millennium, B.C. Diss U. Pa. (Xerox U. Micorfilms 1974)

Jones, A.H.M. The decline of the ancient world. Gen. Hist. Europe ser., ed Denys Hay (Holt, Rinehart & Winston 1966)

Jones, Ernest. "Psychoanalysis and folklore" [orig. 1930]. *In* The study of folklore, ed. Alan Dundes (Prentice-Hall 1965), 88–102

Jones, Tom B. Paths to the ancient past: applications of the historical method to ancient history (London: Collier-Macmillan 1967), II. Decipherment, 46–69

Jorda Cerda, Francisco. "Sobre posibles relaciones del arte levantino espanol." *In* Miscelanes en homenaje al abata Henri Breuil (1877–1961), ed. E. Ripoli Perello. 2 vols. (Barcelona: Inst. Prehist. y Arquelogia 1964–65), I, 167 ff.

Judge, Joseph. "Minoans and Mycenaeans." Nat'l Geographic CLIII/2 (Feb. 1978), 142–85

Judson, Horace Freeland. "Behind the painted mask." The Sciences XXIV/2 (Mar.–Apr. 1984), 26–35

Kaiser, Werner. "Zur vorgeschichtlichen Bedeutung von Hierakonpolis." MDAIK XVI (1958), 189–91

Kantor, Helen J. "Further evidence for early Mesopotamian relations with Egypt." JNES XI/4 (Oct. 1952), 239–50 + 27 plates

Keeler, Dr. Clyde. Adoration of the rising sun [includes transcription of Anubis panel in Anubis Cave (Milledgeville, Ga.: Dec. 1979). Also: ESOP XIV (1985), #344, 75–77

_____ . "The Cuna soul boat" [Egyptian affinities]. ESOP V (1978), II # 114

_____ . "Tree of Life and labyrinth" [Cuna, Pima, Mediterranean, Near-Eastern correspondences]. ESOP V (1978), II #107

_____ . Timeless threads in the fabric of Cuna Indian culture (Milledgeville, Ga.: author 1987)

Kees, Barry J. Horus und Seth als Gotterspaar. 2 vols. (Leipzig: J.C. Hinrichsiche 1923, 1924)

Kelemen, Pal. Art of the Americas, ancient and Hispanic, with a comparative chapter on the Philippines (Thos. Y. Crowell 1969)

Kelley, David H. "Calendar animals and deities." SW Journ. Anthrop. XVI/3 (1960), 317–37 [See Moran & Kelley]

_____ . "Eurasian evidence and the Mayan calendar correlation problem." *In* Mesoamerican archaeology, ed. Norman Hammond (U. Texas 1974), 143

Kemp, Barry J. "Abydos and the royal tombs of the First Dynasty." JEA LII (1968), 13–22

_____ . "The Egyptian 1st Dynasty royal cemetery." Antiquity XLI/161 (Mar. 1967), 22–32

_____ . "Photos of the Decorated Tomb at Hierakonpolis." JEA LIX (1973), 38–43

_____ . "Temple and town in ancient Egypt." *In* Man, settlement and urbanism, ed. Ucko, Tringham, & Dingleby, 657–80

Kendrick, T.D. Late Saxon and Viking art (London: Methuen 1949)

Kenna, Victor E.G. "Cretan and Mycenaean seals." Archaeology XIX/4 (Oct. 1966), 248

Kitchen, Kenneth A. The Third Intermediate Period in Egypt (1100–650 B.C.) (Warminster: Aris & Phillips 1982)

Kirkbride, Diana. "Beidha, an early village in Jordan." Archaeology XIX/3 (June 1966), 199–207

_____ . "Beidha 1967: an interim report." Pal. Expl. Qrtrly. XCIX (July–Dec. 1968), 92–96

_____ . "Five seasons at the Pre-Pottery Neolithic village of Beidha in Jordan." PEQ XCVII (Jan.–June 1966), 8–72

Kluckhohn, Clyde. "The philosophy of the Navaho Indians." Ch. XVII in Ideological differences and world order, ed. F.S.C. Northrop (Yale U. 1949/1963), 356–84

Knorozov, Yuri (pref. Tatiana Proskouriakoff). Selected chapters from the writing of the Maya Indians, tr. Sophie Coe (Peabody Mus. 1967)

Kohl, Philip L. "The balance of trade in southwestern Asia in the mid-third millennium B.C." (+ Lamberg-Karlovsky, Nissen, Oates, Sankalia, Solheim, et al.). Current Anthropology XIX/3 (Sept. 1978), 463–92

_____ . "The northern 'frontier' of the ancient Near East: Transcaucasia and Central Asia compared." AJA XCII/4 (Oct. 1988), 591–96

Konow, Sten & Tuxen, Poul. "The Indus civilization." Ch. 3 in Traditional India, ed, O.L. Chavarria-Aguilar (Prentice-Hall 1964)

Kosok, Paul. Life, land and water in ancient Peru (Long I. U. 1965) [Classifies Cupisnique "Very Early Coastal Chavin" p. 246]

Kramer, Samuel Noah. "Commerce and trade: gleanings from Sumerian literature." Iraq XXXIX/1 (Spr. 1977), 59–66

_____ , tr. Inanna, queen of heaven & earth: her stories & hymns from Sumer (Harper & Row 1983)

_____ , ed. Mythologies of the ancient world (Doubleday Anchor 1961)

Kretschmer, Paul. "Die vorgriechen Sprach-und Volksschichten." Glotta XXIV (1936;1963), 84–217

Krishnamurti, Bh. "The Dravidian identification of Meluhha, Dilmun and Makan." JESHO XXVI/2 (May 1983), 178–90

Kroeber, Alfred Louis. Handbook of the Indians of California. Bur. Ethnol. Smithsonian Inst. Bull. 78 (Gov't Printing Off./Dover 1976)

Kubler, George. The art and architecture of ancient America (Penguin 1962)

Kunst, Jaap. Kulturhistorische Beziehungen zwischen dem Balkan und Indonesien. Koninklijk Instituut voor de Tropen Mededeling CIII, afdeling Culturele en physische anthropologie 46 (Amsterdam: Koniglichen Tropen Institut 1953)

Lacy, A.D. Greek pottery in the Bronze Age (Methuen 1967)

Laird, Carobeth. The Chemehuevis (Banning, Calif. Morongo Reservation: Malki Museum 1976)

Lal, Chaman. Hindu America (Bombay: New Book Co. 1940)

Lamberg-Karlovsky, C.C. "Preshistoric Central Asia" (Review of Masson & Sarianidi, Central Asia, Thames & Hudson 1972). Antiquity XLVII/185 (1973), 43–48

_____ . "The Proto-Elamite settlement at Tepe Yahya." Iran IX (1971), 87–96 + Pl 11

_____ . "The Proto-Elamites on the Iranian plateau." Antiquity LII/205 (July 1978), 114–20

_____ . "Sumer, Elam and the Indus: three urban processes equal one structure?" 4, Harappan civ., ed Possehl (1982), 61–68

_____ . "Tepe Yahya 1971: mesopotamia and the Indo-Iranian borderlands." Iran X (1972), 89–100 + Pl XII

_____ . "Trade mechanisms in Indus-Mesopotamia interrelations." J. Am. Or. Soc. XCII/2 (1972), 222–30

_____ & Tosi, Maurizio. "Shar-i Sokhta and Tepe Yahya: tracks on the earliest history of the Iranian plateau." East & West XC/1-2 (Mar.–June 1973), 21–57

Landes, Ruth. Ojibwa religion and the Midewiwin (U. Wisc. 1968)

Lanning, Edward P. Peru before the Incas (Prentice-Hall 1967)

Lansing, Ambrose. "The Museum's excavations [at Hierakonpolis] 1934–1935." Bull. Met. Mus. of Art XXX/11 (Nov. 1935; Arno 1968), Sec. II 37–45

Lathrop, Donald W. "The tropical forest and the cultural context of Chavin." In Dumbarton Oaks conference on Chavin, ed. Elizabeth P. Benson (Washington, D.C.: Dumb. Oaks Lib. & Coll./ Trustees for Harvard U. 1971), 76–77

Lattimore, Owen. Studies in frontier history: collected papers 1928–1958 (Oxford U. 1964)

Lawrence, Harold G. (Kofi Wangara). "Mandinga voyages across the Atlantic." Ch. 9, African presence in early America (Journ. African Civs. 1987), 202–47

Lear, John. "Ancient landings in America." Sat. Review (18 July 1970), 18–19, 34

Le Breton, Louis. "The early periods of Susa, Mesopotamian relations." Iraq XIX (1957), 79–124

Legge, George Francis. "The carved slates from Hieraconpolis and elsewhere." Procs. Soc. Bibl. Lit. XXII (1900), 125–39 + Pls. 1–9

Legge, James, ed.-tr. The Chinese classics. . . 5 vols. ([reprint] Hong Kong U. 1960, 1970)

Lehmann, Henri. Pre-Columbian ceramics, tr. Galway Kinnell (Viking 1962)

Leemans, W.F. Foreign trade in the Old Babylonian period. . . [Brill 1960], partic. 7. "Some geographical problems," 259–75

——————— . "Old Babylonian letters & economic history. . .with a digression on foreign trade." JESHO XI (1968), 171–226, incl. III. Additional evidence for the Persian Gulf trade & Meluhha," 215–26

Leland, Charles Godfrey. Fusang: or, the discovery of America by Chinese Buddhist priests in the fifth century. Recs. Asian Hist. ser. (London: Curzon Press 1975; N.Y.: Barnes & Noble 1973)

Leroi-Gourhan, Andre. Les signes parietaux du paleolithique superieur franco-cantabrien. Simposio Int. de Arts Ruprestre (Barcelona: Instituto de Prehistoria y Arquelogia 1966)

——————— . Les religions de la prehistoire (paleolithique) (Paris: Prenes Universitaires de France 1984)

——————— . "Le symbolisme des grands signes l'art parietal paleolithique." Bull. Soc. Prehist. Fr. LV (1958), 384–98

Lesko, Leonard H. "Egyptian religion." Ch. 2, Religions of antiquity, ed. R.M. Seltzer (Macmillan 1989), 34–61

[Leventhal, Richard] (AP Nim Li Punit, Belize). "Tomb, hidden in jungle for years, may provide clues to Maya mystery." Winston-Salem Journal (1 June 1986), A21

Levin, Saul. The Indo-European and Semitic languages (U. Press of Am. 1967)

Levy, G. Rachel. Religious conceptions of the Stone Age and their influence upon European thought (Harper Trchbks. Cloister Lib. 1963)

Lewis, Thomas M. Nelson & Kneberg, Madeline. Tribes that slumber: Indians of the Tennessee region (U. Tenn. 1958)

Li, Hui-lin. "Mu-lan-p'i: a case for pre-Columbian transatlantic travel by Arab ships." Harvard Journ. Asiatic Studs. XXIII (1960–61; Johnson Reprint 1971), 114–26

Lieberman, Stephen J. "Of clay pebbles, hollow balls, and writing: a Sumerian view." Am. Journ. Archaeol. LXXXIV/3 (July 1980), 339–58

——————— . The Sumerian loan words in Old-Babylonian Akkadian. I: Proloegomena & evidence. Harvard Semitic ser. 22 (Missoula: Scholars Press/Harvard Semitic Mus. 1977)

Liesegang, Hans. "The mystery of the serpent" (1939). In Pagan and Christian mysteries: papers from the Eranos yearbooks, ed. Joseph Campbell, tr. Ralph Manheim & R.F.C. Hull (Harper Trchbks Bollingen Lib. 1963), 3–69

Limet, Henri. Le travail de metal au pays de Sumer au temps de le IIIe dynastie d'Ur. Bibl. de la Fr. de Philos. et Lettr. d l'U. de Liege CLV (Paris: Soc. d'Edition 'Les Belles Lettr.' 1961) Journ. Cun. Studs. XV/3 (1961), 114–16

Lloyd, Seton. Early highland peoples of Anatolia. Lib. Early Civs., ed. Stuart Piggott (McGraw-Hill/Thames & Hudson 1967)

——————— & Safar, Fuad. "Tell Hassuna: excavations by the Iraq government directorate general of antiquities in 1943 and 1944." Journ. Near Eastern Studs. IV/4 (Oct. 1945), 255–89 + 40 pgs. figs. & plts.

Loewenthal, Rudolf. The Turkic languages and literatures of Central Asia: a bibliography ('s-Gravenhage: mouton 1957)

Loftus, Elizabeth. Memory (Addison-Wesley 1980)

Lopatin, Ivan Alexis. The cult of the dead among the natives of the Amur Basin. Central Asiatic Studs. 6 ('s-Gravenhage: Mouton 1960)

Lopez, Robert S. & Raymond, Irving W., eds./trs. Medieval trade in the Mediterranean world: illustrative documents (Columbia U. 1955), 18–116, 238–39, 248–49, 355–58

Luce, J.V. "Thera and the devastation of Crete: a new interpretation of the evidence." Am. Journ. Archaeol. LXXX/1 (Winter 1976), 9–16

Lumbreras, Luis Guillermo. "Towards a re-evaluation of Chavin." Dumbarton Oaks Conf. on Chavin, ed. E.P. Benson (Dumb. Oaks Lib. & Coll./Harvard U. 1971), esp. figs. p. 15

MacKay, Ernest. Early Indian civ., rev. Dorothy MacKay (N. Delhi: Indological Book Corp. 1976)

Machuch, R. "The origins of the Mandeans and their script." Journ. Semitic Studs. XVI/2 (Aut. 1971), 174—92

Manchen-Helfen, Otto. The world of the Huns: studies in their history and culture, ed. Max Knight (U. Calif. Berkeley 1973)

Mahan, Joeseph. B. Identification of the Tsoyaha Waeno, builders of temple-mounds (msc. Ph.D. diss. U.N.C. 1970)

_____ . The secret: America in world history before Columbus (Columbus, Ga.: author 1983)

Mahler, Jane Gaston. "The art of the Silk Route." IV, East-West in art (Ind. U. 1966), 70—83

Mallowan, Max E.L. Early Mesopotamia and Iran. Lib. Ear. Civs. (Thames & Hudson 1965)

_____ . "The mechanics of ancient trade in western Asia." Iran III (1985), 1—7

Manetho. Aigyptiaka, tr. W.G. Wadell (London: W. Heinemann/Harvard U. 1940)

Marble, Samuel D. Before Columbus: the new history of Celtic, Phoenician, Viking, Black African, and Asian cintacts and impacts in the Americas before 1492 (S. Brunswick & N.Y.: A.S. Barnes/London: Thomas Yoseloff 1980)

Marshak, Alexander. The roots of civilization: the cognitive beginnings of man's first art, symbol & notation (London: Weidenfeld & Nicolson 1972)

_____ . "Upper Paleolithic symbol systems of the Russian plain; cognitive and comparative analysis." Curr. Anth. XX/2 (June 1979), 271—311

Marshall, John, ed. Mohenjo-daro and the Indus civilization: . . .archaeological excavations at Mohenjo-daro. . .between. . .1922 and 1927. 3 vols. [orig. 1931] (Delhi & Varanasi: Indological Book House 1973)

Masson, V.M. "The first farmers in Turkmenia." Antiquity XXXV (1961), 203—13

_____ . "The urban revolution in southern Turkmenia." Ibid. XLII (1968), 178—87

_____ & Sarianidi, V.I. Central Asia: Turkmenia before the Achaemenids, tr. Ruth Tringham. Anc. Peoples & Plcs. 79 (Thames & Hudson 1972)

Martin, Paul S.; Quimby, George I.; & Collier, Donald. Indians before Columbus (U. Chicago 1967)

Massoulard, Emile. Prehistoire et protohistoire d'Egypte (Paris: Institut d'ethnologie 1949)

Masry, Abdullah Hassan. Prehistory in northeastern Arabia: the problem of interregional interaction. Diss. U. Chicago (U. Chicago Lib. 1973)

_____ . "A reply to J. Oates et al., 'Seafaring merchants of Ur?'" Antiquity LII/204 (Mar. 1978), 46—47

Masson, V.M. & Sarianidi, V.I. Central Asia: Turkmenia before the Achaemenids, tr. Ruth Tringham. Anc. Peoples & Places 79 (Thames & Hudson 1972)

Maxwell-Hyslop, Rachel. "Daggers and swords in western Asia: a study from prehistoric time to 600 B.C." Iraq VIII (1946), 1—65 + 6 plates

Mayani, Zacharie. The Etruscans begin to speak, tr. Patrick Evans (Simon & Schuster 1962)

Mazar, Amihay. "The Philistines and the rise of Israel and Tyre." Procs. Israel Acad. Science & Humanities I/7 (1969), 1—22

Mazar, Suzan. "Visions of the alto Magdalena." Archaeology XIII/6 (Nov./Dec. 1989), 28—35

McAlpin, David W. "Toward a Proto-Elamo-Dravidian." Language L/1 (1974), 89—101

McCown, Donald E. "The material culture of early Iran." JNES I/4 (Oct. 1942), 424—49

McGlone, Bill. "An alternative hypothesis for Old World writing in ancient America" [not reliably datable by times flourished in Old World; inter-mixture of parallel foreign scripts among secondary transmitters']. Western Epigraphy I/1 (July 1983), 18—19

McGovern, William Montgomery. The early empires of Central Asia: a study of the Scythians and the Huns and the part they played in world history, with special reference to the Chinese sources (Chapel Hill: U.N.C. 1939)

McNeill, William H. & Sedlar, Jean W., eds. Classical India. Readings in World Hist. 4 (Oxford U. 1969)

_____ , eds. The Classical Mediterranean world Readings in World Hist. 3 (Oxford U. 1969)

Mee, Christopher. "Aegean trade and settlement in Anatolia in the second millennium B.C." Anatolian Studies XXVIII (1978), 121—55

Mellaart, James. "Anatolian trade with Europe and Anatolian geography and culture provinces in the Late Bronze Age." Anat. Studs. XVIII (1968), 187—202

_____ . Catal Huyuk: a Neolithic town [city] in Anatolia (McGraw-Hill 1967)

_____ . Comment on Arkell & Ucko, "Review of predynastic development." Curr. Anth. VI/2 (Apr. 1965), 160—61

_____ . "The earliest settlements in western Asia. . .9th to the end of the 5th millennium B.C.," Ch. VIIa, CAH3 I/1 (1970), 248−303; incl. x. Southern Turkestan, 194−303

_____ . "Excavations at Catal Huyuk. . ." Anatolian Studies XII (1962), 41−65; XIII 1963), 43−103; XIV (1964), 39−119; XV (1965), 135−56; XVI (1966), 165−92

_____ . Excavations at Hacilar. 2 vols. (Edinburgh: Br. Inst. Archaeol. Ankara 1970) Merrillees, R.S. The Cypriot Bronze Age pottery found in Egypt. Studs. in Mediterranean Archaeol. XVIII (Lund: Boktryckeri 1968)

_____ . "Opium trade in the Bronze Age Levant." Antiquity XXXVI (1962), 287−92 + Pls. XLII−III

_____ . The Neolithic of the Near East (Scribner 1975)

Mertz, Henriette. Pale ink (Chicago: Swallow Press 1953)

_____ . The wine dark sea: Homer's heroic epic of the North Atlantic (Chicago: author 1964)

Miller, Molly. The Sicilian colony dates. Studs. in Chronography I (Albany: SUNY 1970)

_____ . The thalassocracies: studs. in chronogr. II (Albany: SUNY 1971)

Miller, Arthur G. The mural painting of Teotihuacan (Dumbarton Oaks/Harvard U. 1973)

Millon, Rene. "The beginnings of Teotihuacan." Am. Antiquity XXVI/1 (July 1960), 1−10

[_____ et al.] "Twilight of the gods" [Teotihuacan]. Time (24 Nov. 1975), 107

Moore, Andrew M.T. "A four-stage sequence for the Levantine Neolithic, ca. 8500−3750 B.C." BASOR CCXLVI/2 (Spring 1982), 1−34

_____ . The Neolithic of the Levant. 2 vols. Diss. Oxfor U. 1978 (Ann Arbor: U. Microfilms Int. #78-70075, 1978)

_____ ; Hillman, G.C.; & Legge, A.J. "The excavation of Tell Abu Hureyra in Syria: a preliminary report." Prehist. Soc. Procs. XLI (Dec. 1975), 50−69

Moorey, P.R.S. "The archaeological evidence for metallurgy & related technologies in Mesopotamia, c.5500−2100 B.C." Iraq XLIV/1 (Spr. 1981), 13−38 + 2 pgs. plates

Moran, Hugh H. & Kelley, David H. The alphabet and the ancient calendar signs, 2nd ed. (Palo Alto: Daily Press 1969)

Moscati, Sabatino, ed. The Celts (N.Y.; Rizzoli 1991)

_____ . The face of the ancient Orient: a panorama of Near Eastern civilization in pre-Classical times, tr. uncredited (Doubleday Anchor 1962)

_____ . An introduction to the comparative grammar of the Semitic languages: phonology & morphology (Wiesbaden: O. Harrassowitz 1964)

_____ . The world of the Phoenicians, tr. Alistair Hamilton. Hist. Civ. ser. (Praeger 1968)

Mosso, Angelo. "Ceramica neolitica di Phaestos e vasi dell'epoca minoica primitiva" (Rome: Accademic de' Lincei Monumenti antichi. . . XIX/2 (1908), 141−218

_____ . La pristoria. I. Escusioni nel Mediterraneo e gli scavi di Creta. . .nuovo ed. con l'aggiunta di tre capitoli (Milan: Treves 1910)

Movius, Hallam L., Jr. "Paleolithic and Mesolithic sites in Soviet Central Asia." Am. Philos. Soc. Procs. XCVII/4 (1953), 383−421

_____ . "The Ptroto-Magdalenian of the Abri Pataud, Les Eyzies. . ." Bericht V. Int. Kongr. fur Vor- und Fruhgeschichte [Hamburg 24−30 Aug. 1958], ed. B. Versu & W. Dehn (Berlin: Gebr. Mann 1961), #185, 561−66 + Pl. 64

_____ & 10 others. Excavation of the Abri Pataud. . . . Am. Sch. Prehst. Res. Bull. 30 (Peabody Mus./Harvard U. 1975)

Muhly, J.D. "Homer and the Phoenicians: the relations between Greece and the Near East in the Late Bronze and Early Iron Ages." Berytus XIX (1970), 19−64

_____ . "Sources of tin and the beginnings of bronze metallurgy." AJA LXXXIX/2 (Apr. 1985), 275−91

_____ . "Tin trade routes of the Bronze Age." Am. Scientist LXI/4 (July−Aug. 1973), 403−13

Mukherjee, B.N. "Ta-Hsia and the problem concerning the advanet of nomadic peoples in Greek Bactria." In Central Asia, ed. Amalendu Guha (Barnes & Noble 1971), 121−29

Murray, Margaret A. "Burial customs and beliefs in the hereafter in predynastic Egypt." JEA XLII (Dec. 1956), 86−96

Murphy, Gerard. Saga and myth in ancient Ireland. Irish life & culture X (Dublin: Colm O Lochlainn 1961)

Murrill, Rupert Ivan. Cranial and postcranial skeletal remains from Easter Island (U. Minn. 1968)

Mutwa, Credo Vusamazulu Mutwa. 8-pg. letter to O.H. Hope (Johannesburg 24 Nov. 1984)

Mylonas, George Emmanuel. "The Luvian invasions of Greece." Hesperia XXXI (1962), 284−309

_____ . Mycenae's last century of greatness. Meyer Found. Lecture 1968. Australian Hum.-Res. Council Occ. Paper 13 (Sydney U. 1968)

Myres, John Linton. Who were the Greeks? (U. Calif. 1930)

Nagy, Gregory. Greek dialects and the transformation of an Indo-European process (Harvard U. 1970)

Nandris, John. "The development and relationships of the earlier Greek Neolithic." Man n.s. V/2 (June 1970), 192−213

Nelson, Harold Hayden. "The naval battle pictured at Medinet Habu." JNES II/1 (Jan. 1943), 40−55

Neugebauer, O[tto]. "The origin of the Egyptian calendar." JNES I/4 (Oct. 1942), 396−403

Neumayer, Erwin. Prehistoric Indian rock paintigs (Delhi: Oxford U. 1983)

Nibbi, Alessandra. Ancient Egypt and some eastern neighbors (Noyes 1981)

_____ . The Sea Peoples and Egypt (Noyes 1974) [but cf. Margaret S. Drower at Sheffield: Bronze Age migrations in the Aegean, ed. R.A. Crossland & Ann Birchell (Noyes 1974), 208]

Nilsson, M.P. The Minoan-Mycenaean religion and its survival in Greek religion, 2nd ed. Skrifter Utgivna av Kungl. Humanistiska Vetenekapssamfundet I Lund IX (Lund: Fleerup 1968)

_____ . The Mycenaean origin of Greek mythology. Sather Class. Lects. VIII (U. Calif. 1932)

Nixon, Ivor Gray. The rise of the Dorians (Praeger 1968)

Oates, Joan. "Prehistory in northeastern Arabia." Antiquity L/197 (Mar. 1976), 20−31

_____ . "Religion and ritual in sixth-millennium B.C. Mesopotamia." World Archaeol. X/2 (Oct. 1978), 117−24

_____ ; Davison, T.E.; Kamilli, D.; & McKerrel, H. "Seafaring merchants of Ur?" Antiquity LI/203 (1977), 221−34

Obermaier, Hugo. "Nouvelles etudes sur l'art represtre du Levant Espagnol." L'Anthropologie XLVII (1937), 477−98

_____ & Wernert, P. "Le edad chaterneria de los pinturas ruprestras del Levante Espanol." Historie Natural (Madrid) XV (1929), 525−37

Obolensky, Dimitri. The Byzantine commonwealth: eastern Europe 500−1453. Praeger Hist. Civ. (Praeger 1971)

O'Bryan, Deric. "The Abandonment of the northern Pueblos in the thirteenth century." Indian tribes of aboriginal America: selected papers XXIXth International Congress of Americanists, N.Y. 1949, ed. Sol Tax (U. Chicago 1952)

Olmstead, A.T. History of the Persian empire (U. Chicago 1948)

Oppenheim, A.L. "The seafaring merchants of Ur." Journ. Am. Oriental Soc. LXXIV (1954), 8−17

Oran, E.D. "The overland route between Egypt and Canaan in the Early Bronze Age (preliminary report)." Israel Expl. Journ. XXIII/4 (1973), 198−205

Oshanin, Lev Vasil'evich. Anthropological composition of the population of Central Asia, and the ethnogenesis of its peoples, ed. Henry Field, tr. Vladimir M. Oshanin. Archael. & Ethnol. 3 vols. People of Central Asia ser. (Cambridge, Mass.: Peabody Mus. 1964)

Ovenden, Michael W. & Rodger, David A. "Megaliths and medicine wheels." Msc. paper submitted to Science (17 July 1978), 7 pgs. + 3 of figs.

Pallotino, Massimo. The Etruscans, rev. ed., tr. J. Cremona, ed. David Ridgway (Ind. U. 1975)

[_____]. "Italians get rare Etruscan exhibit" (AP Viterbo, It.) Winston-Salem Journal 11 Oct. 1990, 11

Palmer, Leonard R. The Greek language (Atlantic Highlands, N.J.: Humanities Press 1980)

_____ . Mycenaeans and Minoans, 2nd ed. (Knopf 1965)

Palol, Pedro de. Arte hispanico de la epoca visigoda (Barcelona: Ediciones Polifrafia 1968)

Paor, Liam de. "A survey of Sceilg Mhichil [Skellig Michael]." Journ. Royal Soc. Antiqs. Ireland LXXXV (1955), 174−87

Parker, Richard A. "The beginning of the lunar month in ancient Egypt." JNES XXIX/4 (Oct. 1970), 217−20

_____ . The calendars of ancient Egypt. Oriental Institue Studs. Ancient Orienral Civ. 26 (U. Chicago 1950)

_____ . "The Sothic dating of the Twelfth & Eighteenth Dynasties." *In* Studies in honor of George R. Hughes. Studs. Anc. Or. Civ. 39 (U. Chicago 1977), 177−89

Parpola, Asko. "New correspondences between Harappan & Near Eastern glyptic art." Ch. 23, S. Asian archaeology, ed. Norman Hammond (Duckworth 1973), 176—95

Parpola, Sino; Parpola, Asko; & Brunswig, Robert, Jr. "The Meluhha village. Evidence of acculturation of Harappan traders in the late erd millennium Mesopotamia?" JESHO XX/2 (May 1977), 129—65

Patterson, George. ". . .The Portuguese on the north-east coast of America, and the first European attempt at colonization there. A lost chapter in American history." Royal Sic. Canada Procs. & Transacts. 1890, VIII (Montreal 1891), 127—73

Payne, Joan Crowfoot. "Lapis lazuli in early Egypt." Iraq XXX/1 (Spr. 1968). 58—61

_____ . "Tomb 100: the Decorated Tomb at Hierakonpolis confirmed." JEA LIX (1973), 31—35

Peet, T. Eric. "Egypt: the predynastic period." Ch. VI, CAH2 I (1928), 238—50

_____ . The cemeteries of Abydos, II., 1911—1912 (EEF Mem. 34 1914)

Pelon, Olivier. 'Aegean religions." Ch. 9, Religions of antiquity, ed. R.M. Seltzer (Macmillan 1989), 151—62

Pendlebury, J.D.S. Aegyptiaca: a catalogue of Egyptian objects in the Aegean area (Cambridge U. 1930)

Perrot, Jean. "Excavations at Eynan ('Ein Mallaha): preliminary report on the 1959 season." Israel Expl. Journ. X/1 (1960), 14 ff.

_____ . "Le gisment Natoufien de Mallaha (Eynan), Israel." L'Anthropologie LXX/5-6 (1966), 437—84

_____ . 'Palestine—Syria—Cilicia." In Courses toward urban life, ed. Braidwood & Willey (Chicago: Aldine 1962), 147—64

_____ . "Le prehistoire palestinienne. Suppl. Dictionnaire de la Bible VIII (1968), 286—446

Persson, Axel W. The religion of Greece in prehistoric times (U. Calif. 1942)

Petitot, Emile F.S. "La femme au serpent, legende des Dene Chippewayans." Melusine (Paris 1884—85), II, 19—21

Petrie, W.M. Flinders. Abydos, Part I, 1902; II, 1903. Eg. Expl. Soc. 22 & 24 (Kegan Paul, Trench, Trubner 1902, 1903) [Pt. III: see Ayrton]

_____ . Corpus of prehistoric pottery & palettes (London: BSAE & ERA 32, 1921)

_____ . Decorative patterns of the ancient world (University College 1930)

_____ . The funeral furniture of Egypt with stone work & metal vases (Aris & Philips 1937)

_____ . The royal tombs of the First Dynasty, 1900—1901. 2 vols. (London & Boston: EEF 1900—01)

_____ & Wace, A.C. Diospolis Parva, the cemeteries of Abadiyeh and Hu, 1898—1899. EEA 20 (London & Boston: K. Paul, Trencn, Trubner 1901)

_____ & Quibell, J.E. (1 ch. F.C.J. Spurrell). Naqada and Ballas (London: Quaritch 1896)

Piette, Edouard. "Les ecritures de l'age glyptique." L'Anthropologie XVI (1905), 1—11

_____ . . . . .Les galets colories du Mas d'Azil (Paris: Mason 1898)

Piggott, Stuart. Prehistoric India (Penguin 1950)

Polybius. Histories, tr. Evelyn S. Shuckburgh (1889). 2 vols. (Ind. U. 1962); also: this tr. abridged by Alvin H. Bernstein as On Roman imperialism (South Bend, Ind.: Regnery/Gateway 1980), & tr. Ian Scott-Kilvert 1979 of F.W. Walbank selections from Buttner-Wobst text as The rise of the Roman Empire (Penguin 1979); etc.

Porada, Edith. Ancient Iran: the art of pre-Islamic times [orig. in German 1962] (London: Methuen 1965)

Porter, Muriel Noe. Tlatilco and the pre-Classic cultures of the New World. Viking Fund Pubs. in Anthrop. 19 (N.Y.: Wenner-Gren Foundation 1953)

Possehi, Gregory L., ed. Ancient cities of the Indus (N. Delhi: Vikas 1979)

Postgate, J. Nichols. The first empires (Oxford U. 1977)

_____ . "The historical geography of the Hamrin Basin." Sumer XXXV/1-2 (1979), 595—91 (numbered backward)

Poussin, de La Vallee. "Buddhism." Ch. 11 in Traditional India, ed. G.L. Chevarria-Aguilar. (Prentice-Hall 1964), 90—108

Prashad, Baini. Animal remains from Harappa. Memoirs Archaeol. Survey of India 51 (Delhi: Mgr. Pubs. 1936) [included horse]

Prior, Daphne. "Shalom, Columbus" [Bat Creek & Metcalf Stones]. The Sciences, XI/5 (May 1971), 14—16

Proskouriakoff, Tatiana. "Olmec and Maya art: problems of their stylistic relation." *In* Conference on the Olmec (Washington, D.C.: Dumbarton Oaks 1968)

Proskouriakoff, Tatiana. "Historical implications of a pattern of dates at Piedras Negras, Guatemala." Am. Antiquity XXV/4 (Apr. 1960), 454—75

Puskas, Ildiko. "Society & religion in the Indus valley civilisation." Ch. 20, S. Asian Archaeology [6th int. conf. 1981], ed. Bridget Allchin (Cambridge U. 1984), 162—65

Quibell, James Edward (notes: Petrie). Hierakonpolis I. ERA Mem. 4 (Quaritch 1900)

_____ & Green, F.W. (Ch. VI Clarke Somer, XIV F. Ll. Griffith). Hierakonpolis II. ERA Mem. 5 (Quaritch 1902)

_____ & Petrie, W.M.F. Hierakonpolis I. ERA Mem. 4 (Quaritch 1900)

Quispel, Gilles. "Gnosticism." Ch. 14. Religions of antiquity, ed. R.M. Seltzer (Macmillan 1989), 259—71

Raban, Avner. "The Thera ships: another interpretation." AJA LXXXVIII/1 (Jan. 1984), 11—19 + Pls. 5-6

Raikes, Robert L. & Dyson, Roberth H., Jr. "The prehistoric climate of Baluchistan & the Indus Valley." Am. Anthropologist LXIII/2 (Apr. 1961), 265—81

Rands, Robert Lawrence/ Some evidences of warfare in classic Maya art. Columbia U. diss. (Ann Arbor: U. Microfilms 1952)

Rankin, H.D. Celts and the Classical world (London & Sydney: Croom Helm/Areopagitica Press 1987)

Rao, S[hikaripur] R[anganatha]. The decipherment of the Indus script (Bombay etc.: Asia Pub. House 1982)

_____ . Lothal & the Indus civilization (N.Y. [Bombay]: Asia Pub. House 1973)

_____ . "Marine archaeology finds submerged Dwarka." Indian & Foreign Review XXV/8 (15 Jan. 1988), 16—17, 27—31

_____ . "A Persian Gulf seal from Lothal." Antiquity XXXVII (1983), 96—99 + Pls. IX--XI

_____ . "Shipping and maritime trade of the Indus people." Expedition VII (1965), 30—37

_____ . "Shipping in ancient India." *In* India's contribution to world thought & culture, ed. Lakesh Chandra (Triplicane, Madras: Vivekananda Rock Memorial Committee 1970), 83—107

Raphael, Max. Prehistoric pottery & civilization in Egypt, tr. Norbert Suterman. Bollingen 8 (Pantheon 1947)

Ratnagar, Shareen. Encounters: the westerly trade of the Harappan civilization (Delhi: Oxford U. 1981)

Rawlinson, H.G. India: a short cultural history (London: Cresset 1937, 2nd ed. 1948; N.Y.: Praeger 1952)

Redford, Donald B. Akhenaten: the heretic king (Princeton U. 1984)

_____ , ed. I. Egypt. Papyrus and tablet (Prentice-Hall 1973)

Reisner, George Andrew. The development of the Egyptian tomb down to the accession of Cheops (Harvard U. 1936)

_____ . Outline of the ancient history of the Sudan, I: Early trading caravans (4000 to 2000 B.C.) (Cairo: Fr. Inst. Or. Arch. 1918)

Renfrew, Colin. Archaeology and language: the puzzle of Indo-European origins (Cambridge U. 1988)

_____ . The emergence of civilisation: the Cyclades and the Aegean in the third millennium B.C. (Methuen 1972)

_____ . "Patterns of population growth in the prehistoric Aegean." *In* Man, settlement and urbanization, ed. Peter J. Ucko,Ruth Tringham, & G.W. Dimbleby (Duckworth 1972), 383—99

_____ . "Systems collapse as social transformation: catastrophe & anastrophy in early state societies." Ch. 21, Tramsformations: mathematical approaches to culture change, ed. Remfrew & Kenneth L. Cooke (Academic 1979), 481—506

Reymond, E.A.E. The mythical origin of the Egyptian temple (Manchester U./Barnes & Noble 1969)

Ridgway, David. "Archaeology in Sardinia and Etruria, 1974—79." Archaeol. Reports for 1979—80, XXVI (1980), 54—70

_____ . "Archaeology in South Italy, 1977—81." Archaeol. Reports for 1981—82 (1982), 64—83

Riley, Carroll L.; Kelley, J. Charles; Penniglan, Campbell W.; & Rands, Robert L., eds. Man across the sea: probs. pre-Columbian contacts (U. Texas 1971)

Roberts, David. "At Casa Malpais, catacombs and collaboration." Smithsonian XXII/12 (Mar. 1992), 28−37

Rolle, Renate. The world of the Scythians, tr. Geyna Walls (London: B.T. Batsford 1989)

Roux, Georges. Ancient Iraq (London: Allen & Unwin 1964; Cleveland: World 1964)

Rowe, Alan. "The famous solar-city of On." Palestine Expl. Qrtrly. XC (July−Dec. 1962), 133−42

Rowley, H[arold] H[enry]. From Joseph to Joshua: biblical traditions in the light of archaeology (London: Br. Acad./Oxford U. 1950)

Rowton, M.B. "Ancient western Asia." Ch. II, CAH3 I/1 (1970), 193−239

_____ . "Autonomy and nomadism in western Asia." Orientalia XLII/1-2 (1973), 247 ff.

_____ . "Enclosed nomadism." JESHO XVII/1 (1974), 1−30

Rudolph, Kurt. "Mystery religions." Ch. 15, Religions of antiquity, ed. R.M. Seltzer (Macmillan 1989), 272−85

Ryan, John. Irish monasticism: origins and early development." (Dublin & Cork: Talbot Press 1931)

Sakellariou, A. "The West House miniature frescoes," tr. Liadain Sherrard. TATAW II, 147−53

Sallust [Gaius Sallustius Crispus]. The Jugurthine War, tr. S.A. Handford (Penguin 1963)

Sambamoorthy, P. History of Indian music (Madras: Indian Music Publishing House 1960)

Samolin, William. "Cultural diffusion from An-yang to the Danube: the role of the Eurasian steppe." III, East-West in art (Ind. U. 1966), 50−69

Sandars, Nancy K. The Sea Peoples: warriors of the ancient Mediterrranean 1250−1150 BC. Anc. Peoples & Places 89 (Thames & Hudson 1978)

Sankalia, H[asmukhal] D[hirajlal]. Prehistory & protohistory in India & Pakistan (U. Bombay 1982)

_____ . Prehistory of India (N. Delhi: Munshiram Manoharlal 1977)

Sarianidi, V.I. The lapis lazuli route in the ancient East, tr. Luba H. Kowalski. Archaeology XXIV/1 (Jan. 1971), 12−15

Sastri, Kallidaikurichi Aiyah Aiyah Nilakanta. New light on the Indus civilization. 2 vols. (Delhi: Ama Ram & Sons 1957, 1965)

Sauneron, Serge. The priests of ancient Egypt, tr. Ann Morrissett. Evergreem Profile 12 (Grover 1980)

_____ . East Turkestan to the twelfth century (Mouton 1964)

Schachermeyr, Fritz. Die Agaische Fruhzeit II: Die Mykenische Zeit und die Gesittning von Thera (Vienna: Osterreich Akad. der Wissenschaft 1976)

_____ . Die Agaische Fruhzeit V: Die Levant im Zeitalter der Wanderungen vom 13. bis zum 11. Jahrhundert V. Chr. Sitzungsderischten der Philosoph.-Historichen (Vienna: Ost. Akad. d. Wiss. 1982)

_____ . "Hornerhelme und Federkronen als Kopfbedeckungen bei den 'Seevolkern' der Agyptischen relifs." Ugaritica VI (1969), 451−59

Schaeffer, Claude Frederic Armand. "Les peuples de la mer et leurs sanctuaires a Enkomi-Alasia aux XII-XI S. AV. N.E." In Alasia I. Mission archeologique d'Alasia, IV. XXe campagne de fouilles a Enkomi-Alasia (1969). Librairie Klincksieck (Paris: Miss. arch. d'Alasia, College de France/Leiden: E.J. Brill 1971), 505−46

Schaeffner, Andre. "Une importante decouvertte archeologique: le lithophone de Ndut Lieng Krak (Vietnam). (Paris: La Revue de Musicologie XXXIII (July 1951), 1−19

Schele, Linda. Maya glyphs: the verbs (U. Texas 1982)

_____ . "The Xibalba shuffle: a dance after death." Ch. 10, Maya iconography, ed. Elizabeth P. Benson & Gillett G. Griffin (Princeton U. 1988), 294−317

_____ & Miller, Mary Ellen. The blood of kings: dynasty and ritual in Maya art (Ft. Worth: Kimbell Art Museum 1986)

_____ & Freidel, David. A forest of kings: the untold story of the ancient Maya (Wm. Morrow 1990)

Scherz, James P. & Price, Joan. The India connection: the Sak and Yuchi tribes of the Old World and the New [msc. prelim. working paper] (Columbus, Ga. 1991)

Schwerdtfeger, Friedrich W. "Urban settlement patterns in northern Nigeria (Hausaland)." In Man, settlement and urbanism, ed. Ucko, P.J.; Tringham, Ruth; & Dimbleby, G.W. Procs. Res. Seminar Archaeol. & Related Subjects, Inst. Archaeol. London U. 5−7 Dec. 1970 (Duckworth 1972), 547−56

Seltzer, Robert M., ed. Religions of antiquity [selections from Encyclopedia of religion, Mircea Eliade ed.-in-chief] (N.Y.: Macmillan 1987/89)

Sethe, Kurt. Urgeschichte und alteste Religion der Agypter. Abhandlungen. . . Kunde des Morgenlandes XVIII/4 (Leipzig 1930; Nendein, Liechtenstein: Kraus Repr. 1966)

Shan hai jing tsien sha [with commentary], ed. Ho Yi-hing 1809 [in Chinese, incorporating Kuo Po's 6th-cent., Wang Chong-king's 16th cent., Wu Zhen-chan's 1667, & Pi Yuan's 1781 glosses) (Taiwan n.d.)

Shao, Paul. Asiatica influences in Pre-Columbian art (Iowa St. U. 1976)

_____ . The origins of ancient American cultures (Ia. U. 1983)

Sharer, Robert. "Did the Maya collapse? a New World perspective on the demise of the Harappan civilization." Ch. 36, Harappan civ., ed. Gregory L. Possehl (1982), 367—83

Sharma, G.R. "India and Central Asia from c.6th century B.C. to 6th century A.D." In Central Asia, ed. Amalendu Guha (Barnes & Noble 1971), 110—20

Shendge, Malati J. The civilized demons: the Harappans in Rgveda (New Delhi: Abhinev 1977)

_____ . "The inscribed calculi and the invention of writing: the Indus view." Journ. Ec. & Soc. Hist. of the Orient XXVIII/1 (Feb. 1985), 50—80

_____ . "The use of seals and the invention of writing." Ibid. XXVI/2 (May 1983), 113—38

Shepherd, Dorothy G. "Iran between East and West." V, East-West in art (Ind. U. 1966), 84—105

Singer, Itamar. "Western Anatolia in the thirteenth century B.C. according to Hittite sources." Anatolian Studies XXXIII (1983), 205—17

Singh, Purushottam. Neolithic cultures of western Asia (Seminar 1974)

Sloley, R.W. "Primitive methods of measuring time with special reference to Egypt." JEA XVII/II (1931), 166—78

Smith, H.S. Comment on Arkell & Ucko, "Review of predynastic development. . ." Curr. Anth. VI/2 (Apr. 1965), 162—63

Smith, Roberta C. "Chinese inscriptions in America (Yu-shi, Yueh-chih, Yuchi)." In Dragon treasures, ed. Donald L. Cyr (Stonehenge Viewpoint 1989), 90—97

_____ . Suggested decipherment of the Alabama Hills solar site inscriptions: an interim report on some California glyphs (Atlanta: author 1987)

Smith, Watson. Kiva mural decorations at Awatovi and Kawaika-a, with a survey of other wall paintings in the Pueblo Southwest (Peabody Mus. 1952)

Snodgrass, Anthony. Archaic Greece: the age of experiment (Dent & Sons 1980)

Soffer, Olga. The Upper Paleolithic of the central Russian plain. Studs. in Archaeol. (Academic 1985)

Solecki, Rose L. An early village site at Zawi Chemi Shanidar. Bibliotheca Mesopotamia 13 (Malibu: Undana 1980)

Soren, David; Khader, Aicha Ben Abed Ben; & Slim, Hedi. Carthage: uncovering the mysteries and splendors of ancient Tunisia (Simon & Schuster 1990)

Soustelle, Jacques. The Olmecs (Doubleday 1984)

Stanley Price, N.P. "Khirokitia and the initial settlement of Cyprus." Levant (1977), 66—89

Steiglitz, Robert R. "Long-distance seafaring in the ancient Near East." Bibl. Archaeologist XLVIII/3 (Sept. 1984), 134—42

Stekelis, Moshe & Yizraely, Tamar. "Excavations at Nahal Oren: preliminary report." Is. Expl. J. XIII/1 (1963), 1—17

Stephens, George. The old-northern runic monuments of Scandinavia and England, now first collected and deciphered. . .with. . .runic [& other ancient] alphabets. . . 4 vols. (London: J.R. Smith/Copenhagen: Michaelsen & Tilge 1866—1901)

_____ . The runes, whence came they (London & Copenhagen: Wms. & Norgate 1894)

_____ . The Ruthwell Cross, Northumbria, from c.A.D. 680, with the runic verses by Caedmon. . . (London: J.R. Smith 1966)

Stone, Merlin. "Goddess worship in the ancient Near East." Ch. 3, Religions of antiquity, ed. R.M. Seltzer (Macmillan 1989), 62—68

Strabo. The geography [Geographia], tr. Horace Leonard Jones. 8 vols. Loeb Classical Library (Heinemann/Putnam's Sons 1929)

Stuart, George E., gen. ed. Peoples and places of the past: the National Geographic illustrated cultural atlas of the ancient world (Nat'l Geographic Soc. 1983)

Stubbings, Frank H. "The Aegean Bronze Age." Ch. III, CAH3 I/1 (1970), 239—47

_____ . Mycenaean pottery from the Levant (Cambridge U. 1951)

_____ . "The recession of Mycenaean civilization." CAH3 II/2 (1975), XXVII 338−58 [Fasc. 39 1965]

Symeonoglou, Sarantis. "A chart of Mycenaean and Late Minoan pottery." AJA LXXIV/3 (July 1970), 285−88

Stewart, Ethel G. The Dene and Na-Dene Indian Migration 1233 A.D.: escape from Genghis Khan to America (Columbus, Ga.: ISAC/Marquette, Mich.: Sperior Heartland 1991)

_____ . "The ferocious enemies of the ancestors of the northern Dene in relation to the Mongols." Anthrop. Journ. Canada XIX/1 (1981), 18−23

_____ . "The Jade Gate of China." Ibid. XVIII/3 (1980), 23−27

_____ . "Kutchin exogamous divisions in relation to eastern Asia." Ibid. XVII/3 (1979), 2−11

_____ . "The thunderbird of the Dene and the Na-Dene." ESOP XV (1986), 113−16

Stigler, Robert; Holloway, Ralph; Solecki, Ralph; Perkins, Dexter, Jr.; & Daly, Patricia. The Old World: early man to the development of agriculture (St. Martin's Press 1974)

Stipcevic, Aleksandar. The Illyrians: history and culture, tre. Srojana Culic Burton (Noyes 1977)

Stuart, George E. "Who were the 'Mound Builders'?" Nat'l Geographic CXLII/6 (Dec. 1972, 782−801

_____ & Stuart, Gene S., photogs. David Alan Harvey & Otis Imboden, pntr. Louis S. Glanzman. The mysterious Maya (Nat'l Geographic Soc. 1977)

Sulimirski, T. "The forgotten Sarmatians." Ch. XII in Vanished civs. of the anc. world, ed. Edward Bacon (Thames & Hudson/McGraw-Hill 1967), 279−98

Sykes, Egerton. "Varangian rune stones in the Mississippi basin." New World Antiquity XVII/11-12 (Nov.−Dec. 1970), 111−16

_____ . "Zimbabwe and the outside world." Ibid., 117−26

Talbot, David N., interviewed by John Gibson. "Saturn's age." Research Communications Network Newsletter 3 (Portland, Ore. (15 Oct. 1977), 1−7 [Misses Tanit relationship but may illuminate it & Saturn "sun" symbolism]

Taylor, Isaac. The alphabet: an account of the origin and development of letters. 2 vols. (London: Kegan Paul, Trench 1883)

Taylor, John H. Egypt and Nubia (Br. Mus./Harvard U. 1991)

Taylour, Lord William. Mycenaean pottery in Italy and adjacent areas (Cambridge U. 1958)

Te-K'un, Cheng. Archaeology in China (Toronto U. 1963)

Thapar, B[al] K[rishen]. Recent archaeological discoveries in India (Paris/Tokyo: Centre East As. Cult. Studs./UNESCO 1985)

Theocharis, Demetrios R., ed. Neolithic Greece (Athens: Nat'l Bank of Greece 1973)

Thomas, Charles. "The interpretation of the Pictish symbols." Royal Archaeol. Inst. Archaeological Journal CXX (London: Dec. 1964), 88−93

Thomas, C.G. "A Mycenaean hegemony? a reconsideration." Journ. Hellenic Studs. XC (1970), 184−92

Thompson, Gunnar. "New World domesticates in the Old World. . . ." In The diffusion issue (Stonehenge Viewpoint 1991), 5−13

_____ . Nu sun: Asian-American voyages 500 B.C. (Fresno: Pioneer Pub. Co. 1989)

Thomsen, Marie-Louise. The Sumerian language. . . (Copenhagen: Akademisk Forlag 1984)

Timreck, T.W., prod./dir./ed. Search for the lost Red Paint People. (PTS: WGBH/NOVA 1987)

Todd, Ian A. Catal Huyuk in prespective (Menlo Park etc.: Cummings 1976)

Tomas, Andrew. "Enigmas of Mayan astronomy." Ancient Skies (Highland Park, Ill. Mar.−Apr. 1987) XIV/1, 1−3

Tosi, Maurizio. "Early urban evolution and settlement patterns in the Indo-Iranian borderlands." In The explanation of culture change, ed. Colin Renfrew (Duckworth 1973), 429−46

_____ . "Excavations at Shar-i Sokhta, a Chalcolithic settlement in the Iranian Sistan. Preliminary report first campaign, Oct.−Dec. 1967." East & West XVIII/1-2 (Mar.June 1968), 9−66; ". . .The 2nd campaign, Sept.−Dec. 1968." XIX/3-4 (Sept.−Dec. 1969), 283−386

Totten, Norman. "Iconography of the Narmer Palette: origin of Egyptian writing." N. Eng. Soc. Studs. Bull. XXXVI/1 (Fall 1978), 3−17

_____ . "Numismatic evidence for pre-Columbian voyages." Ancient Vermont, ed. Warren L. Cook (Rutland, Vt.: Academy Bks. 1978), 44−46

Treistman, Judith M. The prehistory of China: an archaeological exploration Am. Museum Science Bks. (Doubleday 1972)

Tritsch, F.J. "Lycian, Luwian and Hittite." Der Alte Orient XVIII (1950), 494–502

Tschopik, Harry, Jr. Music of the American Indians Southwest: introduction. Am. Mus. Nat. Hist. Ethnic Folkways Lib. P 420, 78–1420 (Folkways Records & Service Corp. 1951)

Uberoi, J.P. Singh. "Between Oxus and Indus: a local history of the frontier 5000 B.C.–1925 A.D." In Central Asia, ed. Amalendu Guha (Barnes & Noble 1971), 181–99

Vagnetti, Lucia di. "Un [IIIC:1] vaso Miceneo da Pantalica." Studi Micenei ed Egeo-Antaloci XXVI (1968), 132–35

Vaillant, G.C. Aztecs of Mexico: origin, rise & fall of the Aztec nation [1944], rev. Suzannah B. Vaillant (Doubleday 1962/Penguin Pelican 1965), esp. Ch. 4, "The Toltecs of Tula," 83–95

Van Buren, E. Douglas. "New evidence conerning an eye-divinity." Iraq XVII (1955), 164–75

_____ . "The rosette in Mesopotamian art." Zeitschrift fur Assyriologie XLV (1939), 99 ff.

Van Sertima, Ivan, ed. African presence in early America (incorporating Journ. African Civs VIII/2) (Rutgers U. 1987)

Vats, Madho Sarup. Excavations at Harappa...1920–21 & 1933–34.... (Delhi: Archaeological Survey Mgrs. Pub. 1940)

Velde, H. Te. Seth, god of confusion: a study of his role in Egyptian mythology and religion, tr. G.F. van Baaren-Pape (Brill 1967)

Vercoutter, Jean. L'Egypte et le Mond Egeen prehellenique (Cairo: Institut franca a d'archeologie orientale 1956)

Vermeule, Emily Townsend. "The fall of the Mycenaean empire." Archaeology XIII/ 1 (Mar. 1960), 66–75

_____ . Greece in the Bronze Age (U. Chicago 1964)

Verrill, L. Ruth & Keeler, Clyde. "A Viking saga in Tennessee?" [Thruston Tablet]. Bull. Ga. Acad. Science XIX/4 (Sept. 1961), 78–82

Vining, Edward Payson. An inglorious Columbus; or, evidence that Hwui Shan and a party of Buddhist monks from Aghanistan discovered America in the fifth century A.D. [also incls. tr. East bks. Shan hai jing, except XIII] (D. Appleton 1885)

Wace, A.J.B. & Thompson, M.S. Prehistoric Thessaly: ...recent excavations and explorations in north-eastern Greece from Lake Kopais to the border of Macedonia (Cambridge U. 1912)

Wainright, Gerald A. "The Red Crown in early prehistoric times." JEA IX/1-2 (1923), 26–33

_____ . "Caphtor, Keftiu, and Cappadocia." Pal. Expl. Qrtrly. LXIII (Oct. 1931), 203–16

_____ . "Keftiu." JEA XVII/I (May 1931), 26–43

_____ . "Some Sea-Peoples and others in the Hittite archives." JEA XXV (1939), 148–53

_____ . "The Teresh, the Etruscans and Asia Minor." Anat. Studs. IX (1959), 197–213

Wales, Horace Geoffrey Quaritch. Angkor and Rome: a historical comparison (London: Bernard Quaritch 1965)

_____ . The Indianization of China and of Southeast Asia (Quaritch 1967)

_____ . The making of Greater India, 2nd ed. (Quaritch 1961)

_____ . Prehistory and religion in Southeast Asia (Quaritch 1957)

_____ . The Mountain of God: a study in early religion and kingship (Quaritch 1953)

Ward, William A. "The H'iw-ass, the H'iw-serpent, and the god Seth." JNES XXXVII/1 (Jan. 1978), 23–24

_____ . "The supposed Asiatic campaign of Narmer." Melanges de l'Universite Saint-Joseph de Bayrouth XLV (1979), 296–310

Wardwell, Allen. "The brilliance of Mayan culture is seen in a dark new light." N.Y. Times (20 July 1986), H 29

Warren, Peter M. The Aegean civilizations. Making of the Past (London: Elsevier-Phaidon 1975)

_____ . "Crete, 3000–1400 B.C.: immigration and the archaeological evidence." In Bronze Age migrations in the Aegean [1st Sheffield colloq. on Aegean prehistory, Mar. 1970], ed. R.A. Crossland & Ann Birchall (Noyes 1971), 41–50

_____ . "Knossos: new excavations and discoveries." Archaeology XXXVII/4 (July/Aug. 1984), 48–55

_____ . "The miniature fresco from the West House at Akrotiri, Thera, and its Aegean setting." Journ. Hellenic Studs. XCIX (1979), 115–29

Warren, William Fairfield. The earliest cosmologies: the universe in thought by the ancient Hebrews, Babylonians, Rgyptians, Greeks, Iranians, & Indo-Aryans (N.Y.: Eaton & Mains 1909)

Washburn, Dorothy K. "A study of the Red on Cream and Cream on Red designs on Early Neolithic ceramics from Nea Nikomedeia." AJA LXXXVIII/3 (July 1984), 305–24

Waters, Frank & Fredericks, Oswald White Bear. Book of the Hopi: the first revelation of the Hopi's historical and religious world-view of life (N.Y.: Ballantine Bks. 1963)

Weaver, Muriel Porter. The Aztecs, Maya, and their predecessors: archaeology of Mesoamerica (N.Y./London Seminar Press 1972), 50–52, 59–60

Weigall, Arthur. A history of the pharoahs. 2 vols. (Dutton 1925)

Weinberg, Saul S. "Halafian and Ubaidian influence in Neolithic Greece." Bericht uber den V. Int. Kong. fur Vor- und Furhgeschichte Hamburg 24–30 Aug. 1958, ed. Gerhard Bersu & Wolfgang Dehn (Berlin: Gebr. Mann 1961), #282: 858

_____ . "The Stone Age in the Aegean." Ch. X, CAH3 I/1 (1970), 557–618

Weinfield, Mosche. "Israelite religion." Ch. 6, Religions of antiquity, ed. R.M. Seltzer (Macmillan 1989), 96–121

Weinstein, James M. "The Egyptian empire in Palestine: a reassessment." BASOR CCXLI (Winter 1981), 1–28

Weisgerber, Gerd. "Makan & Meluhha—3rd millennium BC copper production in Oman &. . .contact with the Indus valley." Ch. 14, S. Asian Archaeology [6th int. conf. 1981], ed. Bridget Allchin (Cambridge U. 1984), 196–201

Wente, Edward F. "On the chronology of the Twenty-first Dynasty." Journ. Near Eastern Studs. XXVI/3 (July 1967), 155–76

_____ & Van Siclen, Charles C. III. "A chronology of the New Kingdom." In Studies in honor of George R. Hughes. Oriental Inst. Studs. in ancient Or. civ. 39 (U. Chicago 1976), 217–61

Wheeler, Robert E. Mortimer. Civilisations of the Indus Valley and beyond. Library Early Civs. (McGraw Hill 1966)

_____ . The Indus civilization. Cambridge Hist. India supplement, 3rd ed. (Cambridge U. 1968)

Wicke, Charles R. Olmec: an early art style of precolumbian Mexico (U. Ariz. 1971)

Williams, Roger. A key into the language of America: or, an help to the language of the natives of that part of America, called New-England (London 1643)

Wilson, John A. The burden of Egypt: an interpretation of ancient Egyptian culture (U. Chicago 1951)

_____ . "Civilization without cities." In City invincible: a symposium on urbanization & cultural dev. in the anc. N. East held at the Oriental Inst. . .Dec. 4–7, 1958, ed. Carl Hermann Kraeling & Robert M. Adams (U. Chicago 1960), 124–64

Winkler, Hans Alexander. . . .Rock-drawings of southern Upper Egypt. . . 2 vols. Sir Robert Mond desert expedition (London: EES/Oxford U. 1938, 1939)

Winter, Nancy A. "News letter from Greece" (Kilian's excavation at Tiryns 1980–81), AJA LXXXVI/4 (Oct. 1982), 543–44

Wittgenstein, Ludwig. Remarks on Frazer's Golden Bough, tr. A.C. Miles, ed. Rush Rhees (Brynmill/ Humanities Press 1979)

Wright, Arthur F. The Sui dynasty: the unification of China, A.D. 581–617 (Knopf 1978)

Wright, Gary A. Obsidian analyses and prehistoric Near Eastern trade 7500–3500 B.C. U. Mich. Archaeol. & Anth. Papers XXXVII (U. Mich. 1969)

Wright, George Ernest. The pottery of Palestine from the earliest times to the end of the Early Bronze Age (Ann Arbor: Edwards Bros. 1937)

Wright, Henry T. & Johnson, Gregory A. "Population, exchange, & early state formation in south-western Iran." Am. Anthropologist LXXVII/2 (June 1975), 267–89

Wuthenau, Alexander von. Altamerikanische Tonplastic [Caucasian & Black et al. races in Meso-america]. Kunst der Welt ser. (Baden-Baden: Holle 1965)

_____ . "Unexpected African faces in pre-Columbian America." Ch. 2 in African presence in early America, ed. Ivan Van Sertima (Journ. African Civs. 1987), 56–75

Yakar, Jak. "Hittite involvement in western Anatolia." Anat. Studs. XXVI 1976), 117–28

_____ . "Northern Anatolia in the Early Bronze Age." Tel Aviv II/4 (1975), 133–45

Yeivin, Sh. [Samuel]. "The ceremonial slate-palette of King Narmer." Studs in Egyptology & Linguistics in honor of H.J. Polotsky (Jerusalem: Israel Expl. Soc. 1964), 22–53

_____ . "Early contacts between Canaan and Egypt." Israel Expl. Journ. X/4 (1964), 193–203

_____ . "Further evidence of Narmer at 'Gat.'" Oriens Antiques (Rome: Centre per le Antichita e la Storia dell'Arte del Vicino Oriente) II (1963), 205–13

Yoshida, Nobuhiro. "Ogam letters at Oshima, Japan: inscribed stones reused for stairway" [report of Yoshikazu Anno team disc. Oshima Is., reprinted from Petrograph News 25 (6 Dec. 1991) *in* La. Mounds Soc. Newsletter 45 (14 Feb. 1992), 1

_____ . Semitic inscriptions [Proto-Shumerian & cuneiform] found in Japan [6-pg. pamphlet] (Kitakyusyu-city, Japan 1991)

_____ . "Petroglyphs at Yuya-cape!" The Petrograph News [Japanese/English] #22 (Kitakyusyu-city 21 Jan. 1991), 1; also: reports of petroglyph discoveries at Izumo, Shimane & Tottori prefectures, & a pass near Keelung, Taiwan, pp. 1, 3–4

Yurko, Frank. "Merenptah's Palestinian campaign." SSEA Journ. VIII (1978), 70

Zettl, Helmut. "More on archaeoastronomy." Ancient Skies XIV/3 (July–Aug. 1987), 4

Zimmer, Heinrich. Myths and symbols in Indian art and civilization, ed. Joseph Campbell (Harper Trcjbks./Bollingen Lib. 1946)

Zvelebil, Marek, ed. Hunters in transition: Mesolithic societies of temperate Eurasia & their transition to farming. New Directions Archaeol. (Cambridge U. 1986)

Zyhlarz, Ernest. "The countries of the Ethiopian empire of Kush and Egyptian Old Ethiopia in the New Kingdom." Kush VI (1958), 7 ff.

Index